D0110147

Securing Liberty

Securing Liberty

Debating Issues of Terrorism and Democratic Values in the Post-9/11 United States

David Cole, editor

International Debate Education Association

New York, London & Amsterdam

Published by
The International Debate Education Association
400 West 59th Street
New York, NY 10019
Copyright © 2011 by Open Society Institute

All rights reserved. No part of this publication may be reproduced or
transmitted in any form or by any means, electronic or mechanical,
including photocopy, or any information storage and retrieval system,
without permission from the publisher.

For permission to use in all or in part, please contact: idea@idebate.org

This book is published with the generous support of the Open Society
Foundations.

Library of Congress Cataloging-in-Publication Data

Securing liberty : debating issues of terrorism and democratic values in
the post-9/11 United States / David Cole, editor.
    p. cm.
 ISBN 978-1-61770-021-7
 1. Civil rights—United States. 2. Human rights—United States. 3.
  Terrorism—Government policy—United States. 4. National
security—United
  States. I. Cole, David, 1958-
  JC599.U5S397 2011
  323.0973—dc22
                                    2011015253

Design by Kathleen Hayes
Printed in the USA

◤ IDEBATE Press

Contents

Acknowledgements

I would like to thank Christian Pangilinan and Zachary Warren for invaluable research assistance in preparing this volume.

Introduction

Everything Changed

The terrorist attacks of September 11, 2001, altered the American landscape in many ways. Approximately three thousand lives were lost. New York City's two tallest buildings fell. Within a month, the United States was bombing Afghanistan, beginning a war that continues a decade later. At home, Congress enacted the USA PATRIOT Act within weeks of the attack, granting the executive broad new surveillance powers while eliminating judicial review and other safeguards. In an effort to coordinate domestic security operations, the Department of Homeland Security was formed, absorbing part or all of 22 different government agencies; it is now the third-largest federal bureaucracy in the United States, after the departments of Defense and Veterans Affairs. In short, the "national security state" was born, as untold resources were redirected to the task of making the nation safe from future attacks. On May 1, 2011, U.S. forces located and killed Osama bin Laden, but the transformations he triggered will long outlive him—as will, apparently, the war in Afghanistan.

The world changed as well. The United Nations Security Council approved resolutions requiring nations around the world to adopt and implement counterterrorism measures, including systems to track and stem the flow of funds to organizations and individuals that the Security Council declared to be "terrorist"—without affording those designated any opportunity to challenge the label. The United States was targeted on September 11, but other mass attacks followed—in Indonesia, the

United Kingdom, Spain, Jordan, and India, to name only a few. Many nations were prompted to strengthen their own counter-terrorism laws. The United Kingdom, for example, authorized indefinite detention without charge of foreign citizens suspected of terrorist involvement—a measure its own highest court subsequently declared incompatible with the European Convention on Human Rights.

In the wake of the attacks, defenders of expanded government power to fight terrorism argued that the attacks were a wake-up call, demonstrating to the United States and the world the increased vulnerability of citizens to deadly attacks on a large scale carried out by small groups of committed individuals. Commentators and government officials raised the specter of terrorists employing chemical, biological, or nuclear weapons. Defending against such catastrophic threats posed new challenges. Many nations have long had access to weapons of mass destruction, but, as they are also responsible for protecting civilian populations, they can presumably be deterred from using such weapons by threats of retaliation; non-state terrorist groups have no such constraints. And suicide bombers have shown that desperate individuals will sacrifice even their own lives to strike a blow for their cause. The potential threats seem limitless, and the vivid and horrifying images of September 11 made what had been previously unthinkable all too imaginable.

The United States' Response

The United States responded to the attacks by adopting what then-attorney general John Ashcroft called a "paradigm of prevention." He argued that it was not enough to capture terrorists after the fact, we must seek to prevent the next attack. To do so, Ashcroft argued, the government had to act aggressively against all who might pose a threat, in order to incapacitate them before they are able to act against us. Many were persuaded by this view, and it soon became conventional wisdom that the FBI and other law enforcement agencies had spent too much time investigating completed crimes and not enough time gathering intelligence to forestall future crimes. The charge is overstated—law enforcement has always been as interested in preventing and deterring crime before it happens as in catching criminals after the fact. And state and federal laws have long made it a crime to plan for or prepare to commit crimes, so there was never a need to wait until a bomb exploded to bring criminal charges. After the attacks of September 11, however, the notion that those bound to protect the nation had failed to "connect the dots" in advance led inexorably to the idea that the government must become "forward-leaning" in its approach to terrorism.

The impetus toward prevention is understandable. All other things being equal, preventing a terrorist act is preferable to responding after the fact—all the more so when the threats include weapons of mass destruction and the attackers are difficult to detect, willing to kill themselves, and seemingly unconstrained by any considerations of law, morality, or human dignity that we can recognize. There is nothing wrong with prevention itself as a motive or a strategy—think, for example, of preventive medicine. In the realm of ordinary criminal law enforcement, preventive policing, which emphasizes direct police involvement with communities to identify and solve potential problems before they lead to criminal conduct, is sensible, effective, and often more humane than imposing lengthy prison sentences. Thus, prevention is a perfectly acceptable goal in many contexts, and is surely permissible in counterterrorism.

Moreover, there are many ways to deter or prevent terrorism that pose little or no concerns from the standpoint of civil liberties. Airport metal detectors and X-ray machines are preventive measures, as are concrete barriers and increased security around government buildings and other vulnerable targets. More careful screening of individuals and cargo entering the country is also a preventive measure. Expanding and improving our ability to analyze and understand intelligence data may help identify and interdict threats before they can be carried out. Developing positive ties to communities and nations that might have individuals sympathetic to terrorist causes may simultaneously reduce the likelihood that such individuals will act on their sympathies and help to identify potential bad actors so that they can be monitored. Providing foreign aid to countries with dire economic and humanitarian needs may reduce the likelihood that extremists and terrorists will find fertile recruiting ground among desperate people. Many of these preventive measures are relatively uncontroversial, in large part because they do not necessitate substantial sacrifices with respect to liberty, privacy, or equality.

The Perils of Prevention

In the wake of 9/11, however, the United States did not limit itself to such responses. It also sought to employ the government's most coercive powers—the power to monitor, abduct, detain, interrogate, and even kill—in "preventive" fashion, using these tactics against individuals and groups based on speculation about what they might do rather than evidence about what they had done. When a democratic state deploys its harshest coercive measures based on speculative predictions about future behavior, it all too often sacrifices some of its most fundamental commitments to the rule of law. In the absence of a focus on objective conduct, for example, suspicion may be predicated on race, ethnicity, or religious affiliation, leading to discriminatory profiling. Because accurate predictions are so difficult, mistakes will be made, subjecting innocents to wrongful surveillance, detention, or worse. Fair process will be short-circuited, as it is difficult to square with predictive guesswork rather than objective assessments of fact.

Much of the Bush administration's "war on terror" was explicitly justified in preventive terms. He launched a war, the most extreme deployment of coercive force, against Iraq on preventive grounds. Iraq had neither attacked us nor threatened to attack us, but President Bush argued that Saddam Hussein might have weapons of mass destruction that he might at some point give to terrorists who might use them against us. It turned out that Saddam Hussein didn't have such weapons, and there was no evidence that he would have turned the weapons over to terrorists even if he had them—but using the preventive rationale, we declared war on pure (and baseless) speculation.

On similar preventive grounds, President Bush authorized the National Security Agency (NSA) to intercept millions of phone calls between persons suspected of being associated with al Qaeda abroad and individuals here at home, without judicial approval and in apparent contravention of a federal criminal law. He created secret prisons run by the CIA into which the United States "disappeared" suspected terrorists—abducting them, detaining them, and denying to the world that they were in U.S. custody. To get high-value suspects to talk, President Bush authorized the CIA to use cruel, inhuman, and degrading methods, and torture itself—including extended sleep deprivation, stress positions, slamming suspects into walls, and waterboarding (temporarily asphyxiating an individual by pouring water over a towel wrapped around his mouth and nose, creating the sensation of drowning). He authorized the CIA to kidnap other suspects and "render" them to security services in countries, Egypt and Syria among them, known for routinely using torture during interrogations. He opened a prison camp at Guantánamo Bay, where the military held more than 775 men, many without objective evidence that they were fighting against us. The president initially refused to acknowledge that they had any legal rights, much less access to a U.S. court to challenge the legality of their detention. He established "military commissions" in which military officers could try and execute terrorists for war crimes based on secret evidence that the defendant had no opportunity to see or rebut—and even on the basis of evidence obtained through torture. President Bush contended that he could authorize these and other actions as commander in chief even where Congress had made them illegal. And he insisted that the Geneva Conventions—international treaties governing the treatment of civilians and combatants in armed conflict—did not protect fighters for al Qaeda or the Taliban at all. All these measures were undertaken in the name of preventing another terrorist attack—and, indeed, by the end of President Bush's second term, no more terrorist attacks had been perpetrated on U.S. soil.

The President Retreats

Many of these measures proved highly controversial—and the president was never able to prove that they were, in fact, necessary to foil a follow-up terrorist attack. Indeed, by the time

President Barack Obama succeeded him, President Bush had been forced to retreat on many of these policies, without any apparent increase in terrorist attacks. In *Rasul v. Bush* (2004) and *Boumediene v. Bush* (2008), the Supreme Court rejected his contention that he could detain suspected terrorists at Guantánamo Bay indefinitely without any access to court to challenge their detentions, and ultimately ruled that not even the president and Congress acting together could deny court review to the detainees. In *Hamdan v. Rumsfeld* (2006), the Court declared that President Bush's military commissions were illegal under domestic law and the Geneva Conventions, dismissing the president's contention that the Conventions do not apply to the conflict with al Qaeda.

When a secret Justice Department memo authorizing waterboarding and other illegal interrogation tactics was leaked to the *Washington Post* in 2004, the administration quickly rescinded the memo as it apparently could not defend in public what it had done in secret. (As detailed in Chapter 4, however, the Justice Department continued to authorize illegal interrogation tactics in secret even after appearing to abandon them in public.) Congress, under the leadership of Senator John McCain, forbade the use of cruel, inhuman, and degrading treatment against all detainees. International condemnation of rendition to torture seems to have led the Bush administration to halt that practice, although the secrecy surrounding the program makes certainty difficult. After the NSA spying program's existence was disclosed, the president halted it until Congress amended the law to authorize electronic surveillance with greater oversight. And Congress added checks and balances to some of the most controversial PATRIOT Act provisions. Even after all these reforms were adopted, there were no further terrorist attacks on the United States, calling into question the administration's claims that the extreme measures it initially adopted were actually necessary for U.S. security.

President Obama — Continuity or Change ?

When President Obama took office in 2009, he introduced further reforms to bring our security policy in line with our commitments to liberty, equality, human dignity, and the rule of law. On his second day in office, he issued executive orders prohibiting the use of "enhanced interrogation techniques," the Bush administration's euphemism for the torture and cruel treatment that it had authorized. He ordered the closure of the CIA's secret prisons, and promised to close the prison camp at Guantánamo Bay within a year. Shortly thereafter, he ordered a temporary halt to military commissions at Guantánamo, appointed an interagency task force to review all Guantánamo cases, and released several previously secret Justice Department memos that had continued to authorize coercive interrogation tactics. Most important, President Obama sounded a very different overall theme on national security, arguing in a speech at the National Archives in May 2009 that the United States can and must defend itself within the confines of the rule of law and that our country will be stronger, not weaker, for doing so. Whereas President Bush had dismissed legal restrictions as an obstacle to be disregarded in the name of security, President Obama insisted that we must pursue security in ways that also preserve our liberty.

As is often the case, however, that goal proved easier to proclaim than to accomplish. Even when Obama's own party controlled both houses of Congress, legislators objected to moving any Guantánamo detainees inside U.S. borders, even if the detainees would be housed in the most secure facilities.

Congress repeatedly barred the president from spending any money to relocate Guantánamo detainees to the United States, effectively blocking his effort to close the camp—a goal everyone from former President Bush to Defense Secretary Robert Gates and former Defense Secretary Colin Powell agreed was desirable from a foreign policy standpoint. When Attorney General Eric Holder announced plans to try men accused of planning and facilitating the 9/11 attacks, including the alleged principal architect of the attack, Khalid Sheikh Mohammed, in a New York civilian courtroom, the plan was roundly criticized. Congress ultimately barred a civilian criminal trial, and Holder was forced to charge Khalid Sheikh Mohammed before a military commission in Guantánamo—an untested forum that may well cause many more complications than a civilian trial would have.

Meanwhile, President Obama continued some of his predecessor's controversial policies. He asserted the right to detain suspected al Qaeda and Taliban members without criminal trial. He invoked the "state secrets privilege" in several lawsuits seeking to hold U.S. officials accountable for unconstitutional and criminal conduct, including rendition to torture. He opposed court review of those detained at Bagram Air Force Base in Afghanistan, even though some of the detainees there, like many at Guantánamo, were captured in foreign lands far from any battlefield. He defended as constitutional a federal law that makes it a crime to advocate for human rights and peace if one does so in conjunction with a group designated as "terrorist"—even if the individual's purpose in doing so is to encourage the group to forgo violence and to pursue peaceful avenues for political change. His administration also opposed efforts to reform the USA PATRIOT Act to implement greater safeguards for Americans' privacy, and authorized the "targeted killing" of radical cleric Anwar al-Awlaki, a U.S. citizen far from any battlefield, on grounds that he was associated with al Qaeda and planning future attacks.

History confirms that sacrificing liberties in times of crisis is not a partisan issue. Republican president Abraham Lincoln, one of the most revered champions of equality and liberty in all of U.S. history, unilaterally suspended the writ of habeas corpus during the Civil War, thereby denying those detained by Union forces any access to court to challenge their detention. The Constitution grants the power to suspend habeas corpus to Congress, not the president, but Lincoln argued that the emergency justified his otherwise illegal action. President Franklin Delano Roosevelt, a progressive Democrat, was responsible for interning in camps some 120,000 people of Japanese descent during World War II, solely because of their Japanese ancestry. Some 70,000 of them were American citizens. None were individually found to pose a risk of espionage or treason. President Bill Clinton, a Democrat, supported and signed the Anti-Terrorism and Effective Death Penalty Act of 1996, a law that radically restricted habeas corpus review for all prisoners, criminalized speech as a form of "material support to terrorism," and established deportation for foreign nationals based on secret evidence that they had no opportunity to confront or rebut.

Does Sacrificing Liberty Increase Security?

Thus, history suggests that balancing liberty and security is no simple matter. Reasonable people will value liberty and security differently and therefore will be inclined to adopt different trade-offs between the two. Moreover, the very idea of "balance" is misleading; the values sought to be weighed against one another are incommensurable. How does one quantify the value of liberty, of privacy, or of equal treatment as measured against the costs of a terrorist attack?

More to the point, sacrificing rights often does not in fact increase security, and may make us less safe. When President Bush authorized torture, for example, he argued that his interrogators obtained information that they could not have learned using lawful, noncoercive interrogation tactics. But the CIA's own inspector general, reviewing the program, found no evidence that the tactics had resulted in information that could not have been gleaned through legal means. As Ali Soufan, a seasoned U.S. interrogator, argues in Part 2, developing rapport is a much more effective technique for obtaining reliable information. There is no conclusive evidence that coercive interrogation worked.

What we can and do know is that the strategy of coercive interrogation has entailed tremendous costs. The interrogation policy eventually led to the Abu Ghraib torture scandal, in which all the world saw graphic photographic evidence of the demeaning ways that U.S. soldiers treated Arab and Muslim detainees. Those revelations, in turn, provided a powerful recruiting tool for al Qaeda, as extremist websites prominently featured the images to stoke anti-American sentiment around the world. Polls suggested that, in short order, the United States went from being the object of the world's sympathy on the day after 9/11 to a country more widely resented than ever.

In addition, the desire to use evidence obtained by torture to hold terrorists accountable led the Bush administration to establish military commissions that fell drastically short of fundamental fairness guarantees. A fair trial cannot be based on evidence obtained through torture, period. Eventually, Congress reformed the commission rules to make clear that coerced confessions could not be used. But that, in turn, creates major obstacles to holding Guantánamo detainees accountable for their alleged wrongs. Once a defendant has been tortured, trying him becomes extremely difficult because fundamental rules of due process and fair play demand that the government not benefit in any way from information it learned through its torture, and it is often difficult or impossible to establish that none of the government's evidence is tainted.

Are We Safer?

Has the "war on terror" in general made us safer or more vulnerable? It is difficult to say. But there are reasons to doubt that many of the measures have been effective. According to the July 2007 National Intelligence Estimate, al Qaeda by that time had fully reconstituted itself in Pakistan's border regions. Terrorist attacks worldwide grew dramatically in frequency and lethality after 2001, with suicide bombings particularly on the rise. New terrorist groups, from al Qaeda in Iraq to the small groups of young men who bombed subways, buses, and commuter trains in London and Madrid, have multiplied. And only a small number of individuals have been convicted of engaging in or conspiring to engage in a terrorist act since 9/11.

Consider the measurable results from one of the most extensive domestic preventive campaigns conducted by the United States in the wake of 9/11. Using immigration law, the Bush administration after 9/11 called in 82,000 foreign nationals for fingerprinting, photographing, and "special registration" simply because they came from predominantly Arab or Muslim countries—on the theory that it might find a terrorist. It sought out another 8,000 young men from the same countries for more extensive FBI interviews, again based solely on the fact that they were young men who had come from predominantly Arab and Muslim countries. And immigration officials placed more than 5,000 foreign nationals, virtually all Arab or Muslim, in preventive detention in the first two years after 9/11, again in hopes that they would identify a terrorist. Yet *not one of these individuals stands convicted of a terrorist crime.* The government's record, in what is surely the largest campaign of ethnic profiling since the Japanese internment during World War II, is 0 for 95,000.

But how can we account for the fact that the United States has been free of a terrorist attack since 9/11? One cannot ultimately prove what combination of factors contributed to this fortunate result. Could it have been the military response in Afghanistan (notably not a "preventive war," but an act of self-defense)? Information obtained from lawful surveillance and interrogation? Information obtained from illegal surveillance and interrogation? Increased airport security measures? Increased spending on intelligence analysts, and increased coordination of intelligence agencies? The detention of suspected al Qaeda and Taliban fighters at Guantánamo and Bagram? All of the above? Some of the controversial preventive measures undertaken may have helped disrupt a terrorist attack, identify a potential terrorist, or deter someone from committing a terrorist act in the first place. We can never know for sure.

Debating Our Future

This is what makes the debates that this book seeks to foster so challenging. The competing values at stake are vital, but impossible to quantify. So much that we might want to know is unknowable. Yet we must nonetheless act—and judge our actions—in the face of this uncertainty. At the end of the day, the debates must be guided by an exploration of our fundamental values. As Senator McCain said in opposing the use of any cruel, inhuman, or degrading interrogation tactics against suspected terrorists, it's not about who they are; it's about who we are.

This volume highlights six issues for debate and presents competing views on each issue. It asks whether ethnic or religious profiling of Arabs and Muslims is constitutional or effective. It explores the question of when, if ever, a state official is justified in employing torture or otherwise illegal coercive interrogation tactics in an attempt to avert an impending disaster. It examines whether the United States is obliged to investigate and consider criminal prosecution of those who authorized torture for intelligence-gathering purposes. It examines the issue of preventive detention in the conflict with al Qaeda, asking whether the United States should be required to try al Qaeda members on criminal charges or release them, or whether it is appropriate to detain them in military custody without criminal charges. It uses the controversy over President Bush's authorization of sweeping warrantless electronic surveillance to assess the extent and limits of the president's executive power as commander in chief: Can the president ignore valid criminal laws if he believes they interfere with his execution of the war effort? Finally, the volume examines the question of what Christian Parenti calls the surveillance society: Has the United States sacrificed fundamental protections of privacy in essentially unwarranted ways or has it simply adapted to the increased threat that terrorism poses? Reasonable people can and have come down on opposite sides of all of these questions. They are hard questions without obvious answers. Your task is to explore their nuances, to recognize the difficult issues that lurk behind each of the debates, and to struggle, for yourself, with finding the answer that would reflect the United States at its best.

The United States and the world after 9/11 will never be the same. The attacks of that day have compelled us to confront new tensions between liberty and security for a decade. The debates will continue as the current generation of high school and college students grows up, graduates, and takes on the responsibility of leadership and stewardship that our democracy assigns to "We the People." It is all the more essential, therefore, that young people grapple with these issues. The debates covered here will continue to be defining issues for generations to come, and the choices we make will determine the kind of country—and world—we live in.

PART 1:
Profiling

Should law enforcement authorities engaged in counterterrorism pay special attention to Arab and/or Muslim men? The terrorist attacks of September 11, 2001, after all, were perpetrated by 19 men, all Arab Muslims. Al Qaeda, the organization that planned and coordinated the attacks, is composed almost entirely of Arab Muslims. Yet, the overwhelming majority of Arabs and Muslims have no connection to or affinity with terrorism, much less al Qaeda. In the wake of the terrorist attacks, the Bush administration rounded up thousands of Arab and Muslim immigrants and subjected them to preventive detention; none turned out to be terrorists. It also required all non-permanent resident immigrants from a list of predominantly Arab and Muslim countries to report to immigration offices for fingerprinting and interviews; again, none turned out to be terrorists. At the same time, most of those convicted since September 11 of supporting terrorist groups or attempting to engage in terrorist activity have been Arab and/or Muslim.

Is profiling on the basis of race, religion, or national origin consistent with the constitutional commitment to equal protection of the law? Is it effective? Is it good policy? K. Shiek Pal reviews the legal and policy landscape regarding profiling and identifies the costs and benefits of such tactics. Stuart Taylor argues that national-origin profiling is rational and necessary to preserve the safety of airline travel. David Harris contends that profiling is bad policing and that more effective and less costly ways are available to maintain our security without compromising principles of equality.

Racial Profiling as a Preemptive Security Measure After September 11: A Suggested Framework for Analysis

by K. Shiek Pal*

Abstract

The events of September 11, 2001, marked the beginning of the United States' renewed war on terror, and introduced racial and ethnic profiling as a tool in that struggle. This paper reviews the body of law and policy concerning profiling prior to and after September 11, and through statistical analysis the impact of preemptive profiling of individuals "of Middle Eastern appearance" to both society and those affected. The author draws attention to the collateral costs associated with broad population screening, and the disproportionate burden borne by the targeted group. Several courses of possible refinement and future research are developed.

Introduction

September 11, 2001, marked a tragic day in the nation's history and ended an era of American innocence and isolation. Americans were no longer absolutely secure in the belief that they were safe within their own borders, and similarly many Americans were no longer secure in the belief that race or ethnic origin would not deprive them of the same civil liberties afforded other Americans. The casualties of September 11 included a massive loss of innocent life, financial loses in the billions, and also the loss of the bedrock American value that race or ethnicity should not be a factor in predicting criminal behavior. This development undermines an extensive body of law and public policy enacted over decades that delineated the appropriate consideration of race in such areas as jury selection, profiling, and internment.[1]

The question of racial and ethnic profiling after September 11 focuses on two new issues: the preemptive use of profiling as a prophylactic against terrorism and the identification of the so-called "of Middle Eastern appearance" (OMEA) group as the primary target of such profiling.[2] The OMEA group is broadly defined to include any individuals whose physical characteristics could plausibly serve as a proxy for Arab, Middle Eastern, or Muslim affiliations.[3] This proxy is theoretically used to identify threats against the United States emanating from extremist Islamic terrorists and is premised on the idea that all prospective terrorists representing this threat will fall into this category.[4] However, the use of preemptive profiling is a dangerous proposition because it carries inherent costs that must be evaluated against the potential benefits that would be derived from a foiled terrorist plot. These costs include the proportion of OMEA citizens falsely identified as threats and the associated harms of social stigma and further deprivation of civil liberties through detention, intensive interrogation, and invasive searches. This paper assesses these social costs as a means of evaluating the appropriate role of profiling under the current federal guidelines.

Preemption

Preemption is controversial because it involves morally ambiguous questions of acceptable loss and calculated risk. However, in a global society increasingly susceptible to nontraditional forms of devastating attacks oriented at amassing massive casualties, preemption offers an inevitable and effective method of protection. Categorically discounting preemption compromises a state's ability to defend its citizens against enemies who do not adhere to similarly defined boundaries, and therefore preemption appears to be an inevitable future policy decision. The distinction between preemption and prevention turns on immediacy—preemption employs various tools to terminate a perceived threat prior to its effectuation, whereas prevention takes a less aggressive and more protracted approach to create an environment where such threats are less likely. Preemption becomes necessary because prevention is not a viable option in situations where the harm is imminent and there is insufficient time to implement a more comprehensive response.[5] The tools of preemption are more controversial than those of prevention because of the greater associated risks and costs. One such preemptive tool employed by authorities in the war against terrorism is racial profiling.

Preemption Through Racial Profiling

The concept of racial profiling—attributing a predisposition for certain behavior to an individual's racial or ethnic heritage—arouses impassioned debate and moral outrage because it necessarily implicates a belief that race determines conduct in some discernable part.[6] This notion fundamentally contradicts cherished bedrock values of equality in the American democratic system, and the Associated Press quoted President Bill Clinton's description of profiling as "a morally indefensible, deeply corrosive practice." However, in a world where any incremental advantage in winning a war against terrorism must be considered, there must be room to incorporate the benefits of preemptive profiling if it sufficiently advances the cause of security. The controversy arises when entire classes of people are treated as suspects based merely and solely on their racial or ethnic heritage. This type of race-based assumption harkens back to periods of American history when discriminatory laws and policies resulted in a stratified citizenship wherein people were denied rights and liberties because of the color of their skin. Considering the costs borne by the targeted group on behalf of the overall society is important in evaluating the actual preemptive mechanism used to screen the group because of the legal, social, and philosophical principles that argue for equal treatment between races, with limited narrow exceptions.

Defining the Problem

Proponents of profiling as a means of preempting terrorism point to the demographic commonalities of the September 11 hijackers, who were uniformly Muslim males of a certain age and primarily of Saudi origin.[7] The basic argument of these proponents is that, given these commonalities, it is ineffective to allocate scarce resources towards screening passengers outside this defined group, particularly when the process of randomized searches results in very young children or elderly women being selected for such scrutiny.[8] By noting that a broadly disseminated threat is emanating from a specific "identifiable" group (i.e., Muslim terrorists), those in favor of such profiling distinguish the measures they endorse from a mere assumption of criminality based on race.[9] While it is true that the threat effectuated on September 11 can be attributed to a group of men sharing some identifiable characteristics, it is equally true that there are also additional, less easily discernable factors that distinguish this particular subset of Muslim men from all those that would be captured under a more targeted screening process focusing on the general profile (young Muslim men of Middle Eastern appearance.) These additional factors include religious extremism, political ideology, and adherence to a socioreligious cultural war known as a jihad.[10] Thus the fundamental problem with a preemptive profiling system using the OMEA standard is that this does not reflect these salient additional factors and therefore improperly captures far more innocent people than intended.

DOJ Guidelines on Racial Profiling

The U.S. Department of Justice has issued guidelines on racial profiling that prevent the use of race in routine domestic investigative procedures but allow for particularized suspect descriptions incorporating racial characteristics.[11] The guidelines state that "general enforcement responsibilities should be carried out without any regard to race or ethnicity,"[12] and that "stereotyping certain races as having a greater propensity to commit crimes is absolutely prohibited."[13] These provisions guard against the most common notions of racial profiling, such as discriminatory traffic stops or targeted searches of minorities. However, these guidelines do not completely constrain the use of racial/ethnic profiling in combating terrorism insofar as there is substantial latitude for national security applications.[14] Specifically, the guidelines use contradictory language and examples in delineating the scope of permissible racial profiling in the war on terror. Compare the following excerpts from the guidelines:

> In investigating or preventing threats to national security or other catastrophic events (including the performance of duties

related to air transportation security), or in enforcing laws protecting the integrity of the nation's borders, federal law enforcement officers may not consider race or ethnicity except to the extent permitted by the Constitution and laws of the United States.[15]

Given the incalculably high stakes involved in such investigations, federal law enforcement officers who are protecting national security or preventing catastrophic events (as well as airport security screeners) may consider race, ethnicity, alienage, and other relevant factors.[16]

Because terrorist organizations might aim to engage in unexpected acts of catastrophic violence in any available part of the country (indeed, in multiple places simultaneously, if possible), there can be no expectation that the information must be specific to a particular locale or even to a particular identified scheme.[17]

This latter excerpt carves out an exceptionally broad set of circumstances wherein the precautions enunciated in the first excerpt do not seem to apply. The elasticity in defining national security exceptions to the general prohibition against racial profiling creates an ambiguous environment without clear delineations of appropriate and inappropriate behavior. The danger identified by the Bush administration, and that which the administration sought to foreclose by issuing these guidelines, is that the unchecked use of racial profiling would completely destabilize the notions of transparent authority, accountability, and equality for many racial and ethnic minorities.[18] However, the lack of precise language in determining the extent to which such profiling may be applied in certain limited (but again, not clearly defined) situations results in an ongoing threat of racial profiling being used in an abusive manner against targeted groups.

The inherent inconsistency in the terms and conditions presented in these guidelines poses a problem for law enforcement agents, civil rights activists, legal theorists, and targeted minorities because it allows virtually unregulated profiling to occur under the exception for national security. The weakness of the guidelines and the glaring loopholes contribute to the opaque nature of the discussion of preemptive profiling. Evaluating the social costs of profiling and reconsidering the guidelines through the lens of those bearing these costs allow for a more comprehensive analysis of what measures are needed to effectively implement any form of racial consideration.

The Costs of Racial Profiling . . . and the Costs of Not Racially Profiling

In evaluating the costs and benefits of preemptive racial profiling in a security context, a comprehensive understanding of each of the potential outcomes for every person identified as being part of the suspect class and subjected to profiling is essential. An analysis of the probabilities of each outcome given certain factors provides a basis to evaluate whether the costs outweigh the benefits. But as discussed below, there is ample room for subjective weighting of the various outcomes, and therefore a clear quantifiable answer may not be feasible. The process by which the weighting takes place may ultimately be more instructive.

In considering the probabilities of how preemptive racial profiling will affect both security and civil rights, two factors must be incorporated into the analysis—the accuracy of the screen used in the profiling process, and the actual correlation between race and criminality (i.e., the percentage of people in the profiled group who are actually terrorists).[19] Each factor has two possible outcomes, positive and negative. Assume *arguendo* an extremely exaggerated hypothetical case wherein one out of every ten thousand Middle Eastern Arabs is actually a terrorist (0.0001 percent) and that an extraordinarily effective screening mechanism is developed (incorporating racial profiling) that is 98 percent accurate;[20] multiplying out the possibilities produces four potential outcomes for each person subjected to the screen, as displayed in Table 1.

Table 1. Projections of Terrorists and Non-Terrorist Identified

	Terrorist	Not Terrorist	Total
Positive	.98	199.98	200.96
Negative	.02	9799.02	9799.04
Total	1	9.999	10.000

These results indicate that 98 percent of actual terrorists will be identified as such, and that only 2 percent of innocent Arab passengers will be falsely identified as terrorists. The respective probabilities of falling into each category are displayed in Table 2.

Table 2. Possible Projections of True and False Positives and Negatives

Category	Description	Probability of Occurrence
True Positive	Actual terrorist identified as such	0.000098
False Positive	Innocent passenger identified as terrorist	0.019998
True Negative	Innocent passenger identified as such	0.979902
False Negative	Actual terrorist identified as innocent	0.000002

The correlation numbers used are extremely exaggerated given the overall global population of people meeting the basic

OMEA definition and the relatively small subgroup of terrorist extremists. But as demonstrated in Table 2, these numbers still produce an extremely high number of false positives—ten thousand false positives for every false negative.

The Trade-off in Errors—Designing a Better System

The purpose of this type of analysis is to measure the accuracy of a screening system as depicted by the relative proportions of the type I and type II errors generated by it. The practical comparison is between false positives (type I errors) and true positives, i.e., how many innocent people are caught up in the additional security measures for each true terrorist actually apprehended. But the comparison that best illuminates the possibilities for improving the system is between the false positives and false negatives (type II errors). Generally, American society prefers false negatives to false positives.[21] But this preference cannot be sustained in the context of terrorism because of the devastating consequences of events such as September 11. Therefore finding the appropriate balance between the two types of errors is essential.

Given the criminal disposition of the terrorist, there are no associated harms inherent in the true positive category—the threat is successfully identified and controlled. However, there are substantial associated harms with the false negatives—those terrorists that slip through the system and ultimately engage in criminal behavior with massive casualties. Thus an appropriate comparison might be between the two groups with the greatest associated harms—the harms borne by the false positives in order to minimize the potential harms caused by the false negatives. Thus the crux of the deliberation is the balance between false positives and false negatives, and how each of these outcomes is weighed. The remainder of this paper focuses on how to consider and derive this balance.

THE ASSOCIATED COSTS AND EFFECTS—WHAT MATTERS MORE?

One false negative is not worth the same amount as one false positive because the false negative left unto itself will lead to massive casualties, whereas the false positive may lead to a weakened state of support or security among the wider racial/ethnic pool from which the false positive is drawn but will not produce greater casualties in and of itself. In evaluating false positives, a distinction must be made between casualties and other harm, so that the erroneous assumption that false positives create no harm is not perpetuated. Rather the harm to false positives must be carefully considered and balanced as a cost against the benefits to be derived from minimizing the false negatives.

False positives (innocent travelers who are identified as risks) can face a range of consequences, depending on the severity of the misidentification, contextual security concerns, and length of time required to rectify the false identification. However, even the most onerous and severe of these outcomes cannot rationally be equated to the loss of life resulting from a false negative. At the same time, these costs can be extremely painful and burdensome for those who have to bear them and cannot be minimized.

But substantial false positives will necessarily accompany each true positive and any false negatives. Recalibrating the screening process to reduce the false negatives correspondingly increases the number of false positives. Finding the appropriate and ideal balance between the two extremes is the challenge in devising such a system. Further complicating this calibration is the political impossibility of acknowledging the necessity of incurring any false positives or false negatives to each respective constituency, and therefore this is a calculation that must be sheltered from public scrutiny because the reality of each outcome is socially repugnant.

But the overwhelming numbers of false positives bear the costs of such a system, therefore these costs need to be carefully evaluated. The false positives here are the innocent travelers who are eyed with suspicion, or perhaps removed from a flight because their ethnic appearance causes distress among other "non-OMEA" passengers, such as reported by the IndUS newswire. In a more extreme case, a false positive can be placed on a no-fly list or detained for a lengthy period due to mistaken identity, irregularities in immigration status, or outstanding questions about social connections or affiliations.[22] For the false positives, the intensity of their experience is compounded by the lack of distinction between true and false positives in the eyes of those witnessing the screening process. These are just some of the costs of a preemptive system of racial profiling—others are less tangible and include the effects on the psyche, security, and comfort of American citizens who fall, rightly or wrongly, into the OMEA pool. These are the costs that need to be examined and weighed.

A false negative (an actual terrorist that is not identified as such) carries the most substantial harm because a consummated terrorist act could result in the loss of hundreds or thousands of innocent lives. The impossibility of truly quantifying the impact of such losses makes potential false negatives devastating to society and makes the overall tolerance for such false negatives nearly zero, irrespective of the actual number of casualties for a given incident. The purpose in considering, let alone implementing, a system of preemptive racial profiling is precisely to address the heightened intolerance for such casualties. In the aftermath of September 11, there was popular rhetoric arguing that in a time of war, citizens should be willing to sacrifice their own civil liberties for the sake of national security, but interestingly, this rhetoric was not being generated by the same segments of society that would have to bear the requisite costs or make those sacrifices.[23]

Therefore the balancing must turn on properly valuing the false positives. Given the premium placed on saving innocent lives, there is a legitimate question as to whether there are any limits on what an acceptable cost would be for a mechanism to prevent such losses. However, the system is not fail-proof, and therefore it seems logical that there should be some cap on the cost for a system that is less than 100 percent effective. It is even more so when the costs are borne disproportionately by one constituency although the benefits are shared by all. Thus, the key consideration in evaluating preemptive profiling is how to weigh the false positives because that is where the social costs of the program will be borne.

The effects of a false positive identification carry associated costs that have prolonged effects. These costs range from the pervasive awareness of a being in an inferior tier of citizenship, to a loss of faith in the security and identity of an America where equality is not predicated on race, and a lingering bitterness that corrupts the integration of different races and ethnicities into a unified society. This type of long-term effect magnifies the weight that needs to be attributed to the costs of false positives. An apt comparison might be to death row prisoners who are acquitted before execution—they still bear the costs of time served, emotional trauma, social stigma, and resentment against the system. These costs are not alleviated by the eventual acquittal.

Further complicating the current situation is the fact that the compromised civil rights are not limited to one isolated individual, but rather an entire class of people broadly (and vaguely) defined to be "of Middle Eastern appearance," which in practice encompasses not only those of Arab descent, but also South Asians, Mediterranean peoples, some Latinos, and generally "brown" people.[24] The fundamental problem with the OMEA description is that the particularized threat against America comes not from a narrow ethnic group, but rather an extreme subset of one of the world's major religions—one that has a sizable following in this country.[25] The OMEA description is not well designed to serve in a future prophylactic capacity but rather is premised entirely upon some selected characteristics of the group of terrorists who successfully attacked America on 11 September 2001.[26] The danger of relying on this description is that the source of the threat is broader than that narrow group, and as previously noted, the description itself is vague and overbroad. Thus, the OMEA description is simultaneously overbroad and too narrow by failing to capture Muslim extremists from other ethnicities but including non-Muslim, non-Arab, non-extremist people, as well as the vast majority of peaceful, law-abiding Arab Muslims.

Our society has historically rejected state conduct that broadly targets an entire class of people based on their appearance, but here that appearance seems to have a stronger predictive value (although still miniscule) than in other contexts.[27] Similar arguments and considerations have previously been made in support of racial profiling in other security contexts, for example, in drug trafficking or urban street crime.[28] Courts have generally disallowed or severely limited the use of such tactics because of the lack of evidence of a reliable predictive value based on race or ethnicity, as weighed against the substantial intrusion upon civil liberties embodied by these types of policing measures.[29] However, the use of racial profiling to prevent terrorism may be distinguishable from these other cases because of the ethnopolitical and religious foundations of the threat against America.[30] As previously discussed, the more nuanced argument considers the use of race or ethnicity in the terrorism context as an example of "preemptive suspect description" based on an articulated threat rather than traditional profiling. However, the DOJ guidelines on racial profiling outline a slightly more stringent standard for this approach by noting that there must be an explicit, temporally limited threat in order to look for a suspect.[31]

But even within the hypothetical situation outlined in the guidelines, there is sufficient ambiguity to complicate the use of profiling in a controlled and limited manner. For example, there are no restrictions on how specific information must be or how imminent a threat must be before profiling can be appropriately used. The guidelines cite an example of a credible threat against an airline from a terrorist organization in "the next week" and use this threat to justify an undefined period within which the strict prohibitions on racial profiling can be bent or suspended.[32] This is a critical point to understand the difficulties of instituting such a program because the ambiguity of the terms combined with the elasticity of the loophole create a situation where civil rights can be substantially diverted for an extended period without proper oversight or accountability—the only requirement is a "credible threat" against national security, and in the contemporary global war on terror, such threats are frequent.

Given the historical burdens of racial prejudice and discrimination in this country, there should be a clearly compelling state reason to employ profiling tactics, and those tactics should be narrowly constructed so as to minimize the costs borne by the profiled group in terms of the compromise that members of that group must make in their civil liberties. The DOJ guidelines meet the compelling reason by noting that a credible threat is required, but by failing to precisely outline the minimal thresholds, the guidelines are not narrowly tailored enough to be acceptable. There are no limits within the guidelines that would restrict the use of profiling if even a minimal argument can be mounted, as evidenced in the previous example. This results in undue costs being borne by the target group, which in this case would be the OMEA group—and more specifically the false positives within the OMEA group.

Balancing the Costs of Racial Profiling

Part of these costs on OMEA passengers come in the insecurity of knowing that there are no clear parameters for the circumstances under which profiling can be instituted. This undermines the ability of OMEA citizens to be secure in their faith in the protections of the system because the decisions as to when the conditions are appropriate for profiling are somewhat arbitrary. This insecurity is a substantial cost because it is only borne by the targeted group, as opposed to all citizens broadly or those engaging in illicit conduct. The costs of profiling also bear a linear relationship to the effectiveness of the profiling system, insofar as the most minimal forms of profiling may not make a discernible difference to the overall effectiveness of the security process, whereas greater degrees of profiling may yield substantial results. Thus the challenge is to determine the equilibrium point between the costs and the effectiveness of profiling.

Balancing more onerous forms of profiling against the benefits of apprehending a terrorist implicate the mathematical calculations of the likelihood of successfully achieving a true positive. Here the probability analysis indicates a far greater likelihood of yielding false positives than true positives, which means that in sheer numbers there will be far more innocent OMEA members subjugated to the higher scrutiny (and consequently greater harm) than there will be actual terrorists apprehended. However, it also seems probable that these measures will be much more valuable in preventing or impeding terrorists, and offer greater payouts from a utilitarian perspective. Thus in order to implement a screening system that is even moderately effective, it seems clear that the costs borne by the OMEA group will be at least at the intermediate level discussed above, if not greater. Any system that requires a lower level of intrusion will not be effective.

The burden placed on all OMEA members will need to be balanced against the benefits of preventing even a single terrorist activity. Because of the difficulty in quantifying the value of a life as compared to varying degrees of harm associated with the practical costs of racial profiling, there is not a clear or easy answer as to whether the potential benefits justify these costs. Theoretically, there can be another level of analysis that attempts to quantify not just the value of a saved life against the infringement of civil rights, but seeks to determine *how many* lives must be saved in order to impose the highest level of scrutiny. It may be difficult to argue that saving one solitary life justifies the costs borne by an entire group of citizens, but it is equally difficult to enunciate a rationale by which to measure how many lives are necessary to balance that equation.

On the other hand, if an innocent life is lost in a terrorist act, it is extremely difficult to explain to the victim's family that there were additional screening measures which could have been taken and that might have reduced the likelihood of that act by 0.0001 percent, but that those measures were not taken because the costs imposed upon the OMEA class were not deemed to be proportionate. In that type of scenario, a plausible argument can be made that no cost is too great and no imposition unwarranted if it furthers the objectives of national security and contributes to the safety of innocent civilians. It is impossible to articulate to the family of a victim the rationale that the life of their loved one was not valuable enough to outweigh the civil rights of another group. At that point, lives and rights become two separate and unrelated issues, and the notion of balancing them in an equation seems devoid of human emotion.

Ultimately, the political decision determining which side of this balance should be given preference will depend entirely on which constituency the authorities would prefer to answer to—the OMEA population or those who lose loved ones in a terrorist act that could *perhaps* have been made more difficult by imposing these measures. This decision necessarily requires consideration of earlier historical lessons, but also turns significantly on the nature of a new modern threat that perhaps undermines the traditional analysis of balancing rights and lives because the perpetrators themselves devalue lives (including their own) to such a great degree. Perhaps the degree of danger we face as a society, and the level of commitment on the part of those who threaten us, requires addressing our fundamental values as a nation in order to defend ourselves. But if so, then the question of how far we are willing to deviate from our values, and for how long, must be answered in the interests of preserving the continuity and integrity of our most cherished freedoms.

Conclusion

There is no right answer as to whether the potential payoffs of racial profiling justify its costs, but the key to making that determination is posing the right questions such that an informed decision can be made. Here, those questions turn on the measurement and balancing of the costs and benefits borne by each of the affected parties. This analysis indicates that even the most highly developed profiling system will still result in massive amounts of false positives for each true positive. But the false positives in this case may be an acceptable cost given the enormous benefit of identifying the true positives and preventing false negatives. An alternative approach is to broaden the screening process by incorporating other nonracial factors into the process such that race is only one measure. These more informative measures can include travel patterns, professional or familial connections, criminal records, financial history, and affiliations with other groups/individuals. Race can be an effective element in such a portfolio of criteria, and the other factors can reduce the false positives. In fact, race can even be used as an *exclusionary* factor to draw conclusions about individual passengers whose overall passenger profile may otherwise arouse suspicion. For example, computerized data indicating frequent travel between Pakistan and the United States is a trigger for further scrutiny, but can be partially mitigated if racial data supports family connections that would explain regular visits. This additional information can then help distinguish those cases that require further investigation from benign ones.

The costs of racial profiling realized upon the false positives cannot be diminished or minimized in pursuit of a most critical goal, namely eliminating the false negatives. The key is striking a balance on a macro level that ensures the overall integrity of the system for all parties. There will always be individual cases of false positives, but as long as the system works on the group level, that might be an acceptable and necessary consequence. But creating a system that fails to incorporate some measures to defend the rights of the OMEA group is inappropriate because it does not consider the burden of the false positives and is therefore not balanced. To make this system work, at the very least the OMEA definition must be redrawn more precisely, and race should only be one of several contributing factors—not a dangerously determinative one. The tremendous costs associated with racial profiling and the disproportionate burden of these costs on the false positives appear to outweigh the incremental security benefits. Therefore, notwithstanding the fact that there could be some marginal improvement in security, ultimately the social costs of a preemptive profiling system are not sustainable, and the system cannot be recommended without the aforementioned adjustments.

ENDNOTES

1. Randall Kennedy, *Race, Crime & the Law* (New York: Pantheon Books, 1997), 3–28, 174–175.

2. John Derbyshire, "At First Glance: Racial Profiling, Burning Hotter," *National Review Online*, October 5, 2001, http://www.nationalreview.com/derbyshire/derbyshire100501.shtml.

3. *Ibid.*

4. *Ibid.*

5. A related argument has been raised in the context of using torture under similar circumstances. Alan M. Dershowitz, "Tortured Reasoning," in *Torture: A Collection*, ed. Sanford Levinson (New York: Oxford University Press, 2004), 258–259. (Dershowitz discusses the hypothetical case of a suspect tortured to reveal the location of a "ticking bomb" that would otherwise harm hundreds of civilians.)

6. Department of Justice (DOJ), "Fact Sheet on Racial Profiling," http://www.usdoj.gov/opa/pr/2003/June/racial_profiling_fact_sheet.pdf.

7. Michael A. Smerconish, *Flying Blind* (Philadelphia: Running Press, 2004), 14–18.

8. *Ibid.*, 51–55.

9. *Ibid.*, 58–60.

10. *Ibid.*, 38.

11. DOJ, "Fact Sheet on Racial Profiling," 6. There is an open question as to the extent to which these guidelines are binding upon law enforcement officers or can actually be enforced. For the purposes of this analysis, it is assumed *arguendo* that these guidelines will be implemented and enforced as written. The jurisprudential basis for the guidelines is enunciated in *Brown v. Oneonta*, 221 F.3d 329, 337–338 (2d Cir. 2000). In *Oneonta*, a woman was assaulted in her home and only managed to see the forearm of her assailant. In her description to the police, she noted that the assailant was a Black male with a cut on his forearm. The police then canvassed the town for all Black males, and given that the town was predominantly White, the canvass resulted in a majority of the town's Black population being questioned. The court held that the use of race in this manner was not illegal because it was based on an eyewitness account of the actual perpetrator and was particularized to the suspect (through the description of the forearm cut) and because the search was geographically and temporally limited in scope. The court specifically noted that even though the police canvass resulted in a large number of Black men being questioned, the racial commonality of these men was directly and relevantly associated with the victim's eyewitness account. Most importantly, this use of race does not infer any type of generalized tendencies or greater proclivities for criminal behavior to Black men, but rather uses race only as a means of identifying one specific suspect. The manner in which the information was obtained, and the subsequent canvass conducted, did not incorporate any broad generalizations of criminality upon Black men but rather

was oriented to collecting the most salient information required to make a timely arrest.

12. DOJ, "Fact Sheet on Racial Profiling," 2.

13. *Ibid.*, 3.

14. *Ibid.*, 5-6.

15. *Ibid.*, 5.

16. *Ibid.*, 5.

17. *Ibid.*, 5.

18. *Ibid.*, 1 (comments from Attorney General John Ashcroft, 28 February 2002).

19. There is another complicating factor in this particular case that has been excluded from the analysis for illustrative purposes. This factor is the lack of clarity inherent in the OMEA designation. Theoretically, the profile relied upon to screen out potential Islamic terrorists is Arab or Middle Eastern males, between the ages of eighteen and fifty, who are Muslim. But using visual assessments will not always capture religious affiliation and will be over-inclusive by capturing other ethnicities that are frequently mistaken for Arab, such as South Asians and other Mediterranean peoples. Moreover, examining basic passport data will still lead to errors in identification along religious lines and possibly even ethnic lines. These inherent problems with this particular profile make it particularly problematic in terms of generating excessive false positives, but for the purposes of illustration, the discussion of analysis above assumes an accurate ethnic identification and then conducts the rest of the analysis from that assumption.

20. Note that for illustrative purposes, extreme numbers were deliberately used in these hypothetical calculations. The realistic numbers would be far more conservative, and accordingly the results of this analysis would be much more dramatic. The hypothetical numbers portray the best-case scenario—in actuality the percentage of actual terrorists is much lower and screening mechanisms are far less reliable. Thus the number of false positives would be much greater.

21. Paul Rosenzweig, "Civil Liberty and the Response to Terrorism," *Duquesne Law Review* 42 (2004): 663, 680 (citing *Winship,* 397 U.S. 357, 372 (1970)).

22. American Civil Liberties Union of Northern California (ACLUNC), "Caught In the Backlash: Arshad Chowdhury," http://www.aclunc. org/911/backlash/chowdhury.html.

23. Compare Peggy Noonan, "Profiles Encouraged," *Wall Street Journal*, 19 October 2001, http://www.peggynoonan.com/article.php?article=72 (editorial advocating that citizens be proactive when seeing "mid-eastern looking" men acting in "suspicious" manners) with Raywat Deonandian, "Profile This!" http://podium.deonandian.com/profiling. html.

24. Derbyshire.

25. *Ibid.*

26. *Ibid.*

27. Mathias Risse and Richard Zeckhauser, "Racial Profiling" *Philosophy & Public Affairs* 32 (2004):132.

28. Kennedy, 13.

29. *Ibid.*, 147.

30. Smerconish, 14–19.

31. DOJ, "Fact Sheet on Racial Profiling," 4.

32. *Ibid.*, 6.

***K. Shiek Pal** is an attorney in Washington, D.C., with degrees from Trinity College, Boston University, Harvard, and Georgetown. He has worked in the private and public sectors, including the U.S. Department of Justice and the District of Columbia Department of Education.

Pal, K. Shiek. 2005. Racial profiling as a preemptive security measure after September 11: A suggested framework for analysis," *Kennedy School Review* 6: 119–129.

Used by Permission.

Politically Incorrect Profiling: A Matter of Life or Death

by Stuart Taylor, Jr.*

What would happen if another 19 well-trained Al Qaeda terrorists, this time with 19 bombs in their bags, tried to board 19
airliners over the next 19 months? Many would probably succeed,
blowing up lots of planes and thousands of people, if the forces
of head-in-the-sand political correctness prevail—as they did
before September 11—in blocking use of national origin as a factor in deciding which passengers' bags to search with extra care.

But a well-designed profiling system might well catch all 19.
Such a system would not be race-based; indeed, most Arab-
Americans would not fit the profile. It would factor in suspicious
behavior, along with national origin, gender, and age. It could
spread the burden by selecting at least one white (or black, or
Asian) passenger to be searched for every Middle Easterner so
selected. And it should be done politely and respectfully.

We have no good alternative. For the foreseeable future, the
shortage of high-tech bomb-detection machines and the long
delays required to search luggage by hand will make it impossible to effectively screen more than a small percentage of checked
bags. The only real protection is to make national origin a key
factor in choosing those bags. Otherwise, federalizing airport
security and confiscating toenail clippers will be futile gestures.

I revisit this issue in part because research since my September 22 column reinforces my conviction that national-origin profiling may be the only way (in the short term) to avoid hundreds or thousands of deaths. At the same time, critics have persuaded me that the "racial" profiling of "Arab-looking" people that I previously advocated would be less effective than profiling based on apparent origin in any of the nations known to be exporters of anti-American terrorism—not only nations in the Arab world, but also most, or all, of the nations in the Muslim world. Millions of Arab-Americans would not fit the profile because their American roots would be apparent—from their accents and speech patterns—to trained security screeners.

We have heard a great deal about the hurt feelings of Middle Eastern passengers who have been searched and (in some cases) rudely treated on flights or unjustifiably ejected from airliners. We have heard far less about the dangers of not searching. The reason is that "large and important parts of the American news media practice a virulent form of political correctness that is indistinguishable from censorship," in the words of Richard Cohen, the mostly liberal *Washington Post* columnist.

Opponents of national-origin profiling claim it would be more effective to focus solely on suspicious behavior. They are wrong. Competent terrorists know how to avoid the suspicious- behavior trap. They are not likely to buy one-way tickets the next time. Or to pay in cash. Or to fly from Afghanistan to Pakistan to New York. Or to hang around airport security checkpoints with video cameras. These people are not stupid.

The hardest thing to hide if you are an Islamic terrorist is your Islamic-world origin, as evinced by speech patterns, facial characteristics, skin color, or (to a lesser extent) dress and travel documents. Sure, there is always the risk that the next attack will come from another homegrown Timothy McVeigh, or a Swedish Girl Scout, or (more likely) a mush-headed leftist French coed recruited by Al Qaeda. But there are a lot more Islamic terrorists than there are Timothy McVeighs. And not many people from outside the Islamic world appear eager to volunteer for suicide missions. Many Arab-Americans—if not their purported leaders—now seem to understand this. In a *Detroit Free Press* poll of 527 local Arab-Americans, 61 percent supported extra scrutiny of people with Middle Eastern features or accents.

Political pressure from Arab-American and liberal groups spurred the Clinton and Bush Administrations to bar use of national origin as a profiling component before September 11. In 1996, President Clinton put Vice President Al Gore in charge of a White House commission to recommend improvements in airliner security. But from the start, according to *The Boston Globe*, "debate over the program focused on civil liberties, not effectiveness." The Gore commission declared, "No profile should contain or be based on . . . race, religion, or national origin." Accordingly, the Federal Aviation Administration, in unveiling its Computer-Assisted Passenger Screening program, stressed that the Justice Department's Civil Rights Division—an ultraliberal bastion—had certified that the CAPS criteria "do not consider passengers' race, color, national or ethnic origin, religion, or gender," or even "names or modes of dress." That left few criteria for flagging possible terrorists other than reservation histories—as any competent terrorist would have known.

The FAA bent even further to avoid offending hypersensitive passengers by restricting CAPS to the checked baggage—not the carry-ons or persons—of passengers whose papers the computers flagged as suspicious. European nations and Israel, by contrast, have long subjected those who fit their profiles to questioning and manual searches. And Israel's El Al has shut out terrorists since 1968.

The politically correct approach to profiling achieved its goal of minimizing complaints, which plunged from 78 in 1997 to 11 in 1998, 13 in 1999, and 10 last year, according to Transportation Department data. It did not work so well at preventing mass murder. On September 11, the CAPS system flagged only six of the 19 Middle Eastern hijackers for extra scrutiny, which was apparently confined to the bags of the two who checked luggage. None of the 19 men or their carry-ons appear to have been individually searched. And the FAA's 1999 decision to seal CAPS off from all law enforcement databases—after complaints from liberal groups that criminal records were error-prone—may help explain why the FBI had not told the FAA that two of the 19 were on its watch list of suspected terrorists.

It's unclear whether national-origin profiling would have prevented the hijackings, in part because FAA rules did not bar small knives—although some airlines have suggested that they would have confiscated any box cutters they detected. But politically correct profiling virtually guaranteed that the hijackers' weapons would go undetected.

The Bush Administration's profiling policy, if any, is cloaked in politically cowardly and dangerous ambiguity. The FAA and Attorney General John D. Ashcroft have implied opposition to national-origin profiling, even as Ashcroft's subordinates have detained with minimal explanation more than 1,000 people, mostly Middle Easterners against whom there appears to be scant evidence of terrorist activity. The Administration should have the courage to preach what it practices.

Some arguments repeatedly advanced by opponents of national-origin profiling illustrate the weakness of their logic:

You are suggesting that all Middle Easterners are terrorists. Nonsense. Obviously, only a minuscule number are terrorists. But any passenger might be a terrorist. That's why we all go through security screening. The logic of profiling is to identify for more-careful screening those small groups who, based on historical experience, seem much more likely than others to include suicide bombers (or just bombers). History tells us that all 19 of the September 11 suicide bombers, and most or all other terrorists known to have murdered planeloads of people have been Middle Eastern men. Millions of others clamor to join this jihad.

What about all the white male American terrorists? The list is not long: Timothy McVeigh, Ted Kaczynski, a handful of anti-abortion extremists, a few others. In all, they have killed fewer than 200 people—less than 5 percent of the number killed on September 11 alone, not to mention the more than 600 Americans and thousands of others previously killed (mostly overseas) by Middle Eastern terrorists.

Profiling will foster racist hysteria. The opposite is more likely. The disgraceful ejections of Middle Easterners from airliners since September 11 were spurred less by racism than by well-founded fears of the ease with which weapons could be smuggled aboard. The best way to prevent such episodes is to give crews and passengers confidence that any would-be terrorists have been carefully searched.

Once you start profiling, there's no stopping point. Yes, there is. The police's stopping of people for "driving while black," for example, has rightly been discredited because the costs—both to those searched and to the long-term interests of law enforcement—far exceed any benefits. Stopping people for "driving while Arab" would be similarly unwarranted. Flying while Middle Eastern poses a dramatically different cost-benefit calculus.

If considered unblinkingly, this is not a close call. It has nothing to do with prejudice. It is a matter of life or death.

*Stuart Taylor, Jr., is a journalist who has written regularly for the *National Journal*, *Newsweek*, and the *New York Times*. He is a graduate of Harvard Law School and a Nonresident Senior Fellow at the Brookings Institution.

Taylor, Stuart. 2001. Politically incorrect profiling: A matter of life or death. *National Journal*, November 3.

Reprinted with permission from National Journal, November 3, 2001. Copyright 2011 by National Journal Group, Inc. All rights reserved.

Racial Profiling Revisited: "Just Common Sense" in the Fight Against Terror?

*by David A. Harris**

We have all heard, many times, that the events of September 11 "changed everything." Many political issues that had stood front and center in the national debate before that day abruptly assumed back-burner status; others disappeared altogether.

Racial profiling—an issue of broad national concern before September 11—did not become less important nor did it disappear. Instead, it was recast and dramatically changed. Before September 11, polling data had shown that almost 60 percent of Americans—not just African Americans and Latinos, but all Americans—understood what racial profiling was, thought it was an unfair and unwise law enforcement tactic, and wanted it eliminated. After September 11, that same percentage, including those minority citizens most often subjected to past profiling, said that they thought some racial or ethnic profiling in the context of airport searches was acceptable and even necessary as long as the group profiled consisted of Arabs, Muslims, and other Middle Easterners.

This is not particularly hard to understand. After all, the 19 suicide hijackers who attacked the World Trade Center and the Pentagon on September 11 were all young Arab Muslims from the Middle East. And the group claiming responsibility for the attacks, al-Qaeda, draws its legitimacy from an interpretation of Islam that cites the wrongs done to Muslims in the Middle East by nonbelievers. Therefore, most people say it simply makes sense to focus our law enforcement energies on Arab and Middle Eastern men; like it or not, they are the people who constitute the real threat to us, and no amount of political correctness will change that.

But just because it is easy to understand this reasoning does not mean it is correct. No matter how intuitively obvious it may seem, the use of racial and ethnic profiling, even in today's circumstances, is a huge mistake that jeopardizes the strength of our antiterrorism initiatives. When we look at what we have learned about racial profiling on highways and city streets over the last few years, we see there is good reason to avoid using this tool to fight al-Qaeda—to refuse to take the easy, quick-fix path of racial profiling.

In times of great national fear and real threat, it is tempting to say that we must do everything we can to make ourselves safe, even if that means sacrificing individual liberties we normally seek to preserve. But we should not restructure our society and the principles that make it great without asking whether these changes would, in fact, make us any safer.

What We Knew Before September 11

Before September 11, a national consensus had emerged about racial profiling: It is a biased and unfair police practice that Americans wanted eliminated. This consensus resulted, in no small part, from the data released in the mid-1990s that substantiated, for the first time, the stories told by African Americans and

Latinos of being stopped, searched, and treated like suspects by the police. The data proved to a majority of Americans that these were not just stories or excuses used by criminals trying to escape wrongdoing, but manifestations of a real phenomenon, something we could observe and measure.

For example, in data submitted by the Maryland State Police to a federal court, African Americans comprised more than 70 percent of all drivers stopped and searched, even though they represented just 17 percent of all drivers on the road. (Report of John Lamberth, *Wilkins v. Maryland State Police et al.*, Civil No. MJG–93–468 (D. Md. 1996).) To be sure, not every police department, and not every police officer, used racial or ethnic profiling. But it was common enough that most minority men and women, of all ages, professions, and classes, had either experienced it first-hand, or had close relatives or friends who had

The availability of these data brought about an important shift in the public debate. Fewer defenders of the police denied the existence of racial profiling. Rather, they insisted that such profiling was not racist; it was just common-sense crime fighting. Defenders of profiling argued that because African Americans and Latinos were disproportionately represented among those arrested and imprisoned, smart police officers focused their enforcement efforts on these racial and ethnic groups. The fact that this resulted in disproportionate numbers of stops, searches, and arrests of African Americans and Latinos was, according to a spokesman for the Maryland State Police, simply "the unfortunate byproduct of sound police policy." (Michael Fletcher, *Driven to Extremes: Black Men Take Steps to Avoid Police Stops*, Wash. Post., March 29, 1996, at A1.)

In order to advance the debate, researchers and scholars needed to confront the assumption head-on. Did racial profiling, in fact, make for better and more productive law enforcement? It was already clear that racial profiling existed, given the data from the mid-1990s. Many Americans were already aware of the high social costs of profiling: the distrust of police, cynicism about the courts and the law, an unwillingness to believe police officers testifying as witnesses in court. These factors were often dismissed as just the costs of fighting crime and drugs, since it was assumed that profiling did, indeed, fight crime. Thus the importance of testing the assumption. Did racial profiling really help police officers find the bad guys more often?

Data that became available in the late-1990s made such testing possible for the first time. These data, from police departments of all kinds from all over the country, allowed the study of "hit rates"—the success rates for police stops and searches using racial profiling as opposed to those stops and searches using traditional, nonracial criteria that focus simply on observation of suspicious behavior. Hit rates indicate the rate at which police find what they seek— drugs, guns, people with arrest warrants, and the like—when they execute a stop and search. In these studies, stops and searches of Caucasians were not counted as profiling because they were based not on race, but on observed behavior that appeared suspicious. Stops and searches of African Americans and Latinos, on the other hand, may have been based on some suspicious behavior, but were driven, overwhelmingly, by race or ethnic appearance. This is why, in all of these studies, African Americans and Latinos were stopped in numbers greatly disproportionate to their presence on the highways, roads, or city sidewalks. With these data broken down by racial categories for each of the police departments studied, I was able to make an apples-to-apples, side-by-side comparison of police behavior within particular police departments, both with and without the variable of race or ethnicity. (*See* David A. Harris,

Profiles in Injustice: Why Racial Profiling Cannot Work, chapter 4 (The New Press, 2002).)

The results of these hit rate studies were striking, all the more so for their consistency across many different jurisdictions and law enforcement agencies. The data on hit rates show that target-ing law enforcement using racial or ethnic appearance does not, in fact, improve policing. It actually makes policing worse—less successful, less productive, less likely to find guns, drugs, and bad guys. Contrary to what the proponents of profiling might expect, hit rates were not higher using racial profiling. In fact, hit rates for race-based stops were lower—significantly lower—than the hit rates for traditional, nonprofile-based policing. That is, when police used racial and ethnic profiling to target black and brown populations as suspicious, the results they got were uniformly poorer than the results they got when they stopped whites simply on the basis of suspicious behavior. Racial profil-ing, then, doesn't improve policing; it pulls it down, delivering less bang for the law enforcement buck. Even if we ignore the high social costs—distrust of all government, including police and the legal system; exacerbation of existing problems such as residential segregation and employment discrimination; and destruction of valuable law enforcement initiatives such as com-munity policing—racial profiling as a means to crime reduction simply does not deliver

A Little History

The use of race or ethnic appearance as a proxy to tell police officers who the likely criminals might be did not begin recently. Some trace profiling back all the way to the slave patrols, which were empowered to stop and demand an explanation from any black person unaccompanied by a white person, as well as to search blacks' dwellings for contraband, such as books. But it was in the 1980s that certain segments of law enforcement certainly honed the tactic to perfection. Racial profiling was not an accident, and it was not the result of a few bad apples in policing. It was the predictable outcome of a number of decisions by the U.S. Supreme Court that allowed police to use traffic enforcement as a convenient and universally available means to make end runs around the requirements of the Fourth Amendment. And it was the federal government, through the Drug Enforcement Administration, that deliberately made use of these opportunities.

As far back as 1973, the U.S. Supreme Court confronted the possibility that police officers might use arrests, traffic stops, and other traditional enforcement mechanisms as pretexts to do what would otherwise be forbidden by the Fourth Amendment in the absence of probable cause or a warrant or both. In *Robinson v. U.S.*, 414 U.S. 218 (1973), the Supreme Court allowed police to perform a full search incident to a traffic arrest, despite the lack of any reason to fear the presence of weapons or the destruction of evidence, the two traditional rationales for searches incident to a valid arrest. The real intentions of the police officer in making the arrest, that is, whether the arrest might be nothing but an excuse for a search or seizure for which there was no supporting evidence at all, did not matter. All that was important, the Court said, was that there was valid probable cause for the arrest.

Robinson set the stage for a series of decisions through the 1970s, 1980s, and 1990s that increased police discretion and the ability to use stops and searches as pretexts to do what would otherwise be impermissible under the Fourth Amendment. These cases reached their high-water mark in *Whren v.*

U.S., 517 U.S. 806 (1996). In *Whren*, the Court resolved an argument that had split the federal circuits and state courts: Could police officers use traffic enforcement as an excuse to stop drivers for investigation of other crimes when there was no evidence of these crimes? Since the mid-1980s, the use of traffic enforcement as a pretext to investigate drugs and drug trafficking on the roads had been championed by the federal government itself. The federal Drug Enforcement Administration had been using a profile to spot potential drug couriers in airports; the Supreme Court's cases and those from lower courts encouraged the DEA to try to engraft this method onto traffic enforcement on highways across the country. A DEA program called Operation Pipeline was set up in the 1980s to spread the gospel of highway drug courier profiling nationwide. The DEA trained tens of thousands of state and local police officers in the tactics of profiling through Operation Pipeline; these officers then went back to their own departments to train others and to set up specialized drug interdiction units. The DEA says that none of its training encouraged the police to use race as part of its profiles, but training materials sometimes showed otherwise. For example, one training video shows officers making several mock stops; in each one, the driver stopped has a Hispanic surname. The DEA and other federal agencies were also disseminating intelligence in the 1980s and 1990s that blamed trafficking in particular drugs on identified ethnic groups.

The *Whren* case can, thus, be seen as the Supreme Court's final word and official blessing of these practices. The parties confronted the Court with the question of pretext stops and their use as tools in racial profiling—the briefing of the case is replete with references to these issues—but the justices were unimpressed. In a unanimous opinion, the Court said that unlimited police discretion to make traffic stops—even the use of this power in a racially biased manner—had no place in the Fourth Amendment analysis. The Court dismissed them as nothing more than the possible grounds for a lawsuit based on the Equal Protection Clause.

As a result, racial profiling became a national topic of conversation in the mid- and late-1990s not simply because of occasional overzealous law enforcement. On the contrary, profiling was an entirely predictable outcome of U.S. Supreme Court decisions that broadened police power and discretion to make traffic and pedestrian stops and searches to the point that this discretion was for all practical purposes unlimited. That police took advantage of the authority these decisions gave them is understandable. Indeed, it would have been surprising if they had not.

More Than One Way to Skin a Cat

What *Whren* and recent cases such as *Atwater v. Lago Vista*, 533 U.S. 924 (2001) (Fourth Amendment is no barrier to arrest and accompanying search of woman for offense that carries no possible sentence of incarceration), make clear is that any changes in police use of racial profiling will almost certainly not come from the courts. The few successful private lawsuits regarding these practices, such as those in New Jersey and Maryland, are not nearly so numerous as those that have failed. (*E.g., Nater et al. v. Vogel*, 106 F.3d 415 (11th Cir. 1997); *Chavez v. Illinois State Police*, 251 F.3d 612 (7th Cir. 2001); *see also* Daryl Kelly, *Federal Racial Profiling Suit Is Dismissed*, L.A. Times, March 19, 2002.) Thus, traditional litigation strategies, although certainly a tool that should not be ignored, do not represent the best method for attacking these issues.

Yet the inhospitability of the courts to opponents of racial profiling is, perhaps surprisingly, where the story grows more encouraging. Lack of success in using judicial routes to create change has forced opponents of profiling to find other avenues: the use and mobilization of public opinion and concerted pushes for legislative measures. These efforts have met with surprising success. By the beginning of 2002, 15 state legislatures had enacted some kind of law concerning racial profiling. These laws ranged from simple requirements that police departments collect data on some or all of their traffic stops to laws that require new antiprofiling policies, training, and other initiatives, in addition to data collection. Besides these new laws, hundreds of police departments have, on their own and without any state law requirement, begun to collect data to track their traffic and other stops and searches, and have revised their policies. In a way, this is far more important than state legislative action. It shows that these police departments have recognized the fact that *it is in their own interest* to face the issue of profiling head-on and to forthrightly collect information on police practices, regardless of what it may or may not show.

It is this last set of changes—police departments themselves deciding that it is important to take some action on profiling—that points the way to the future. By getting beyond the old questions of whether or not profiling exists, as it surely does in many places, and whether anything should be done about it, the public debate can move to instituting better ways of policing. Many individuals involved in policing have long characterized modern law enforcement using a stark dichotomy. We can have good, tough, effective law enforcement that brings down the crime rate or we can have "kinder, gentler" policing that respects citizens and their rights, but we cannot have both. The example used to illustrate this "either-or" approach is New

York City. During the 1990s Mayor Rudolph Giuliani and the New York Police Department used tough, zero tolerance law enforcement against low-level, quality-of-life crimes. The crime rate dropped an astonishing seven years in a row. But while New York accomplished much in the way of crime reduction, it was not alone. Although New York City, with its nationally ambitious mayor and its role as media capital of the world, got most of the attention, it was only one of many major American cities that saw a dramatic fall in crime rates. And most of these cities did not use New York City's zero tolerance model. In fact, a number of large cities, from San Diego to Boston, used entirely different methods that produced drops in crime that were the same or greater than those seen in New York—and did so with less man-power on a per capita basis. And, unlike New York, these cities put their anticrime initiatives together in cooperation with their minority communities, instead of in opposition to them. Now, as New York deals with a backlash of distrust between police and minority communities, these other cities have built partnerships between their police and minority communities that can serve as the basis for strong efforts to reduce crime far into the future.

It is examples such as these that demonstrate that we should reject the "either-or" dichotomy. The idea that we can have either effective policing or policing that respects citizens, but not both, is a myth. We can—we must—have both. Police depart-ments nationwide are taking concrete steps to make this happen. They are not following pie-in-the-sky academic theory, but instead using solid management tools and putting the police accountability at the top of their agenda. Among the approaches employed are:

- the collection of analysis of data on traffic and pedestrian stops and the aftermath of those stops, including consent searches and their results;

- early warning systems, designed to help supervisors manage officers under their charge and to spot officers who may need more training or who should be taken out of policing in order to avoid further problems down the road;

- greater supervisory responsibility of police middle management—chiefly sergeants and lieutenants—for the actions of those officers under their commands doing line policing;

- improvement of the conduct of police officers during traffic stops;

- better training designed to ferret out and combat pre-existing biases and to show officers how bias-free policing improves police performance;

- changes in police organizational incentive structures, to promote the type of policing that is both effective and respectful; and

- the use of technology, such as video and audio recording and real-time data tracking systems, to observe and make records of police actions on the street.

(David A. Harris, *Profiles in Injustice: Why Racial Profiling Cannot Work*, chapter 7 (The New Press, 2002).)

In short, there is more than one way to skin the law enforcement cat. Avoiding racial and ethnic profiling will improve policing, and, along with other accountability-based reforms, can take it beyond the demonstrably false, "either-or" myth.

What About Now?

Since September 11, of course, much has changed in our national discussion of policing strategy, not least the shift in focus from anticrime to antiterrorism. Given all that we now know—a lethal attack upon thousands of innocent civilians by al-Qaeda, a Muslim organization in which the weapons of mass destruction were airplanes hijacked and flown by 19 Muslim Arab men from the Middle East—how is it possible to ignore the fact that being Arab or Muslim means that one is more likely to be involved in terrorism? Doesn't it just make sense to use a racial or ethnic profile that singles out Arabs, Muslims, and other Middle Easterners for greater attention, including more frequent stops and searches? Isn't anyone suggesting tactics to the contrary simply suffering from blindness of political correctness? Syndicated columnist Kathleen Parker has given voice to this way of thinking. "When a police officer apprehends and searches an African American only because he's black, assuming no other mitigating factors, that's unjustified racial profiling. When an airport security guard searches a male of Middle Eastern extraction following a historical terrorist attack by males of Middle Eastern extraction, that's common sense." Parker wrote that "a terrorist attack of such enormous proportions, followed by a declaration of war, makes racial profiling a temporary necessity that no patriotic American should protest." (Kathleen Parker, *All Is Fair in This War Except for Insensitivity*, Chi. Trib., Sept. 26, 2001, at 19.)

To a large extent, that is the way things have gone. In the wake of the attacks of September 11, Arabs and other Middle Easterners were removed from planes. Others were repeatedly searched and questioned. More serious, the U.S. Department of Justice detained hundreds of Arabs and Muslims—not one of whom has been linked to the September 11 attacks. The department also undertook the "voluntary" questioning of 5,000, and then another 3,000, young Arab men who were, according to the U.S. attorney general, not suspects, in the hope of learning something, anything, that might help. (Law enforcement professionals reacted by quietly refusing to take part in the questioning and commenting that this tactic differed markedly from established methods for conducting antiterrorism investigations.) The government has also announced an "absconder initiative" in which it will focus its deportation efforts on 6,000 men from Middle Eastern nations who have violated their visas—despite the fact that they make up only the tiniest fraction of all the hundreds of thousands of violators.

These actions may seem intuitively correct, but it is not at all clear that they are, in fact, the right way to proceed. If we look at what has happened in the past with racial profiling, we will see that there are real reasons to hesitate to take the profiling path now. In fact, using racial or ethnic profiles to protect ourselves against al-Qaeda operatives will likely have an effect opposite of what we desire. Our antiterrorism cause will be set back, not advanced.

First, think of what we might call the gold standard of traditional policing: the observation of suspicious behavior. Veteran police officers know there is no substitute for this. It's not what people look like that tells the savvy officer who is suspicious; it's what people do that matters. Using a racial or ethnic profile to decide whom to regard as suspicious cuts directly against this experience-based principle. Some people do look different than the majority, of course, and we know that those in the majority often tend to see people who are different as threatening or suspicious. The net result is that those who look different, especially in some skin-deep way that we equate with danger, come under immediate suspicion without any suspicious behavior; our law enforcement agents shift their attention from what counts—how people behave—to what doesn't: what they look like. We could not make a bigger mistake than to take our eyes so completely off the ball.

A second point is related to the first. If we use racial and ethnic profiles, instead of behavioral clues, to decide which people we think should be treated as suspects, we will greatly enlarge our suspect pool. This is true whether our profiles are based only on race or ethnicity (a very unlikely event) or if race or ethnicity is just one characteristic among many in a multifactor profile. This means that our enforcement resources will be spread thinner than they would if they were part of an effort focused on suspicious behavior. This is not a trivial consequence. On the contrary, our enforcement resources will be stretched to address many more individuals, and, therefore, they will be that much less effective. This points to one of profiling's inherent flaws: It is always overinclusive. Judging whether individuals are suspicious based on their racial or ethnic characteristics means that many people who would not otherwise draw the attention of law enforcement get swept into the dragnet. Of course, this is exactly what happened to African Americans and Latinos profiled during the war on drugs. It wasn't just the drug dealer on the corner, but the minister, the doctor, and the businessman who were stopped, searched, and treated like suspects. Many more minorities were stopped because of their color than would have been the case had police simply looked for suspicious behavior. In the antiterrorism context, not even the FBI has unlimited manpower. Even with the aid of state and local antiterrorism task forces, little can hold us back more completely than increasing the enforcement burden beyond what focusing on behavior would call for.

If focusing on suspicious behavior is the gold standard in policing, an accompanying principle is the importance of collecting and using information and intelligence. If we are to avoid attacks in the future by al-Qaeda operatives based on our own soil, we need to do much better in the intelligence arena than we did before September 11. And that, of course, means we will have to get information from those likely to know the Arab, Muslim, and Middle Eastern men we might suspect. This information is going to have to come not from the population at large, but from the Middle Eastern communities themselves; there is simply no avoiding this. It stands to reason, then, that what we need most right now are good, solid relations with the Arab and Muslim communities in the United States. Profiling that focuses on Arab and Muslim heritage will effectively communicate to these very same communities that we regard all of their members not as our partners in law enforcement and terror prevention, but just the opposite: as potential terrorists. When every young Arab or Muslim man is effectively labeled a potential terrorist, when many are detained indefinitely on petty immigration violations, and even those who have come forward to help have been rewarded with incarceration, it is not hard to imagine the result: alienation and anger toward the authorities at a time when we can least afford it.

The interesting thing about the "common sense" of profiling Middle Easterners is how roundly and quickly many law enforcement professionals rejected it. Attorney General John Ashcroft's directive ordering the "voluntary" questioning of 5,000 Middle Eastern men was met by skepticism in a number of major police departments. (Fox Butterfield, *Police Are Split on Questioning of Mideast Men*, N.Y. Times, Nov. 22, 2001.) Command staff quickly recognized the damage that this questioning would do to their long-term efforts to build crime-fighting partnerships with their Middle Eastern communities. Some departments quietly refused to take part or were happy to leave the task to FBI agents; a few police officials publicly rejected the Department of Justice's requests that they take part. Eight former FBI officials, including the former chief of both the FBI and CIA, William H. Webster, went on record with his doubts about the law enforcement value of these tactics; one former official called the wholesale questioning "the Perry Mason School of Law Enforcement." (Jim McGee , *Ex-FBI Officials Criticize Tactics on Terrorism*, Wash. Post., Nov. 28, 2001.) Little wonder, then, that senior U.S. intelligence officials circulated a memorandum early in the fall that warned about the dangers of profiling. This memorandum, first reported in the *Boston Globe*, urged law enforcement and intelligence agents to balk at racial profiling. Profiling would fail, the memorandum said; the only way to catch terrorists was the observation of suspicious behavior. (Bill Dedman, *Airport Security: Memo Warns Against Use of Profiling as Defense*, Boston Globe, Oct. 12, 2001.) Too bad that this warning never seems to have penetrated to the senior levels of the Department of Justice leadership.

Despite all of this, many continue to argue that it doesn't make sense to screen anyone at airports besides young Arab and Middle Eastern men. After all, why waste time and resources stopping or searching anyone else when we already know exactly who the "real" suspicious people are? This argument shows a serious misunderstanding of the nature of what we are up against in al-Qaeda. The most important thing for us to realize about this organization is that beyond its vicious and murderous elements, it has also shown itself to be intelligent, patient, and thoroughly adaptable. These are the qualities that make it a formidable enemy. The attack on the World Trade Center on September 11 was not the first but the second assault on this landmark. When the first attack in 1993 failed to accomplish their goal, the terrorists pulled back and spent eight years devising an entirely new method of attack—planned to the smallest detail and then practiced so that it could be carried out almost perfectly. Despite our important military successes in Afghanistan, this set of qualities remains very much alive in the al-Qaeda structure. In the aftermath of September 11, we began to harden cockpit doors, to check carry-on bags for even the smallest potential weapons, and to profile Middle Eastern men. Al-Qaeda's answer was Richard Reid—a non-Arab, non-Middle Easterner from England; a British citizen with a valid British passport and a bomb in his shoe. Clearly, they knew what we were looking for, and they did not repeat what they had done in the past.

Those who insist that it is a waste of time to look at any non-Arab, who want all Arabs carefully screened and searched despite the lack of any suspicious behavior, seem to have missed this point entirely. Terrorists generally, and al-Qaeda specifically, will always look for new weaknesses to use as their point of attack. Just such a weakness became glaringly obvious in mid-January 2002 when the government announced that it could not meet the deadline for having all bags aboard airliners electronically screened for explosives. Instead, the authorities said, they would use a group of other stopgap measures such as partial bag matching. It is much more likely that the next attack on an airplane will come not in the form of a suicide hijacking, but through efforts to bring an explosive aboard a plane—either in the checked baggage of an al-Qaeda suicide soldier who boards the plane and avoids detection through bag matching, or in the luggage of an innocent passenger. Who can forget the foiled terrorist attempt some years ago to bomb a plane by putting explosives in the luggage of the terrorist's unsuspecting pregnant girlfriend? And, as some federal law enforcement officials have already said, the next face of a terrorist we will see is unlikely to be a Middle Easterner; instead, we may see someone from Asia, Malaysia, the Philippines, or even a European country. Thus, random searches and searches of non-Arabs are, in fact, extremely important security tactics. Without them, we create a weak point that begs to be exploited by our enemies.

Those who insist on the "commonsense" approach of focusing on Middle Eastern men would, of course, have us ignore all of this. They want a fast food solution—something convenient and comforting for "us" that only inconveniences "them." But there is little reason to think that type of profiling will see any greater success than profiling for drugs and other crimes did. If we go down that failed path we will likely reap the same kind of reward: poor results and the alienation of our citizens from the police at a time when we most need cooperation between the two. Ironically, if we keep ourselves focused on traditional methods of police procedures—surveillance of suspicious behavior and the collection and effective use of intelligence—we do not have to fail. We can do a better job of policing, even as we do right by our fellow citizens.

*David A. Harris is a law professor at the University of Pittsburgh Law School, where he teaches and studies policing and national security. He is author of two books, *Profiles in Injustice: Why Racial Profiling Can't Work* (2002) and *Good Cops: The Case for Preventive Policing* (2005).

Harris, David. 2002. Racial profiling revisited: 'Just common sense' in the fight against terror? *Criminal Justice* 17 (2) (Summer). http://www.americanbar.org/publications/criminal_justice_magazine_home/crimjust_cjmag_17_2_profiling.html.

Copyright 2002© by the American Bar Association. Reprinted with permission. This information or any or portion thereof may not be copied or disseminated in any form or by any means or stored in an electronic database or retrieval system without the express written consent of the American Bar Association.

Discussion Questions

1. Is there a constitutionally significant difference between profiling based on national origin and profiling based on race or religion?

2. Is there a constitutionally significant difference between taking race, national origin, or religion into account as factors in deciding whom to focus on for more intensive investigation and using such factors as the exclusive bases for such treatment?

3. How should the law treat the use of race, religion, or national origin as criteria in looking for a suspect in a specific crime who has been identified using those descriptive criteria? Is it different when those factors are used to make educated guesses about who may commit crimes in the future?

4. What are the benefits of profiling? What are the costs? Can we achieve the benefits in ways that do not have the same costs?

PART 2:

The Use of Torture in Exceptional Circumstances

Is torture ever warranted? If torturing a single individual could elicit information about a ticking time bomb that would allow police to defuse the bomb and save the lives of one hundred, one thousand, or even one million innocent civilians, wouldn't it be indefensible *not to torture*? This question, a staple hypothetical of philosophy class discussions for years, became a much less hypothetical, and much more real, question in the wake of the terrorist attacks of September 11, 2001. Arguing that it was critical that we prevent the next terrorist attack, that "enhanced interrogation" is an essential tool for intelligence gathering when time is short, and that high-level al Qaeda suspects were resistant to other forms of interrogation, officials in the

Bush administration authorized coercive interrogation tactics up to and including waterboarding, a tactic that previously had been recognized (including by the United States itself) as torture. The Bush administration argued that the tactics obtained valuable intelligence and saved lives. But is torture ever justified? And, if so, what does that say about the international treaty, signed and ratified by the United States and virtually every other country in the world, which states unequivocally that torture is never justified under any circumstance, including in national emergencies? Charles Krauthammer argues that torture is sometimes warranted and that to oppose torture where doing so would lead to hundreds of innocent civilian deaths is moral squeamishness. Ali Soufan, a professional interrogator for the FBI, argues that torture doesn't work; it gets bad intelligence and undermines the kind of rapport-building that practice shows produces good intelligence. Michael Posner, a prominent human rights lawyer, argues that the prohibition is absolute for good reasons and that the "ticking time bomb" hypothetical is fundamentally misleading.

The Truth About Torture

ONE SIDE DEPLOYS PIETIES. THE OTHER SIDE, EUPHEMISMS. IT'S TIME TO BE HONEST ABOUT DOING TERRIBLE THINGS.

by Charles Krauthammer*

During the last few weeks in Washington the pieties about torture have lain so thick in the air that it has been impossible to have a reasoned discussion. The McCain amendment that would ban "cruel, inhuman, or degrading" treatment of any prisoner by any agent of the United States sailed through the Senate by a vote of 90–9. The Washington establishment remains stunned that nine such retrograde, morally inert persons—let alone senators—could be found in this noble capital.

Now, John McCain has great moral authority on this issue, having heroically borne torture at the hands of the North Vietnamese. McCain has made fine arguments in defense of his position. And McCain is acting out of the deep and honorable conviction that what he is proposing is not only right but is in the best interest of the United States. His position deserves respect. But that does not mean, as seems to be the assumption in Washington today, that a critical analysis of his "no torture, ever" policy is beyond the pale.

Let's begin with a few analytic distinctions. For the purpose of torture and prisoner maltreatment, there are three kinds of war prisoners:

First, there is the ordinary soldier caught on the field of battle. There is no question that he is entitled to humane treatment. Indeed, we have no right to disturb a hair on his head. His detention has but a single purpose: to keep him *hors de combat*. The proof of that proposition is that if there were a better way to keep him off the battlefield that did not require his detention, we would let him go. Indeed, during one year of the Civil War, the two sides did try an alternative. They mutually "paroled" captured enemy soldiers, i.e., released them to return home on the pledge that they would not take up arms again. (The experiment failed for a foreseeable reason: cheating. Grant found that some paroled Confederates had reenlisted.)

Because the only purpose of detention in these circumstances is to prevent the prisoner from becoming a combatant again, he is entitled to all the protections and dignity of an ordinary domestic prisoner—indeed, more privileges, because, unlike the domestic prisoner, he has committed no crime. He merely had the misfortune to enlist on the other side of a legitimate war. He is therefore entitled to many of the privileges enjoyed by an ordinary citizen—the right to send correspondence, to engage in athletic activity and intellectual pursuits, to receive allowances from relatives—except, of course, for the freedom to leave the prison.

Second, there is the captured terrorist. A terrorist is by profession, indeed by definition, an unlawful combatant: He lives outside the laws of war because he does not wear a uniform, he hides among civilians, and he deliberately targets innocents. He is entitled to no protections whatsoever. People seem to think that the postwar Geneva Conventions were written only to protect detainees. In fact, their deeper purpose was to provide a deterrent to the kind of barbaric treatment of civilians that had become so horribly apparent during the first half of the 20th century, and in particular, during the Second World War. The idea was to deter the abuse of civilians by promising combatants who treated noncombatants well that they themselves would be treated according to a code of dignity if captured—and, crucially, that they would be denied the protections of that code if they broke the laws of war and abused civilians themselves.

Breaking the laws of war and abusing civilians are what, to understate the matter vastly, terrorists do for a living. They are entitled, therefore, to nothing. Anyone who blows up a car bomb in a market deserves to spend the rest of his life roasting on a spit over an open fire. But we don't do that because we do not descend to the level of our enemy. We don't do that because, unlike him, we are civilized. Even though terrorists are entitled to no humane treatment, we give it to them because it is in our nature as a moral and humane people. And when on rare occasions we fail to do that, as has occurred in several of the fronts of the war on terror, we are duly disgraced.

The norm, however, is how the majority of prisoners at Guantánamo have been treated. We give them three meals a day, superior medical care, and provision to pray five times a day. Our scrupulousness extends even to providing them with their own Korans, which is the only reason alleged abuses of the Koran at Guantánamo ever became an issue. That we should have provided those who kill innocents in the name of Islam with precisely the document that inspires their barbarism is a sign of the absurd lengths to which we often go in extending undeserved humanity to terrorist prisoners.

Third, there is the terrorist with information. Here the issue of torture gets complicated and the easy pieties don't so easily apply. Let's take the textbook case. Ethics 101: A terrorist has planted a nuclear bomb in New York City. It will go off in one hour. A million people will die. You capture the terrorist. He knows where it is. He's not talking.

Question: If you have the slightest belief that hanging this man by his thumbs will get you the information to save a million people, are you permitted to do it?

Now, on most issues regarding torture, I confess tentativeness and uncertainty. But on this issue, there can be no uncertainty: Not only is it permissible to hang this miscreant by his thumbs. It is a moral duty.

Yes, you say, but that's an extreme and very hypothetical case. Well, not as hypothetical as you think. Sure, the (nuclear) scale is hypothetical, but in the age of the car- and suicide-bomber, terrorists are often captured who have just set a car bomb to go off or sent a suicide bomber out to a coffee shop, and you only have minutes to find out where the attack is to take place. This "hypothetical" is common enough that the Israelis have a term for precisely that situation: the ticking time bomb problem.

And even if the example I gave were entirely hypothetical, the conclusion—yes, in this case even torture is permissible—is telling because it establishes the principle: Torture is not always impermissible. However rare the cases, there are circumstances in which, by any rational moral calculus, torture not only would be permissible but would be required (to acquire life-saving information). And once you've established the principle, to paraphrase George Bernard Shaw, all that's left to haggle about is the price. In the case of torture, that means that the argument is not *whether* torture is ever permissible, but *when*—i.e., under what obviously stringent circumstances: how big, how imminent, how preventable the ticking time bomb.

That is why the McCain amendment, which by mandating "torture never" refuses even to recognize the legitimacy of any moral calculus, cannot be right. There must be exceptions. The real argument should be over what constitutes a legitimate exception.

Let's take an example that is far from hypothetical. You capture Khalid Sheikh Mohammed in Pakistan. He not only has already killed innocents, he is deeply involved in the planning for the present and future killing of innocents. He not only was the architect of the 9/11 attack that killed nearly three thousand people in one day, most of them dying a terrible, agonizing, indeed tortured death. But as the top al Qaeda planner and logistical expert he also knows a lot about terror attacks to come. He knows plans, identities, contacts, materials, cell locations, safe houses, cased targets, etc. What do you do with him?

We have recently learned that since 9/11 the United States has maintained a series of "black sites" around the world, secret detention centers where presumably high-level terrorists like Khalid Sheikh Mohammed have been imprisoned. The world is scandalized. Black sites? Secret detention? Jimmy Carter calls this "a profound and radical change in the . . . moral values of our country." The Council of Europe demands an investigation, calling the claims "extremely worrying." Its human rights commissioner declares "such practices" to constitute "a serious human rights violation, and further proof of the crisis of values" that has engulfed the war on terror. The gnashing of teeth and rending of garments has been considerable.

I myself have not gnashed a single tooth. My garments remain entirely unrent. Indeed, I feel reassured. It would be a gross dereliction of duty for any government *not* to keep Khalid Sheikh Mohammed isolated, disoriented, alone, despairing, cold and sleepless, in some godforsaken hidden location in order to find out what he knew about plans for future mass murder. What are we supposed to do? Give him a nice cell in a warm Manhattan prison, complete with Miranda rights, a mellifluent lawyer, and his own website? Are not those the kinds of courtesies we extended to the 1993 World Trade Center bombers, then congratulated ourselves on how we "brought to justice" those responsible for an attack that barely failed to kill tens of thousands of Americans, only to discover a decade later that we had accomplished nothing—indeed, that some of the disclosures at the trial had helped Osama bin Laden avoid U.S. surveillance?

Have we learned nothing from 9/11? Are we prepared to go back with complete amnesia to the domestic-crime model of dealing with terrorists, which allowed us to sleepwalk through the nineties while al Qaeda incubated and grew and metastasized unmolested until on 9/11 it finished what the first World Trade Center bombers had begun?

Let's assume (and hope) that Khalid Sheikh Mohammed has been kept in one of these black sites, say, a cell somewhere in Romania, held entirely incommunicado and subjected to the kind of "coercive interrogation" that I described above. McCain has been going around praising the Israelis as the model of how to deal with terrorism and prevent terrorist attacks. He does so because in 1999 the Israeli Supreme Court outlawed all torture in the course of interrogation. But in reality, the Israeli case is far more complicated. And the complications reflect precisely the dilemmas regarding all coercive interrogation, the weighing of the lesser of two evils: the undeniable inhumanity of torture versus the abdication of the duty to protect the victims of a potentially preventable mass murder.

In a summary of Israel's policies, Glenn Frankel of the *Washington Post* noted that the 1999 Supreme Court ruling struck down secret guidelines established 12 years earlier that allowed interrogators to use the kind of physical and psychological pressure I described in imagining how KSM might be treated in America's "black sites."

"But after the second Palestinian uprising broke out a year later, and especially after a devastating series of suicide bombings of passenger buses, cafes and other civilian targets," writes Frankel, citing human rights lawyers and detainees, "Israel's internal security service, known as the Shin Bet or the Shabak, returned to physical coercion as a standard practice." Not only do the techniques used "command widespread support from the Israeli public," but "Israeli prime ministers and justice ministers with a variety of political views," including the most conciliatory and liberal, have defended these techniques "as a last resort in preventing terrorist attacks."

Which makes McCain's position on torture incoherent. If this kind of coercive interrogation were imposed on any inmate in the American prison system, it would immediately be declared cruel and unusual, and outlawed. How can he oppose these practices, which the Israelis use, and yet hold up Israel as a model for dealing with terrorists? Or does he countenance this kind of interrogation in extreme circumstances—in which case, what is left of his categorical opposition to inhuman treatment of any kind?

But let us push further into even more unpleasant territory, the territory that lies beyond mere coercive interrogation and beyond McCain's self-contradictions. How far are we willing to go?

This "going beyond" need not be cinematic and ghoulish. (Jay Leno once suggested "duct tape" for Khalid Sheikh Mohammed. See photo.) Consider, for example, injection with sodium pentathol. (Colloquially known as "truth serum," it is nothing of the sort. It is a barbiturate whose purpose is to sedate. Its effects are much like that of alcohol: disinhibiting the higher brain centers to make someone more likely to disclose information or thoughts that might otherwise be guarded.) Forcible sedation is a clear violation of bodily integrity. In a civilian context it would be considered assault. It is certainly impermissible under any prohibition of cruel, inhuman, or degrading treatment.

Let's posit that during the interrogation of Khalid Sheikh Mohammed, perhaps early on, we got intelligence about an imminent al Qaeda attack. And we had a very good reason to believe he knew about it. And if we knew what he knew, we could stop it. If we thought we could glean a critical piece of information by use of sodium pentathol, would we be permitted to do so?

Less hypothetically, there is waterboarding, a terrifying and deeply shocking torture technique in which the prisoner has his face exposed to water in a way that gives the feeling of drowning. According to CIA sources cited by ABC News, Khalid Sheikh Mohammed "was able to last between two and 2 1/2 minutes before begging to confess." Should we regret having done that? Should we abolish by law that practice, so that it could never be used on the next Khalid Sheikh Mohammed having thus gotten his confession?

And what if he possessed information with less imminent implications? Say we had information about a cell that he had helped found or direct, and that cell was planning some major attack and we needed information about the identity and location of its members. A rational moral calculus might not permit measures as extreme as the nuke-in-Manhattan scenario, but would surely permit measures beyond mere psychological pressure.

Such a determination would not be made with an untroubled conscience. It would be troubled because there is no denying the monstrous evil that is any form of torture. And there is no denying how corrupting it can be to the individuals and society that practice it. But elected leaders, responsible above all for the protection of their citizens, have the obligation to tolerate their own sleepless nights by doing what is necessary—and only what is necessary, nothing more—to get information that could prevent mass murder.

Given the gravity of the decision, if we indeed cross the Rubicon—as we must—we need rules. The problem with the McCain amendment is that once you have gone public with a blanket ban on all forms of coercion, it is going to be very difficult to publicly carve out exceptions. The Bush administration is to be faulted for having attempted such a codification with the kind of secrecy, lack of coherence, and lack of strict enforcement that led us to the McCain reaction.

What to do at this late date? Begin, as McCain does, by banning all forms of coercion or inhuman treatment by anyone serving in the military—an absolute ban on torture by all military personnel everywhere. We do not want a private somewhere making these fine distinctions about ticking and slow-fuse time bombs. We don't even want colonels or generals making them. It would be best for the morale, discipline, and honor of the Armed Forces for the United States to maintain an absolute prohibition, both to simplify their task in making decisions and to offer them whatever reciprocal treatment they might receive from those who capture them—although I have no illusion that any anti-torture provision will soften the heart of a single jihadist holding a knife to the throat of a captured American soldier. We would impose this restriction on ourselves for our own reasons of military discipline and military honor.

Outside the military, however, I would propose, contra McCain, a ban against all forms of torture, coercive interrogation, and inhuman treatment, except in two contingencies: (1) the ticking time bomb and (2) the slower-fuse high-level terrorist (such as KSM). Each contingency would have its own set of rules. In the case of the ticking time bomb, the rules would be relatively simple: Nothing rationally related to getting accurate information would be ruled out. The case of the high-value suspect with slow-fuse information is more complicated. The principle would be that the level of inhumanity of the measures used (moral honesty is essential here—we would be using measures that are by definition inhumane) would be proportional to the need and value of the information. Interrogators would be constrained to use the least inhumane treatment necessary relative to the magnitude and imminence of the evil being prevented and the importance of the knowledge being obtained.

These exceptions to the no-torture rule would not be granted to just any nonmilitary interrogators, or anyone with CIA credentials. They would be reserved for highly specialized agents who are experts and experienced in interrogation, and who are known not to abuse it for the satisfaction of a kind of sick sadomasochism Lynndie England and her cohorts indulged in at Abu Ghraib. Nor would they be acting on their own. They would be required to obtain written permission for such interrogations, from the highest political authorities in the country (cabinet level) or from a quasi-judicial body modeled on the Foreign Intelligence Surveillance Court (which permits what would ordinarily be illegal searches and seizures in the war on terror).

Or, if the bomb was truly ticking and there was no time, the interrogators would be allowed to act on their own, but would require post facto authorization within, say, 24 hours of their interrogation, so that they knew that whatever they did would be subject to review by others and be justified only under the most stringent terms.

One of the purposes of these justifications would be to establish that whatever extreme measures are used are for reasons of nothing but information. Historically, the torture of prisoners has been done for a variety of reasons apart from information, most prominently reasons of justice or revenge. We do not do that. We should not do that. Ever. Khalid Sheikh Mohammed, murderer of 2,973 innocents, is surely deserving of the most extreme suffering day and night for the rest of his life. But it is neither our role nor our right to be the agents of that suffering Vengeance is mine, sayeth the Lord. His, not ours. Torture is a terrible and monstrous thing, as degrading and morally corrupting to those who practice it as any conceivable human activity including its moral twin, capital punishment.

If Khalid Sheikh Mohammed knew nothing, or if we had reached the point where his knowledge had been exhausted, I'd be perfectly prepared to throw him into a nice, comfortable Manhattan cell and give him a trial to determine what would be fit and just punishment. But as long as he had useful information, things would be different.

Very different. And it simply will not do to take refuge in the claim that all of the above discussion is superfluous because torture never works anyway. Would that this were true. Unfortunately, on its face, this is nonsense. Is one to believe that in the entire history of human warfare, no combatant has ever received useful information by the use of pressure, torture, or any other kind of inhuman treatment? It may indeed be true that torture is not a reliable tool. But that is very different from saying that it is *never* useful.

The monstrous thing about torture is that sometimes it does work. In 1994, 19-year-old Israeli corporal Nachshon Waxman was kidnapped by Palestinian terrorists. The Israelis captured the driver of the car used in the kidnapping and tortured him in order to find where Waxman was being held. Yitzhak Rabin, prime minister and peacemaker, admitted that they tortured him in a way that went even beyond the '87 guidelines for "coercive interrogation" later struck down by the Israeli Supreme Court as too harsh. The driver talked. His information was accurate. The Israelis found Waxman. "If we'd been so careful to follow the ['87] Landau Commission [which *allowed* coercive interrogation]," explained Rabin, "we would never have found out where Waxman was being held."

In the Waxman case, I would have done precisely what Rabin did. (The fact that Waxman's Palestinian captors killed him during the Israeli rescue raid makes the case doubly tragic, but changes nothing of the moral calculus.) Faced with a similar choice, an American president would have a similar obligation. To do otherwise—to give up the chance to find your soldier lest you sully yourself by authorizing torture of the person who possesses potentially lifesaving information—is a deeply immoral betrayal of a soldier and countryman. Not as cosmically immoral as permitting a city of one's countrymen to perish, as in the Ethics 101 case. But it remains, nonetheless, a case of moral abdication—of a kind rather parallel to that of the principled pacifist. There is much to admire in those who refuse on principle ever to take up arms under any conditions. But that does not make pure pacifism, like no-torture absolutism, any less a form of moral foolishness, tinged with moral vanity. Not reprehensible, only deeply reproachable and supremely impracticable. People who hold such beliefs are deserving of a certain respect. But they are not to be put in positions of authority. One should be grateful for the saintly among us. And one should be vigilant that they not get to make the decisions upon which the lives of others depend.

Which brings us to the greatest irony of all in the torture debate. I have just made what will be characterized as the pro-torture case contra McCain by proposing two major exceptions carved out of any no-torture rule: the ticking time bomb and the slow-fuse high-value terrorist. McCain supposedly is being hailed for defending all that is good and right and just in America by standing foursquare against any inhuman treatment. Or is he?

According to *Newsweek*, in the ticking time bomb case McCain says that the president should disobey the very law that McCain seeks to pass—under the justification that "you do what you have to do. But you take responsibility for it." But if torturing the ticking time bomb suspect is "what you have to do," then why has McCain been going around arguing that such things must never be done?

As for exception number two, the high-level terrorist with slow-fuse information, Stuart Taylor, the superb legal correspondent for *National Journal*, argues that with appropriate legal interpretation, the "cruel, inhuman, or degrading" standard, "though vague, is said by experts to codify . . . the common-sense principle that the toughness of interrogation techniques should be calibrated to the importance and urgency of the information likely to be obtained." That would permit "some very aggressive techniques . . . on that small percentage of detainees who seem especially likely to have potentially life-saving information." Or as Evan Thomas and Michael Hirsh put it in the *Newsweek* report on McCain and torture, the McCain standard would "presumably allow for a sliding scale" of torture or torture-lite or other coercive techniques, thus permitting "for a very small percentage—those High Value Targets like Khalid Sheikh Mohammed—some pretty rough treatment."

But if that is the case, then McCain embraces the same exceptions I do, but prefers to pretend he does not. If that is the case, then his much-touted and endlessly repeated absolutism on inhumane treatment is merely for show. If that is the case, then the moral preening and the phony arguments can stop now, and we can all agree that in this real world of astonishingly murderous enemies, in two very circumscribed circumstances, we must all be prepared to torture. Having established that, we can then begin to work together to codify rules of interrogation for the two very unpleasant but very real cases in which we are morally permitted—indeed morally compelled—to do terrible things.

*Charles Krauthammer is a columnist for the *Washington Post*, a contributing editor to *The Weekly Standard* and *The New Republic*, and a commentator for the Fox News Channel. He was formerly a member of the President's Council on Bioethics.

Krauthammer, Charles. 2005. The truth about torture. *Weekly Standard*, December 5.

Used by Permission.

Testimony of Ali Soufan

TESTIMONY OF ALI SOUFAN*

BEFORE THE SENATE JUDICIARY COMMITTEE,
SUBCOMMITTEE ON ADMINISTRATIVE OVERSIGHT AND
THE COURTS

*"What Went Wrong: Torture and the Office of Legal
Counsel in the Bush Administration"*

MAY 13, 2009

Mr. Chairman, Committee members, thank you for inviting me to appear before you today. I know that each one of you cares deeply about our nation's security. It was always a comfort to me during the most dangerous of situations that I faced, from going undercover as an al Qaeda operative, to unraveling terrorist cells, to tracking down the killers of the 17 U.S. sailors murdered in the USS Cole bombing,[1] that those of us on the frontline had your support and the backing of the American people. So I thank you.

The issue that I am here to discuss today—interrogation methods used to question terrorists—is not, and should not be, a partisan matter. We all share a commitment to using the best interrogation method possible that serves our national security interests and fits squarely within the framework of our nation's principles.

From my experience—and I speak as someone who has personally interrogated many terrorists and elicited important actionable intelligence—I strongly believe that it is a mistake to use what has become known as the "enhanced interrogation techniques," a position shared by many professional operatives, including the CIA officers who were present at the initial phases of the Abu Zubaydah interrogation.[2]

These techniques, from an operational perspective, are ineffective, slow and unreliable, and as a result harmful to our efforts to defeat al Qaeda. (This is aside from the important additional considerations that they are un-American and harmful to our reputation and cause.) [...]

[...]I wish to do my part to ensure that we never again use these harmful, slow, ineffective, and unreliable techniques instead of the tried, tested, and successful ones—the ones that are also in sync with our values and moral character. Only by doing this will we defeat the terrorists as effectively and quickly as possible.

Most of my professional career has been spent investigating, studying, and interrogating terrorists. I have had the privilege of working alongside, and learning from, some of the most dedicated and talented men and women our nation has—individuals from the FBI, and other law enforcement, military, and intelligence agencies.

In my capacity as a FBI Agent, I investigated and supervised highly sensitive and complex international terrorism cases, including the East Africa bombings, the USS Cole bombing, and the events surrounding the attacks of 9/11. [...]

I personally interrogated many terrorists we have in our custody and elsewhere, and gained confessions, identified terror operatives, their funding, details of potential plots, and information on how al Qaeda operates, along with other action-able intelligence. [...]

There are many examples of successful interrogations of terrorists that have taken place before and after 9/11. Many of them are classified, but one that is already public and mirrors the other cases, is the interrogation of al Qaeda terrorist Nasser Ahmad Nasser al-Bahri, known as Abu Jandal.[3] In the immediate aftermath of 9/11, together with my partner Special Agent Robert McFadden, [...]I interrogated Abu Jandal.

Through our interrogation, which was done completely by the book (including advising him of his rights), we obtained a treasure trove of highly significant actionable intelligence. For example, Abu Jandal gave us extensive information on Osama Bin Laden's terror network, structure, leadership, membership, security details, facilities, family, communication methods, travels, training, ammunitions, and weaponry, including a breakdown of what machine guns, rifles, rocket launchers, and anti-tank missiles they used. He also provided explicit details of the 9/11 plot operatives, and identified many terrorists who we later successfully apprehended.

The information was important for the preparation of the war in Afghanistan in 2001. It also provided an important background to the 9/11 Commission report; it provided a foundation for the trials so far held in Guantánamo Bay; and it also has been invaluable in helping to capture and identify top al Qaeda operatives and thus disrupt plots. The approach used in these successful interrogations can be called the Informed Interrogation Approach. Until the introduction of the "enhanced" technique, it was the sole approach used by our military, intelligence, and law enforcement community.

[…]

The Informed Interrogation Approach is based on leveraging our knowledge of the detainee's culture and mindset, together with using information we already know about him. The interrogator knows that there are three primary points of influence on the detainee:

> First, there is the fear that the detainee feels as a result of his capture and isolation from his support base. People crave human contact, and this is especially true in some cultures more than others. The interrogator turns this knowledge into an advantage by becoming the one person the detainee can talk to and who listens to what he has to say, and uses this to encourage the detainee to open up.
>
> In addition, acting in a non-threatening way isn't how the detainee is trained to expect a U.S. interrogator to act. This adds to the detainee's confusion and makes him more likely to cooperate.
>
> Second, and connected, there is the need the detainee feels to sustain a position of respect and value to interrogator. As the interrogator is the one person speaking to and listening to the detainee, a relationship is built—and the detainee doesn't want to jeopardize it. The interrogator capitalizes on this and compels the detainee to give up more information.
>
> And third, there is the impression the detainee has of the evidence against him. The interrogator has to do his or her homework and become an expert in every detail known to the intelligence community about the detainee. The interrogator then uses that knowledge to impress upon the detainee that everything about him is known and that any lie will be easily caught.

For example, in my first interrogation of the terrorist Abu Zubaydah, who had strong links to al Qaeda's leaders and who knew the details of the 9/11 plot before it happened, I asked him his name. He replied with his alias. I then asked him, "how about if I call you Hani?" That was the name his mother nick-named him as a child. He looked at me in shock, said "ok," and we started talking.

The Army Field Manual is not about being nice or soft. It is a knowledge-based approach.[4] It is about outwitting the detainee by using a combination of interpersonal, cognitive, and emo-tional strategies to get the information needed. If done correctly it's an approach that works quickly and effectively because it outwits the detainee using a method that he is not trained, or able, to resist.

This Informed Interrogation Approach is in sharp contrast with the harsh interrogation approach introduced by outside contractors and forced upon CIA officials to use. The harsh technique method doesn't use the knowledge we have of the detainee's history, mindset, vulnerabilities, or culture, and instead tries to subjugate the detainee into submission through humiliation and cruelty. The approach applies a force contin-uum, each time using harsher and harsher techniques until the detainee submits.

The idea behind the technique is to force the detainee to see the interrogator as the master who controls his pain. It is an exercise in trying to gain compliance rather than eliciting cooperation. A theoretical application of this technique is a sit-uation where the detainee is stripped naked and told: "Tell us what you know."

If the detainee doesn't immediately respond by giving infor-mation, for example he asks: "what do you want to know?" the interviewer will reply: "you know," and walk out of the inter-rogation room. Then the next step on the force continuum is introduced, for example sleep deprivation, and the process will continue until the detainee's will is broken and he automatically gives up all information he is presumed to know.

There are many problems with this technique.

A major problem is that it is ineffective. Al Qaeda terrorists are trained to resist torture. As shocking as these techniques are to us, the al Qaeda training prepares them for much worse—the torture they would expect to receive if caught by dictatorships for example. [...]

In addition the harsh techniques only serve to reinforce what the detainee has been prepared to expect if captured. This gives him a greater sense of control and predictability about his experience, and strengthens his will to resist.

A second major problem with this technique is that evidence gained from it is unreliable. There is no way to know whether the detainee is being truthful, or just speaking to either mitigate his discomfort or to deliberately provide false information. [...]

A third major problem with this technique is that it is slow. [...] When we have an alleged "ticking timebomb" scenario and need to get information quickly, we can't afford to wait that long.

A fourth problem with this technique is that ignores the end game. In our country we have due process, which requires evidence to be collected in a certain way. The CIA, because of the sensitivity of its operations, by necessity, operates secretly. These two factors mean that by putting the CIA in charge of interrogations, either secrecy is sacrificed for justice and the CIA's operations are hampered, or justice is not served. Neither is a desirable outcome.

[...]

The case of the terrorist Abu Zubaydah is a good example of where the success of the Informed Interrogation Approach can be contrasted with the failure of the harsh technique approach. I have to restrict my remarks to what has been unclassified. [...] Immediately after Abu Zubaydah was captured, a fellow FBI agent and I were flown to meet him at an undisclosed location. We were both very familiar with Abu Zubaydah and have successfully interrogated al-Qaeda terrorists. We started interrogating him, supported by CIA officials who were stationed at the location, and within the first hour of the interrogation, using the Informed Interrogation Approach, we gained important actionable intelligence.

The information was so important that, as I later learned from open sources, it went to CIA Director George Tenet who was so impressed that he initially ordered us to be congratulated. That was apparently quickly withdrawn as soon as Mr. Tenet was told that it was FBI agents, who were responsible. He then immediately ordered a CIA CTC interrogation team to leave DC and head to the location to take over from us. During his capture Abu Zubaydah had been injured. After seeing the extent of his injuries, the CIA medical team supporting us decided they were not equipped to treat him and we had to take him to a hospital or he would die. At the hospital, we continued our questioning as much as possible, while taking into account his medical condition and the need to know all information he might have on existing threats.

[...]All this happened before the CTC [CIA Counterterrorist Team] team arrived.[5]

A few days after we started questioning Abu Zubaydah, the CTC interrogation team finally arrived from DC with a contractor who was instructing them on how they should conduct the interrogations, and we were removed. Immediately, on the instructions of the contractor, harsh techniques were introduced, starting with nudity. (The harsher techniques mentioned in the memos were not introduced or even discussed at this point.) The new techniques did not produce results as Abu Zubaydah shut down and stopped talking. At that time nudity and low-level sleep deprivation (between 24 and 48 hours) was being used. After a few days of getting no information, and after repeated inquiries from DC asking why all of sudden no information was being transmitted (when before there had been a steady stream), we again were given control of the interrogation. We then returned to using the Informed Interrogation Approach. Within a few hours, Abu Zubaydah again started talking and gave us important actionable intelligence. This included the details of José Padilla, the so-called "dirty bomber."[6] To remind you of how important this information was viewed at the time, the then-Attorney General, John Ashcroft, held a press conference from Moscow to discuss the news. Other important actionable intelligence was also gained that remains classified.

After a few days, the contractor attempted to once again try his untested theory and he started re-implementing the harsh techniques. He moved this time further along the force continuum, introducing loud noise and then temperature manipulation. Throughout this time, my fellow FBI agent and I, along with a top CIA interrogator who was working with us, protested, but we were overruled. I should also note that another colleague, an operational psychologist for the CIA, had left the location because he objected to what was being done.

Again, however, the technique wasn't working and Abu Zubaydah wasn't revealing any information, so we were once again brought back in to interrogate him. We found it harder to reengage him this time, because of how the techniques had affected him, but eventually, we succeeded, and he re-engaged again.

Once again the contractor insisted on stepping up the notches of his experiment, and this time he requested the authorization to place Abu Zubaydah in a confinement box, as the next stage in the force continuum. While everything I saw to this point were nowhere near the severity later listed in the memos, the evolution of the contractor's theory, along with what I had seen till then, struck me as "borderline torture."

[…]I protested to my superiors in the FBI and refused to be a part of what was happening. The Director of the FBI, Robert Mueller, a man I deeply respect, agreed passing the message that "we don't do that," and I was pulled out.

As you can see from this timeline, many of the claims made in the memos about the success of the enhanced techniques are inaccurate. For example, it is untrue to claim Abu Zubaydah wasn't cooperating before August 1, 2002. The truth is that we got actionable intelligence from him in the first hour of interrogating him.

[…]

In summary, the Informed Interrogation Approach outlined in the Army Field Manual is the most effective, reliable, and speedy approach we have for interrogating terrorists. It is legal and has worked time and again.

It was a mistake to abandon it in favor of harsh interrogation methods that are harmful, shameful, slower, unreliable, ineffective, and play directly into the enemy's handbook. It was a mistake to abandon an approach that was working and naively replace it with an untested method. It was a mistake to abandon an approach that is based on the cumulative wisdom and successful tradition of our military, intelligence, and law enforcement community, in favor of techniques advocated by contractors with no relevant experience. The mistake was so costly precisely because the situation was, and remains, too risky to allow someone to experiment with amateurish, Hollywood style interrogation methods—that in reality—taints sources, risks outcomes, ignores the end game, and diminishes our moral high ground in a battle that is impossible to win without first capturing the hearts and minds around the world. It was one of the worst and most harmful decisions made in our efforts against al Qaeda.

For the last seven years, it was not easy objecting to these methods when they had powerful backers. I stood up then for the same reason I'm willing to take on critics now, because I took an oath swearing to protect this great nation. I could not stand by quietly while our country's safety was endangered and our moral standing damaged.

[. . .]

ENDNOTES

1. The USS *Cole* was a United States navy destroyer that was bombed in Yemen on October 12, 2000, by the terrorist group al Qaeda.
2. Abu Zubaydah was an al Qaeda member who was captured in 2002. The CIA initially held him in a secret CIA prison in Thailand. He is currently held in Guantánamo Bay.
3. Abu Jandal is a former bodyguard of Osama bin Laden.
4. Mr. Soufan refers to the U.S. Army's Field Manual 27-10: The Law of Land Warfare. This manual incorporates certain international legal standards on the treatment of prisoners of war.

5. The Counterterrorist Center is an office in the CIA created in the 1980s to act as a counterterrorism unit. The CTC, working with the FBI, pursues terrorists abroad.

6. José Padilla is a U.S. citizen. In 2002, he was arrested in Chicago and held for several years on the charge of planning to use a bomb to spread radioactive material.

*__Ali Soufan__ is chief executive officer of the Soufan Group, LLC, a security consultancy firm. He was previously a supervisory special agent with the Federal Bureau of Investigation, where he investigated terrorist attacks and trained other agents in interrogation techniques.

Statement of Ali Soufan before the Senate Subcommittee on Administrative Oversight and the Courts of the Subcommittee on the Judiciary. May 13, 2009. What went wrong: Torture and the office of legal counsel in the Bush administration. 111th Cong.

The Case for an Outright Ban on Torture

by Michael H. Posner*

Introduction

More than eight years after the attacks of September 11, 2001, the United States continues to debate a wide range of national security policies.[4] Perhaps no issue has stirred greater debate and controversy than the adoption of policies authorizing the use of torture and other coercive interrogation techniques to gather intelligence. And no other aspect of the Bush administration's counterterrorism policies was more damaging to America's internal commitment to uphold the rule of law and to its reputation and standing in the world. As the Obama administration and Congress grapple with these issues, they must recognize that enforcing the ban on torture and cruel treatment is the only effective way to end these abuses. President Barack Obama strongly signaled his intent to follow this approach during his first week in office when he signed an executive order that bans all forms of torture and cruel treatment.[5]

The debate on this issue is set in a broader context, one in which the government has employed security measures to prevent or greatly reduce the risks of future attacks. Preventive measures are essential. The U.S. government has the right, indeed the duty, to protect its people. Since the attacks on 9/11, the government, mindful of this obligation, has devoted significant resources and attention to enhancing airport security and increasing financial and other support for America's front line defenders—police, firefighters, and emergency medical providers. It has taken a series of measures to step up inspections of shipping containers coming into this country. The government also has adopted additional means of protecting other aspects critical to the national infrastructure, such as nuclear power facilities, electrical grids, the water supply, and America's food production and distribution system.

On a parallel track, officials have made efforts to improve and better coordinate intelligence gathering by federal and state governmental entities, having realized that better intelligence can prevent attacks and save lives. The federal government aided this effort by creating a new post, the director of national intelligence. These measures and more were examined by the 9/11 Commission, an independent, bipartisan group established by the president and Congress. The commission made a series of useful recommendations for enhancing the safety of Americans that were prudent, thoughtful, practical, and wise. Everything recommended was rights-neutral and clearly within the bounds of the law.[6]

But the focus of this essay is on another, much more troubling component of this broader context: the government's reliance on and attempt to justify coercive means, torture, or other forms of cruel, inhuman, or degrading treatment as an appropriate way to extract information from suspected members of al-Quaeda and other terrorist groups. Since 2002, reliance on such coercive interrogations by the CIA and other agencies has harmed America's reputation in the world. Rather than enhancing intelligence gathering, it has undermined these efforts. Rather than increasing the nation's security, this reliance has emboldened America's enemies, strained relations with its closest allies, and put its troops around the world at greater risk. The relaxation of rules on interrogations has undermined discipline within the military. As a consequence, the introduction of official cruelty as government policy has made the United States weaker and more vulnerable to attack.

To restore America's reputation and image, to support its troops, and to reaffirm relations with its allies, the U.S. government must, as President Barack Obama has directed, stop all forms of torture and cruelty, adopting a zero-tolerance approach. The use of torture or cruel, inhuman, or degrading treatment in interrogations should never be tolerated, regulated, or justified as a matter of official policy, law, or practice.

The Precedent for Treating Prisoners Humanely

The United States has a proud history of requiring the humane treatment of all enemy prisoners, a tradition dating back to Gen. George Washington. In January 1777, Washington ordered his troops to treat captured British soldiers "with humanity," writing, "Let them have no reason to complain of our copying the brutal example of the British army."[7]

Washington's admonition to his troops reflected a broader commitment by the Founders to set a high ethical standard and to adhere to the rule of law. As Thomas Jefferson later wrote to James Madison, "It has great effect on the opinion of our people and the world to have moral right on our side."[8]

This commitment has been reinforced at key junctures in U.S. history. In the Civil War, Lincoln appointed Columbia law professor Francis Lieber, under sponsorship of the army's general-in-chief, Henry Halleck, to develop a set of minimum standards for the military that forbade suffering, disgrace, cruel imprisonment, want of food, mutilation, death, or other barbarity. The Lieber Code, as it came to be known, required Union forces to treat prisoners of war "with humanity" and to "be strictly guided by the principles of justice, honor, and humanity—virtues adorning a soldier even more than other men, for the very reason that he possesses the power of his arms against the unarmed."[9]

The Lieber Code served as a basis for the development of the law of armed conflict, which the U.S. military has taken a leading role in developing and promoting on the international stage. Influenced by the Lieber Code, Theodore Roosevelt urged at the time of the Philippine-American War that "determined and unswerving effort must be made to find out every instance of barbarity on the part of our troops, to punish those guilty of it, and . . . to prevent the occurrence of all such acts in the future."[10]

The Lieber Code also guided those U.S. officials who, after World War II, took a lead in the international negotiations that led to the promulgation of the Geneva Conventions of 1949. Each of the four Geneva Conventions contains an identical provision, Common Article 3, which specifically prohibits "violence to life and person, in particular murder of all kinds, mutilation, cruel treatment and torture" and "outrages upon personal dignity, in particular humiliating and degrading treatment."[11]

In 1950 Secretary of Defense George Marshall spelled out the application of the humane treatment standard to U.S. officials in a book entitled *The Armed Forces Officer*. In it, he lists twenty-nine propositions that govern American conduct at war, explaining that

> the United States abides by the laws of war. Its Armed Forces, in their dealings with all other peoples, are expected to comply with the laws of war, in the spirit and to the letter. In waging war, we do not terrorize helpless non-combatants, if it is within our power to avoid doing so. Wanton killing, torture, cruelty or the working of unusual hardship on enemy prisoners or populations is not justified under any circumstances. Likewise, respect for the reign of law, as the term is understood in the United States, is expected to follow the flag wherever it goes.[12]

Consistent with General Marshall's words, the U.S. military applied the humane treatment standard of the Geneva Conventions to all prisoners in its custody, even those like the Viet Cong who neither recognized nor abided by the Geneva Conventions and did not qualify as prisoners of war under the Geneva Conventions.

Members of the military still hold to these precedents. Over the last five years, some retired senior U.S. military leaders and Defense Department officials have become increasingly outspoken critics of U.S. interrogation practices. In September 2006, about fifty members of this group wrote a letter to the Senate Armed Services Committee in favor of strict adherence to Common Article 3 in the interrogation of al Qaeda prisoners:

> The framers of the Geneva Conventions, including the American representatives in particular, wanted to ensure that Common Article 3 would apply in situations where a state party to the treaty, like the United States, fights an adversary that is not a party, including irregular forces like al Qaeda. The United States military has abided by the basic requirements of Common Article 3—even to enemies that systematically violated the Geneva Conventions themselves.[13]

The Case Against Torture and Coercive Tactics: Why an Absolute Ban is Essential

The case against torture and official cruelty is clear. For starters, these techniques are an ineffective and even counterproductive way to gather intelligence. As experienced interrogators from the military and intelligence agencies have said repeatedly, these techniques are not the best way to obtain actionable intelligence. Joe Navarro, a twenty-year veteran of the Federal Bureau of Investigation (FBI) with wide experience in counterterrorism investigations, said, "The only thing torture guarantees is pain. It never guarantees the truth. It's a technique that we in the FBI have never used, we don't need . . . . [M]ost of the military interviewers that I've worked with don't subscribe to it."[14]

Navarro teaches interrogators at the CIA and FBI that torture results in fear, contempt, and resistance. Although prisoners may occasionally volunteer useful information when tortured, they will not cooperate in the long run, and far more vital information will then be lost. Instead, an interrogator should "convince an informant to release information, not threaten" and remember "that acts of kindness help to build informants' confidence in the interrogator."[15]

As images and stories of torture and mistreatment by U.S. officials have spread and gained currency since the events of 9/11, potential sources of intelligence and even America's close allies in the world have turned and refused to cooperate with its intelligence-gathering efforts, making America less safe. Reacting to the U.S. government's recent reliance on harsh interrogations, fifteen senior interrogators, interviewers, and intelligence officials in the U.S. military, FBI, and CIA issued a public statement on this matter in June 2008. They concluded that the use of torture and other inhumane and abusive treatment results in false and misleading information, loss of critical intelligence, and has caused serious damage to the reputation and standing of the United States. The use of such techniques also facilitates enemy recruitment, misdirects or wastes scarce resources, and deprives the United States of the standing to demand humane treatment of captive Americans.[16]

Torture and coercive interrogation practices also run counter to the fundamental principles upon which the United States was founded and betray its citizens' religious and ethical ideals as a people. Those who have experienced torture at the hands of their enemies are often the most passionate advocates on this point. For example, Sen. John McCain, who was imprisoned and tortured by the North Vietnamese during the Vietnam War for almost six years, led the fight in Congress in 2005 against the Bush administration's coercive interrogation policy.[17]

As mentioned earlier, torture and cruel treatment also violate U.S. national and international law obligations. The Geneva Conventions are complemented by a set of human rights standards, including a provision in the International Covenant on Civil and Political Rights that bars all forms of torture and cruel, inhuman, and degrading treatment.[18] The Convention Against Torture and Other Cruel, Inhuman or Degrading Treatment or Punishment, which entered into force in 1987 and was ratified by the United States in 1994, elaborated on this standard.[19] All of these international standards serve as a minimum baseline, a floor beneath which the U.S. government cannot sink, and conform with and reinforce U.S. law.

Torture and mistreatment carried out by U.S. soldiers or intelligence agents also invite retaliatory treatment when U.S. citizens are detained abroad. The U.S. military has been a staunch advocate of the Geneva Conventions because these standards protect

American soldiers in the field. If the U.S. government adopts policies that sanction "enhanced interrogation techniques," how can the United States object when similar policies are applied to its own citizens?[20]

Reliance on cruelty also engenders a broader climate of lawlessness and ill discipline by those who engage in such practices. An effective military relies on discipline and adherence to the rules. When commanders begin to relax these rules, especially on something as basic as the treatment of prisoners, soldiers will inevitably take it upon themselves to stretch the meaning of other rules as well. This is a prescription for a breakdown of discipline and control.

The resort to torture also has profound international implications. Because the United States is such a powerful country and has long presented itself to the world as a leader on human rights, a U.S. retreat from those standards has a devastating effect on others—a ripple effect that in recent years has provided a convenient excuse for dictatorial regimes around the world to follow suit. To cite just two examples:

- Former president of Georgia Eduard Shevardnadze stated in October 2002, after being criticized for colluding with Russia in violating the human rights of Chechens, that "international human rights commitments might become pale in comparison with the importance of the anti-terrorist campaign."[21]

- In September 2003, Malaysia's justice minister, Rais Yatim, defended detaining more than one hundred alleged terrorists without trial by citing the U.S. government's detention of individuals at Guantánamo Bay.[22]

In a similar vein, opportunistic governments expressed support for the fight against terrorism after the 9/11 attacks, while presenting their own domestic insurgencies as conflicts perpetrated by terrorist groups analogous to al-Qaeda. For example, Syria and Egypt, both notorious for their human rights abuses, encouraged the United States to emulate their "successful" strategies for fighting terrorism. Syria's minister of information, Adnan Omran, declared that Syria was "ahead [of the United States] in fighting terrorism" and Syrian president Bashar al-Assad invited the United States to "take advantage of Syria's successful experiences."[23] Similarly, Egypt's prime minister, Atef Abeid, responded to criticism of his country's use of torture by rejecting criticism of Egypt's rights record and linking Egypt's challenges to those of the United States:

> The U.S. and U.K., including human rights groups, have, in the past, been calling on us to give these terrorists their "human rights." You can give them all the human rights they deserve until they kill you. After these horrible crimes committed in New York and Virginia, maybe Western countries should begin to think of Egypt's own fight against terror as their new model.[24]

Today, America's longtime pursuit of human rights around the world has been tarnished by prisoner abuses, particularly in the use of coercive interrogations, in the years since 9/11. Intangible but vitally important assets—such as U.S. standing in the world, its soft power, and its moral authority to lead—have been severely damaged. This was put most eloquently by Sen. John McCain:

> We are Americans. We hold ourselves to humane standards of treatment no matter how terribly evil or awful they [enemy combatants] may be. To do otherwise undermines our security, and it also undermines our greatness as a nation. We are not simply any other country. We stand for a lot more than

that in the world: a moral mission, one of freedom and democracy and human rights at home and abroad. . . . The enemy we fight has no respect for human life or human rights. They don't deserve our sympathy. But this is not about who they are. . . .It is about who we are. These are values that distinguish us from our enemies.[25]

Justification for Torture and Coercive Interrogations: The Bush Administration's Global War on Terrorism

James Madison once wrote, "War is in fact the true nurse of executive aggrandizement."[26] His admonition was borne out by the Bush administration's assertions that in a new "global war on terror," war trumps law, and laws become a luxury, not a necessity, binding on the executive.

In the aftermath of the 9/11 attacks, the Bush administration departed from U.S. tradition and instituted draconian policies that allowed for and even encouraged official cruelty, including torture. This shift was part of what Vice President Dick Cheney called the "new normalcy," a concept he believed reflected an "understanding of the world as it is."[27] In an interview five days after the 9/11 attacks, the vice president asserted that to obtain information about al-Qaeda and to prevent future attacks, the U.S. government would

> have to work, though, sort of the dark side, if you will. We've got to spend time in the shadows of the intelligence world. A lot of what needs to be done here will have to be done quietly, without any discussion. [I]t's going to be vital for us to use any means at our disposal, basically, to achieve our objective."[28]

By using this framework and asserting that it was fighting a new kind of enemy, the administration was claiming that existing laws were impediments to fighting this new war. The thrust of the government's approach to the public was essentially this: "Trust us—we will do what is necessary to keep you safe."

In 2002 White House Counsel Alberto Gonzales provided a legal underpinning to the administration's approach to interrogations. He instructed the office of Legal Counsel in the Justice Department (DOJ) to provide a legal definition of torture in order to give legal cover to interrogators from the CIA and other agencies who were fearful that their reliance on "enhanced interrogation techniques" could lead to future criminal prosecutions. In August 2002, the DOJ presented its memo, authored by Jay S Bybee. It concluded that to constitute torture, an act "must inflict pain that is difficult to endure . . . equivalent in intensity to the pain accompanying serious physical injury, such as organ failure, impairment of bodily function or even death."[29]

Four months later, Secretary of Defense Donald Rumsfeld took his cue from the Bybee memo. Frustrated by the military's failure to obtain good intelligence from detainees at Guantánamo,[30] Rumsfeld authorized a series of harsh techniques, including the use of dogs, to intimidate detainees and to get better information. In the spring of 2003, he authorized twenty four new interrogation methods for prisoners at Guantánamo, part of the administration's gloves-off approach to interrogations.[31] Rumsfeld subsequently authorized the extension of these harsh, often illegal techniques for use in the interrogation of prisoners in Afghanistan and Iraq.

On a parallel track, the CIA developed what President Bush called "an alternative set of procedures," which were intended to give the CIA greater latitude questioning high-value detainees in its custody.[32] These "enhanced interrogation techniques," more aggressive and often more abusive, were carried out in secret detention facilities under the CIA's control and reportedly included painful stress positions, temperature manipulation, forced nudity, sexual humiliation, sleep deprivation, physical abuse, and, in some cases, a form of simulated drowning known as waterboarding.

The combination of illegal interrogation rules and secret detentions led to serious abuses. These abuses became front-page headlines in the spring of 2004 when the news media released photographs showing the abuse and humiliation of prisoners at Abu Ghraib prison in Baghdad.[33] But these photos only revealed a small slice of the problem. A 2006 study conducted by Human Rights First revealed that more than one hundred prisoners have died in U.S. custody in Iraq, Afghanistan, and other places. The Pentagon has classified thirty-four of those one hundred cases as criminal homicides. Of those thirty-four, none occurred at Guantánamo and only one at Abu Ghraib prison. Human Rights First also documented that eleven of the one hundred cases were prisoners who literally were tortured to death.[34]

Both Congress and the Supreme Court attempted to check the Bush administration, but they met intense resistance. In 2005 Congress overwhelmingly passed the Detainee Treatment Act with a provision that explicitly prohibits any cruel, inhuman, or degrading treatment of detainees in U.S. custody.[35] Although the president signed the bill into law, he included a signing statement that stripped it of its essential meaning, asserting that there would be compliance with the law so long as it did not compromise national security.[36]

In June 2006, the Supreme Court entered the debate, ruling in *Hamdan v. Rumsfeld* that all detainees in U.S. custody are entitled to humane treatment, as defined by Common Article 3 of the Geneva Conventions.[37] The administration, however, rejected the court's ruling by proposing the Military Commissions Act (MCA) in September 2006. Though ostensibly aimed at bringing the procedures of Guantánamo's military commissions into conformity with the *Hamdan v. Rumsfed* (2006) decision, the MCA included a provision that exempted the CIA, granting it latitude to continue using "enhanced interrogation techniques." At a press conference announcing this new initiative, President Bush made the case for circumventing the court's decision, claiming that he was simply proposing "that there be clarity in the law so that our professionals will have no doubt that that which they are doing is legal. . .[and so that] our professionals [cannot] be held to account based upon court decisions in other countries."[38]

Although there was pushback from Congress, which principally came from Republican senators John Warner, John McCain, and Lindsey Graham, all former military servicemen, Congress ultimately passed the MCA, adding a requirement for the president to issue an executive order spelling out how the CIA would comply with Common Article 3.[39] Again, the administration ignored the clear intent of the congressional directive and sought to avoid any restraints on the CIA. The executive order, issued by the president in July 2007, prohibits torture and asserts that the CIA program "fully complies" with Common Article 3, but significantly limits the circumstances in which acts of abuse are strictly prohibited and only prohibits other forms of cruel, inhuman, or degrading conduct if the purpose of such abuses is to humiliate or degrade.[40] Commenting on this provision, Gen. P. X. Kelley, retired U.S. Marine Crops commandant and Prof. Robert Turner wrote, "The president has given the CIA carte blanche to engage in 'willful and outrageous acts of personal abuse.'" [41]

Responding to the executive order, Congress passed in 2007 a provision as part of the Intelligence Authorization Act for Fiscal Year 2008 that would have required the CIA to follow the army standard. Although the provision passed both chambers of Congress, yet again the administration recoiled, and the president vetoed the bill in March 2008.[42] President Obama explicitly revoked this executive order in January 22, 2009.[43]

In December 2008, a month before Obama took office, the Senate Armed Services Committee released a report placing responsibility for abuses committed in Guantánamo, Abu Ghraib, and other detention centers squarely on the shoulders of top Bush administration officials, including Secretary Rumsfeld. Issued jointly by Senators Carl Levin and John McCain, the report states:

> Secretary of Defense Donald Rumsfeld's December 2, 2002 authorization of aggressive interrogation techniques and subsequent interrogation policies and plans approved by senior military and civilian officials conveyed the message that physical pressures and degradation were appropriate treatment for detainees in U.S. military custody. What followed was an erosion in standards dictating that detainees be treated humanely.[44]

Ticking Bombs and Red Herrings: Why Torture is Never Legitimate

Despite the sound advice of many senior military officers and national security experts and practitioners, some policymakers, academics, and others continue to make the case for some form of officially sanctioned torture or abuse.[45] One such proponent is Prof. Alan Dershowitz. In a series of articles and books in recent years, he has argued that because coercive questioning will inevitably occur in the new national security environment, it should be regulated through the use of torture warrants.[46] Professor Dershowitz believes that torture warrants would not only limit torture but also ensure openness and accountability because oversight and monitoring would be built into the system.[47] His argument for these warrants is based on the notion that in a war against terrorists, it is no longer sufficient for the United States to be on the defensive. Thus he argues, as he did in a March 2003 interview, that the U.S. government needs to have at its disposal a series of aggressive measures, including coercive interrogation techniques, to prevent terrorist acts:

> We should never under any circumstances allow low-level people to administer torture. If torture is going to be administered as a last resort in the ticking-bomb case, to save enormous numbers of lives, it ought to be done openly, with accountability, with approval by the president of the United States or by a Supreme Court justice.[48]

Professor Dershowitz frequently cites this ticking bomb hypothetical to make his point. In such cases, he argues, a torture warrant would actually be a form of protection because it

> puts a heavy burden on the government to demonstrate by factual evidence the necessity to administer this horrible, horrible technique of torture. I would talk about nonlethal torture, say, a sterilized needle under the nail, which would violate the Geneva Accords, but you know, countries all over the world violate the Geneva Accords. . . secretly and hypothetically. . . . If we ever came close to doing it, and we don't know whether this is such a case, I think we would want to do it with accountability and openly and not adopt the way of the hypocrite.[49]

The logic behind the use of torture warrants as a protective measure is flawed. Coercive interrogations tarnish the legal right to a presumption of innocence. With a presumption of guilt instead of innocence comes poor treatment and conditions, and the burden of proof is shifted to the detainee. In these situations, the detainee has the burden of providing information to his interrogators in order to stop the maltreatment. Torture warrants also promote and sustain an environment of hysteria and fear and open the door to more abuse, not less.

Professor Dershowitz has also theorized, "We won't know if he is a ticking bomb terrorist unless he provides us information, and he's not likely to provide information unless we use certain extreme measures."[50] Although this may be an interesting law school exercise, national security experts warn against using this scenario as a basis for making official policy.

They make two points. First, the ticking bomb scenario in this country is rare or almost nonexistent. As such, it is not a sound basis for making law or policy. As Stephen Holmes, a professor at New York University School of Law, writes:

> Although neither realistic nor representative, the hypothetical [ticking bomb] is nevertheless revealing. For one thing, the idea that authorities might get a dangerous terrorist in their custody, after he has planned an attack but before he has executed it, is a utopian fantasy. The elusiveness of these criminal conspirators is intensely frustrating and naturally gives rise, among counter-terrorism officials, to daydreams of superman-style rescues. To set policies on the basis of such far-fetched scenarios would be folly.[51]

However, viewed from the battlefield, stressful situations akin to the ticking bomb seem to occur every hour of every day. As retired major general Paul Easton testified before Congress:

> The argument, the "ticking time bomb," Jack Bauer, the program "24 Hours" gets a lot of press for his solutions to the threats of our Nation. Recently his performance under pressure of the ticking time bomb scenario was favorably received by many

people, with criminal behavior excused for the greater good. . . .[S]quad leaders in Iraq are faced with a ticking time bomb scenario every day. The question is: Do we want our soldiers and Marines to play Jack Bauer?[52]

These stresses of combat, however, rarely if ever lead to situations in which a single interrogation leads to the discovery and dismantling of a ticking time bomb, though movies and television shows like *24* would have us believe otherwise. In Jack Bauer's world on *24*, he and other interrogators often are presented with a detainee or suspect, and the evidence makes it seem as if he has time-sensitive information. That is the world of entertainment; in the real world, the choices are never so clear or simple.

Thus, according to two retired U.S. marine generals, Charles Krulak and Joseph Hoar, it is important for hard and fast rules to be established for interrogations and the battlefield so that interrogators and military personnel know how to react and what they can and cannot do. In 2007 General Krulak, former commandant of the U.S. Marines, and General Hoar, former commander in chief of the U.S. Central Command, wrote "Complex situational ethics cannot be applied during the stress of combat. The rules must be firm and absolute; if torture is broached as a possibility, it will become a reality."[53]

Along these same lines, in September 2006 forty-eight retired generals, admirals, and other senior military leaders wrote a public letter to members of the Senate Armed Services Committee warning that "a flexible, sliding scale that might allow certain coercive interrogation techniques under some circumstances, while forbidding them under others. . . will only create further confusion."[54] If torture is sanctioned, allowed, or even winked at by a high-ranking official, including the president or a Supreme

Court justice, there will be a trickle-down effect with disastrous results—one need only look at Abu Ghraib and its aftermath to see how information and practices can flow down the chain of command, become distorted, and then lead to undesirable, unforeseen results.[55]

Finally, military experts and other national security professionals reject the misguided notion that because other countries or violent extremist groups rely on torture, the United States can too. As Rear Admiral John Huston, a former judge advocate general of the U.S. Navy, testified to Congress in 2005:

> We must not be deterred just because our enemy in a war on terror doesn't comply with the [Geneva] Conventions. Our unilateral compliance will aid in the peace process. Moreover, it should have been understood that violations of the Conventions, or ignoring them, doesn't help bring an end to the war. To the contrary, as we have seen, this only adds ferocity to the fighting and lengthens the war by hardening the resolve of the enemy. Our flagrant disregard for the Conventions only serves as a recruiting poster for this enemy and for our enemies for generations to come.[56]

The experiences of other democratic societies such as Israel and Britain support Admiral Hutson's warning. In 1987 the Landau Commission examined interrogation methods of General Security Services (GSS), a department of the Israeli government that investigates individuals suspected of committing crimes against the security of the country. The commission found that interrogation methods used against those suspects of "hostile terrorist activity" would be allowed so long as the methods were not lied about. Specifically, the commission wrote:

> The means of pressure should principally take the form of non-violent psychological pressure through a vigorous and extensive interrogation, with the use of stratagems, including

acts of deception. However, when these to not attain their purpose, the exertion of moderate measures of physical pressure cannot be avoided.[57]

A study conducted by B'Tselem, a human rights group based in Jerusalem, found that the GSS interrogated 1,000–1,500 Palestinians a year and that 85 percent of those, about 850, were tortured.[58] Such figures and hundreds of petitions to the Supreme Court by detained Palestinians who complained of physical force and psychological pressure led to a change in policy. In September 1999, twelve years after the Landau Commission was appointed, the Israeli Supreme Court banned the use of torture and cruel treatment during interrogations.[59] In its order, Prime Minister Ehud Barak wrote on behalf of the Court, "Indeed, violence directed at a suspect's body or spirit does not constitute a reasonable investigation practice."[60]

Similarly, there has been a shift in thinking in the United Kingdom where, during the height of the troubles in Northern Ireland, coercive interrogation methods were used against suspected members of the Irish Republican Army and others. In recent years, UK officials have relied on noncoercive methods, a shift in policy that has served Britain well. According to Louise Richardson of the University of St. Andrews, who has studied British interrogation practices in-depth, the United States has much to learn about interrogation: "The U.S. is repeating the same mistakes that other democracies [like Britain] have made. They overreact initially by relying on force and over time learn that force is not the most productive response."[61]

Preventing the Slippery Slope: Recommendations for the Obama Administration

In the long run, the struggle against al-Qaeda or other terrorist groups will not be won by resorting to torture and abuse. To the contrary, such methods make Americans less safe and are likely to actually prolong the struggle. As Generals Krulak and Hoar wrote:

> This war will be won or lost not on the battlefield but in the minds of potential supporters who have not yet thrown in their lot with the enemy. If we forfeit our values by signaling that they are negotiable in situations of grave and imminent danger, we drive those undecideds into the arms of the enemy.[62]

In its first days in office, the Obama administration took bold and decisive steps to begin restoring America's reputation. The series of executive orders issued by the administration embraced strong, effective counterterrorism policies, which include the establishment of a single interrogation standard based on humane treatment and the closure of secret prisons, policies that are consistent with the nation's core civil liberties precepts.

As the Obama administration acts to implement these directives and formulates future policy in this important area, its actions will be guided in part by the findings of the Special Interagency Task Force on Interrogations and Transfer Policies. Chaired by the attorney general, the task force will make recommendations to the administration on whether the interrogation practices and techniques outlines in the *Army Field Manual* provide "appropriate means of acquiring the intelligence necessary to protect the nation." If not, the task force is charged with recommending additional or different guidance for other departments or agencies.

President Obama's task force should follow his lead and make recommendations consistent with his commitment to uphold America's legal and ethical values. As President Obama stated in his remarks at the National Archives Museum in May 2009, we Americans "cannot keep this country safe unless we enlist the power of our most fundamental values."[63] To help the president take full advantage of what he described as "our best national security asset," the task force should urge a permanent ban on torture and all forms of cruel treatment by all U.S. agencies.

The president and Congress also should work together to find the appropriate way to review all U.S. government interrogation policies and practices since 9/11. One option proposed by Sen. Patrick Leahy and others would be to establish a commission based on the 9/11 Commission to review the past as a basis for making recommendations on how to avoid future abuses. As Senator Leahy has stated, "We need to be able to read the page before we turn the page."[64]

These steps will serve to enhance national security and to ensure the protection of basic civil liberties. In so doing, they will go a long way toward restoring America's moral standing in the world.

ENDNOTES

[…]

4. The author wishes to thank Emily Stanfield for her extensive research assistance. He also wishes to thank Devon Chaffee, Sharon Kelly, Elisa Massimino, and Gabor Rona for their helpful suggestions. Views expressed are those of the author and do not necessarily represent official views of the U.S. Department of State.

5. President Obama signed three executive orders on January 22, 2009, that put a halt to the CIA's "enhanced" interrogation program, ended secret detentions, guaranteed Red Cross access to prisoners, imposed a one-year deadline for closing the detention facilities at Guantánamo Bay, Cuba, and set a single U.S. standard for all prisoners in U.S. custody—a standard that is contained in the *Army Field Manual on Human Intelligence Collector Operations.* The executive order on lawful interrogations makes clear that every person in U.S. custody must be treated humanely and not subjected to torture or any other forms of cruel, humiliating, or degrading treatment. See White House, "Executive Orders to Date," January 23, 2009, http://www.whitehouse.gov/executive-orders-to-date.

6. National Commission on Terrorist Attacks upon the United States, *The 9/11 Commission Report: Final Report* (Washington, D.C.: Government Printing Office, 2004).

7. David Hackett Fischer, *Washington's Crossing* (New York: Oxford University Press, 2006), 379.

8. Jefferson to James Madison, Monticello, April 19, 1809, in *The Works of Thomas Jefferson, Federal Edition,* Vol. 11, ed. Paul Leicester Ford (New York: G. P. Putnam's Sons, *1905), 107.*

9. Frances Lieber, *Instructions for the Government of Armies of the United States in the Field* (Washington, D.C.: Government Printing Office, 1898), sec. 111, art. 76, and sec. 1, art. 4. These instructions were promulgated by Abraham Lincoln as General Orders No. 100, April 24, 1863. See Dietrich Schindler and Jiří Toman, eds., *The Laws of Armed Conflicts* (Boston: Martins Nihjoff, 1988), 3-23.

10. President Theodore Roosevelt, speaking on May 30, 1902, to veterans at Arlington National Cemetery. See Joseph Bucklin Bishop, *Theodore Roosevelt and His Time Shown in His Own Letters* (New York: Charles Scribner's Sons, 1920), 192.

11. "Geneva Convention Relative to the Treatment of Prisoners of War," United Nations, Geneva, 1949.

12. U.S. Office of Information for the Armed Forces, U.S. Department of Defense, *The Armed Forces Officer* (Washington, D.C.: Armed Forces Information Service, 1975), 191.

13. Gen. John Shalikashvili et al., letter to Sen. John Warner and Sen. Carl Levin, September 12, 2006, www.Humanrightsfirst.info/pdf/06913-etn-military-let-ca3.pdf.

14. "'Hardball with Chris Matthews' for November 22," msnbc.msn.com, November 23, 2005, www.msnbc.msn.com/id/10175425.

15. "'Treating Terrorists with Respect," Talkradionews.com, June 2008, http://talkradionews.com/2008/06/treating-terrorists-with-respect.

16. Human Rights First, "Top Interrogators Declare Torture Ineffective in Intelligence Gathering," June 24, 2008, http://www.humanrightsfirst. org/media/etn/2008/alert/313/index.htm.

17. In November 2005, Senator McCain wrote, "Our enemies didn't adhere to the Geneva Convention. Many of my comrades were subjected to very cruel, very inhumane and degrading treatment, a few of them even unto death. But every one of us . . . knew and took great strength from the belief that we were different from our enemies, that we *were* better than them, that we, iif the roles were reversed, would not disgrace ourselves by committing or countenancing such mistreatment of them." See John McCain, "Torture's Terrible Toll," *Newsweek,* November 21, 2005.

18. "International Covenant on Civil and Political Rights," United Nations, New York, 1966, part 3, art. 7

19. American Civil Liberties Union, "FAQ—The Convention Against Torture," April 27, 2006, www.aclu.org/safefree/torture/25353res20060427. html.

20. In a letter to members of the Senate Armed Services Committee in September 2006, a group of retired military leaders wrote: "If degradation, humiliation, physical and mental brutalization of prisoners is decriminalized or considered permissible [by the United States] under a restrictive interpretation of Common Article 3, we will forfeit all credible objections should such barbaric practices be inflicted upon American prisoners." See Shalikashvili et al., letter to Sen. John Warner and Sen. Carl Levin.

21. Naomi Klein, "Bush's War Goes Global," *Globe and Mail* (Toronto), August 27, 2003.

22. Human Rights First, "Defending Security: The Right to Defend Rights in an Age of Terrorism" (preliminary draft), Human Rights First, New York, 2004, 8, www.humanrightsfirst.org/us_law/PDF/behind-the-wire-033005.pdf.

23. Human Rights First, A *Year of Loss: Reexamining Civil Liberties since September 11* (New York: Human Rights First, 2002), 42.

24. Ibid., 43. Egyptian president Hosni Mubarak claimed in 2001 that U.S. policies implemented after September 11 "prove that we were right from the beginning in using all means" to combat terrorism.

25. National Defense Authorization Act for Fiscal Year 2006, H.R. 1815, 109th Cong., 1st sess., Congressional Record 102 (July 25, 2005): S 8792.

26. Alexander Hamilton and James Madison, "Helvidius Number IV," in *The Pacificus-Helvidius Debates of 1793-1794: Toward the Completion of the American Founding,* ed. Morton J. Frisch (Indianapolis, Ind.: Liberty Fund, 2007).

27. White House, "Vice President Cheney Delivers Remarks to the Republican Governors Association," October 25, 2001, http://georgewbush-whitehouse.archives.gov.

28. White House, "The Vice President Appears on Meet the Press with Tim Russert," September 16, 2001, http://georgewbush-whitehouse.archives.gov.

29. Jay S. Bybee, memorandum to Albert R. Gonzales, counsel to the president, August 1, 2002. http://fl1.findlaw.com/news.findlaw.com/hdocs/docs/doj/bybee80102mem.pdf.

30. Commenting on the insulation of these practices from court review, a member of the "working group" assembled by the vice president and his attorney David Addington during the aftermath of September 11 called Guantánamo "the legal equivalent of outer space"—a "lawless" universe. See Michael Isikoff and Stuart Taylor Jr., "The Gitmo Fallout," *Newsweek,* July 17, 2006.

31. Donald Rumsfeld, memorandum to the commander, U.S. Southern Command, April 16, 2003, www.gwu.edu/~nsarchiv/NSAEBB/NSAEBB127/03.04.16.pdf.

32. White House, "President Discusses Creation of Military Commissions to Try Suspected Terrorists," September 6, 2006. http://georgewbush-whitehouse.archives.gov.

33. "Abu Ghraib," Times Topics, *New York Times,* http://topics.nytimes.com/top/news/intemational/countriesandterritories/iraq/abu_ghraib/index.html.

34. Human Rights First, *Command's Responsibility: Detainee Deaths in U.S. Custody in Iraq and Afghanistan* (New York: Human Rights First, 2006), 1.

35. Eric Schmitt, "House Backs McCain on Detainees, Defying Bush," *New York Times,* December 15, 2005.

36. The signing statement stated specifically: "The executive branch shall construe these sections in a manner consistent with the constitutional authority of the President." See White House, "President's Statement on Signing of H.R. 2863, the `Department of Defense, Emergency Supplemental Appropriations to Address Hurricanes in the Gulf of Mexico, and Pandemic Influenza Act, 2006,'" http://georgewbush-whitehouse.archives.gov.

37. Linda Greenhouse, "Justices, 5-3, Broadly Reject Bush Plan to Try Detainees," *New York Times,* June 30, 2006.

38. White House, "Press Conference of the President," September 15, 2006, http://georgewbush-whitehouse.archives.gov.

39. *Military Commissions Act of 2006,* Public Law 109-366, 109th Cong., 2nd sess. (October 17, 2006), 2632, 2637.

40. The language of the executive order specifically reads: "willful and outrageous acts of personal abuse done for the purpose of humiliating or degrading the individual in a manner so serious that any reasonable person, considering the circumstances, would deem the acts to be beyond the bounds of human decency, such as sexual or sexually indecent acts undertaken for the purpose of humiliation, forcing the individual to perform sexual acts or to pose sexually, threatening the individual with sexual mutilation, or using the individual as a human shield; or acts intended to denigrate the religion, religious practices, or religious objects of the individual." See White House, "Executive Order: Interpretation of the Geneva Conventions Common Article 3 as Applied to a Program of Detention and Interrogation Operated by the Central Intelligence Agency," July 20, 2007, http://georgewbush-whitehouse.archives.gov.

41. P. X. Kelley and Robert F. Turner, "War Crimes and the White House: The Dishonor in a Tortured New 'Interpretation' of the Geneva Conventions," *Washington Post,* July 26, 2007.

42. In a statement to the U.S. House of Representatives, the president wrote, "I am returning herewith without my approval...the 'Intelligence Authorization Act for Fiscal Year 2008.' The bill would impede the United States Government's efforts to protect American people effectively from terrorist attacks and other threats because it imposes several unnecessary and unacceptable burdens on our Intelligence Community." He went on to write: "Section 327 of the bill would harm our national security by requiring any element of the Intelligence Community to use only the

interrogation methods authorized in the Army Field Manual on Interrogations. It is vitally important that the Central Intelligence Agency (CIA) be allowed to maintain a separate and classified interrogation program. . . . [M]y concern is the need to maintain a separate CIA program that will shield from disclosure to al Qaeda and other terrorists the interrogation techniques they may face upon capture." See www.fas.org/irp/congress/2008_cr/veto.html.

43. For the full text of President Obama's executive order revoking the Bush order, see www.whitehouse.gov/the_press_office/EnsuringLawfulInterrogations.

44. "Senate Armed Forces Committee Inquiry into the Treatment of Detainees in U.S. Custody," December 11, 2008, http://levin.senate.gov/newsroom/supporting/2008/Detainees.121108.pdf. The report pointedly rejects the administration's notion that using these coercive interrogation techniques keeps the country and its troops safe.

45. For a defense of the Bush administration's post-9/11 interrogation policy, see George Tenet, *At the Center of the Storm* (New York: HarperCollins, 2007).

46. Alan Dershowitz, "Want to Torture? Get a Warrant," January 22, 2002, www.alandershowitz.com/publications/docs/torturewarrants2.html.

47. Ibid.

48. "Dershowitz: Torture Could Be Justified," CNN.com, March 3, 2003, www.cnn.com/2003/LAW/03/03/cnna.Dershowitz.

49. Ibid.

50. Ibid.

51. Stephen Holmes, "Is Defiance of Law a Proof of Success? Magical Thinking in the War on Terror," in *The Torture Debate in America,* ed. Karen J. Greenberg (New York: Cambridge University Press, 2006), 127–128.

52. Senate Committee on Foreign Relations, "Extraordinary Rendition, Extraterritorial Detention and Treatment of Detainees: Restoring Our Moral Credibility and Strengthening Our Diplomatic Standing," hearing, 110th Cong., 1st sess., www.fas.org/irp/congress/2007_hr/rendition2.pdf.

53. Charles C. Krulak and Joseph P. Hoar, "It's Our Cage, Too; Torture Betrays Us and Breeds New Enemies," *Washington Post,* May 17, 2007.

54. Shalikashvili et al., letter to Sen. John Warner and Sen. Carl Levin.

55. Alberto Mora, former general counsel to the U.S. Navy from 2001 to 2005 and a principled dissenting voice on these issues, stated in an interview with *Vanity Fair* magazine, "I will also tell you that there are general-rank officers who've had senior responsibility within the Joint Staff or counterterrorism operations who believe that the number-one and number-two leading causes of U.S. combat deaths in Iraq have been, number one, Abu Ghraib, number two, Guantánamo, because of the effectiveness of these symbols in helping recruit jihadists into the field and combat against American soldiers." See Cullen Murphy and Todd S. Purdum, "Farewell to All That: An Oral History of the Bush White House," *Vanity Fair,* February 2009.

56. "Testimony of John D. Hutson before the United States Senate Committee on the Judiciary Concerning the Nomination of Alberto Gonzales for Confirmation as Attorney General of the United States," January 6, 2005, http://judiciary.senate.gov/hearings/testimony. cfm?id=1345&wit_id=3937.

57. "Background on the High Court of Justice's decision," www.btselem. org/english/Torture/Background.asp.

58. Ibid.

59. "Israel Supreme Court Bans Interrogation Abuse of Palestinians," CNN. com, September 6, 1999, www.cnn.com/WORLD/meast/9909/06/ israel.torture/.

60. A. Barak, "Text of Israeli Supreme Court Decision on GSS Practices," Totse.com, September 6,1999, www.totse.com/en/politics/foreign_ military_intelligence_agencies/ua92170.html.

61. Quoted in Josh Meyer, "CIA Should Tape More, Experts Say," *Los Angeles Times,* December 23, 2007.

62. Krulak and Hoar, "It's Our Cage, Too."

63. Remarks of President Barack Obama, National Archives Museum, Washington D.C., May 21, 2009, www.whitehouse.gov/the_press_office/ Remarks-by-the-President-On-National-Security-5-21-09.

64. Sen. Patrick Leahy, "Take Action: Support a Truth and Reconciliation Commission," Office of Sen. Patrick Leahy, Truth Commission petition, http://ga3.org/campaign/btcpetition?qp_source=btc_dk.

*__Michael H. Posner__ is the assistant secretary of state for the Bureau of Democracy, Human Rights, and Labor in the U.S. Department of State. He was previously the executive director and then president of Human Rights First, a nonprofit human rights organization.

Posner, Michael H. 2010. Yes: Torture violates U.S. and international law and should never be allowed. In *Debating terrorism and counterterrorism,* ed. Stuart Gottlieb, 307–320. Washington, DC: CQ Press. Copyright © [2010] CQ Press, a division of SAGE Publications, Inc.

Discussion Questions

1. Ali Soufan describes the interrogation of Abu Zubaydah, a terror suspect, by a team from the FBI and also by a contractor to the CIA. What are the two interrogation methods Ali Soufan says were used against Zubaydah? Which one did he think was more effective and why? Is rappor-building always likely to be more effective than physical coercion and fear?

2. Charles Krauthammer's opinion piece begins by mentioning the "McCain amendment." The McCain amendment, named for Senator John McCain of Arizona, forbade the use on any person under the custody or control of the United States of "cruel, inhuman, or degrading treatment or punishment." Why does Krauthammer oppose the McCain amendment? How far would he go in allowing torture to prevent terrorist attacks? What basis does he provide for believing that torture "works"?

3. Some commentators support the idea that torture should be permitted in specific, extraordinary circumstances, most notably during "ticking time bomb" scenarios. What are Michael Posner's responses to that argument? What would he advise the president to do if in fact torture appeared to be the only way to save lives?

4. What would you do in a "ticking time bomb" scenario? How should the law treat an individual who tortures in order to save lives?

PART 3:

Accountability

What should be done about the fact that Bush administration officials, including the president himself, authorized illegal interrogation tactics against al Qaeda suspects, including waterboarding, a technique widely considered to be torture? On August 1, 2002, the United States Department of Justice issued two secret memoranda advising the Central Intelligence Agency that it could employ a variety of "enhanced interrogation techniques" against "high-value detainees" being kept in secret prisons overseas. Those memos, and a series of memos that followed them over the next five years, authorized a number of interrogation tactics that would be plainly illegal in the United States, including depriving individuals of sleep, hitting them, slamming them into walls, forcing them into painful stress positions, and waterboarding them. Many experts consider these tactics to be torture; indeed, the United States has previously treated waterboarding as torture when done by others.

When the August 1 memo was leaked to the press, the Bush administration swiftly rescinded it; exposed to public scrutiny, an opinion the government had relied on in secret could no longer be sustained. Yet, the administration continued, in secret, to authorize waterboarding and other coercive techniques. Virtually everyone agrees that these memos, and the tactics they endorsed, were a dark chapter in American history. But much disagreement exists about what, if anything, should be done about them. Should the lawyers who wrote the memos and the officials who approved these tactics be criminally prosecuted, censured by Congress, sanctioned by lawyers' associations, or investigated by a bipartisan commission? In the first essay that follows, I argue that, at a minimum, the United States government has an obligation to investigate and declare illegal the Bush administration's tactics. In the second piece, Human Rights Watch maintains that international law obligates us to prosecute those who authorized torture. In the last contribution, Julian Ku argues that criminal prosecutions of the lawyers would be unwarranted and dangerous. What do you think?

The Torture Memos: The Case Against the Lawyers

by David Cole*

1.

On Monday, August 24, as President Obama began his vacation on Martha's Vineyard, his administration released a previously classified 2004 report by the CIA's inspector general that strongly criticized the techniques employed to interrogate "high-value" al-Qaeda suspects at the CIA's secret prisons.[1] The report revealed that CIA agents and contractors, in addition to using such "authorized" and previously reported tactics as water-boarding, wall-slamming, forced nudity, stress positions, and extended sleep deprivation, also employed a variety of "unau-thorized, improvised, inhumane and undocumented" methods. These included threatening suspects with a revolver and a power drill; repeatedly applying pressure to a detainee's carotid artery until he began to pass out; staging a mock execution; threatening to sexually abuse a suspect's mother; and warning a detainee that if another attack occurred in the United States, "We're going to kill your children."

The inspector general also reported, contrary to for-mer Vice President Dick Cheney's claims, that "it is not possible to say" that any of these abusive tactics—authorized or unauthorized—elicited valuable information that could not have been obtained through lawful, nonviolent means. While some of the CIA's detainees provided useful information, the inspector general concluded that the effectiveness of the coercive methods in particular—as opposed to more traditional and lawful tactics that were also used—"cannot be so easily measured." CIA officials, he wrote, often lacked any objective basis for concluding that detainees were withholding information and therefore should be subjected to the "enhanced" techniques. The inspector general further found no evidence that any imminent terrorist attacks had been averted by virtue of information obtained from the CIA's detainees. In other words, there were no "ticking time bombs."

The same day, Attorney General Eric Holder announced that he was asking John Durham, a federal prosecutor already investigating the CIA's suspicious destruction of its interrogation videotapes, to expand his inquiry to include a preliminary investigation into some of the CIA's most extreme interrogation tactics. Holder simultaneously announced that he would not prosecute "anyone who acted in good faith and within the scope of the legal guidance given by the Office of Legal Counsel regarding the interrogation of detainees."

The latter limitation suggests that Holder has directed the investigation to focus only on those interrogators who engaged in unauthorized conduct, but not on the lawyers and Cabinet officials who authorized the CIA to use specific techniques of brutal physical coercion in the first place. If the inquiry stops there, it will repeat the pattern we saw after the revelation of the abuses at Abu Ghraib, in which a few low-level individuals were prosecuted but no higher-ups were held accountable.

Lost in all the attention given to the CIA inspector general report and Holder's announcement was still another packet of documents released later the same day, from the Justice Department's Office of Legal Counsel (OLC). When these memos, letters, and faxes are considered together with an earlier set disclosed in April 2009, it becomes clear that there is an inherent conflict of interest in the investigation Holder has initiated. Justice Department lawyers were inextricably involved in justifying every aspect of the CIA program. They wrote memo after memo over a five-year period, from 2002 to 2007, all maintaining that any interrogation methods the CIA was planning to use were legal. And now the Justice Department is investigating not itself, but only the CIA, for atrocities in which both were deeply implicated.

While the memos from the Office of Legal Counsel have received less attention than the details of brutal treatment recorded by the CIA inspector general, these memos are the real "smoking gun" in the torture controversy. They reveal that instead of requiring the CIA to conform its conduct to the law, the OLC lawyers contorted the law to authorize precisely what it was designed to forbid. They concluded that keeping suspects awake for eleven days straight, stripping them naked, exposing them to cold temperatures, dousing them with water, slamming them into walls, forcing them into cramped boxes and stress positions for hours at a time, and waterboarding them hundreds of times were not torture, not cruel, not inhuman, not even degrading, and therefore perfectly legal. The memos make clear that true accountability cannot stop at the CIA interrogators, but must extend up the chain of authority, to the lawyers and Cabinet officers who approved the "enhanced interrogation techniques" in the first place.

The OLC's defenders argue that it was difficult to define concretely exactly what constitutes torture or cruel, inhuman, or degrading treatment and that there was little direct precedent to go on. There is some truth to these arguments. Not all physically coercive interrogation is torture. Determining whether tactics qualify as torture under federal law requires difficult distinctions between "severe" and less-than-severe pain and suffering, and between "prolonged" and temporary mental harm. Former Attorney General Michael Mukasey has argued that the lawyers acted in good faith to render their best judgment on these issues in perilous times.

Precisely because many of the questions were so difficult, however, one would expect a good-faith anal0ysis to reach a nuanced conclusion, perhaps approving some measures while definitely prohibiting others. Yet it is striking that on every question, no matter how much the law had to be stretched, the Bush administration lawyers reached the same result—the CIA could do whatever it had proposed to do. And long after federal officials acknowledged that the threat of terror had substantially subsided, the OLC continued to distort the law so as to facilitate brutality.

Most disturbingly, the OLC lawyers secretly maintained their position even as the relevant facts changed, and even after the law developed to underscore that the CIA's tactics were illegal. There was one law for public consumption, but another quite different law operating in secret. For example, when the Justice Department's initial August 2002 memo interpreting the torture statute was leaked to the press in June 2004 and widely condemned, the department publicly issued a replacement memo, dated December 30, 2004, which rejected several interpretations advanced in its earlier memo. But the recently disclosed documents reveal that the department continued in secret to approve all the same interrogation tactics.

In 2005 Congress threatened to restrict CIA tactics further by confirming that every person in US custody was protected against not only torture, but all cruel, inhuman, and degrading treatment. The Bush lawyers drafted yet another secret opinion, concluding that none of the CIA's tactics could even be considered cruel, inhuman, or degrading. And when the Supreme Court ruled in 2006 that the Geneva Conventions, which broadly prohibit all mistreatment of wartime detainees, applied to al-Qaeda, the OLC lawyers wrote still another secret opinion recommending that President Bush issue an executive order that would "authoritatively" establish that the CIA's tactics did not violate the laws of war—simply because the president said so. When considered as a whole, the memos reveal a sustained effort by the OLC lawyers to rationalize a predetermined and illegal result.

2.

History has shown that even officials acting with the best intentions may come to feel, especially in times of crisis, that the end justifies the means, and that the greater good of national security makes it permissible to inflict pain on a resisting suspect to make him talk. History has also shown that inflicting such pain—no matter how "well-intentioned"—dehumanizes both the suspect and his interrogator, corrodes the system of justice, renders a fair trial virtually impossible, and often exacerbates the very threat to the nation's security that was said to warrant the interrogation tactics in the first place.

Knowing that history, the world's nations adopted the Geneva Conventions and the Convention Against Torture (in 1949 and 1984), both of which prohibit torture in absolute terms. The Convention Against Torture provides that "no exceptional circumstances whatsoever, whether a state of war or a threat of war, internal political instability or any other public emergency, may be invoked as a justification of torture."

If laws such as the Geneva Conventions and the Convention against Torture are to work, however, lawyers must stand up for them. That means being willing to say no when asked whether it is permissible to subject a human being to the brutality that the CIA proposed. Yet the OLC lawyers always said yes. Where precedents were deemed helpful, they cited them even if they were inapposite; where precedents were unhelpful, they did not cite them, no matter how applicable. They treated the law against torture not as a universal moral prohibition, but as an inconvenient obstacle to be evaded by any means necessary.

Such an approach to the law is especially alarming in view of the particular role of the Office of Legal Counsel. That office is designed to serve as the "constitutional conscience" of the Justice Department. As Jack Goldsmith, one of the heads of the OLC under President Bush, has said, "OLC is, and views itself as, the frontline institution responsible for ensuring that the executive branch charged with executing the law is itself bound by law." It attracts some of the nation's best lawyers, and its alumni include former Chief Justice William Rehnquist, Justice Antonin Scalia, former Solicitors General Theodore Olson and Walter Dellinger, former Yale Law School Dean and current State Department Legal Adviser Harold Koh, Harvard Law Professor Cass Sunstein, and former Yale University President Benno Schmidt Jr.

Private lawyers are sometimes considered "hired guns," whose obligation is to interpret the law as far as possible to do their client's bidding. We rely on the adversarial system and public airing of arguments and evidence to reach a just result. Lawyers in the Office of Legal Counsel, by contrast, work in a setting that affords no adversarial presentation or public scrutiny. In that position, the lawyer's obligation is to provide objective advice as an "honest broker," not to act as an advocate or a hired gun.

When it comes to covert activities such as the CIA interrogation program, judgments of legality are often uniquely in executive hands, since the judiciary, Congress, and the public may not even know of the activities' existence. In addition, on the question of torture the OLC lawyers were the last—and only—line of defense, since the detainees were denied all recourse to the outside world.

If OLC lawyers had exercised independent judgment and said no to the CIA's practices, as they should have, that might well have been the end of the Bush administration's experiment with torture. Vice President Dick Cheney and his chief counsel, David Addington, would undoubtedly have put tremendous pressure on the OLC to change its views; but had the OLC stood firm, it is difficult to imagine even the Bush-Cheney White House going forward with a program that the OLC said was illegal.

The OLC lawyers had the opportunity, and the *responsibility*, to prevent illegal conduct *before* it occurred. The lawyers involved in drafting the "torture memos"—Jay Bybee, John Yoo, Daniel Levin, and Steven Bradbury—failed to live up to these obligations. In their hands, law became not a constraint on power but the instrument of unconscionable abuse.

3.

The "original sin" in this narrative dates to August 1, 2002, when the OLC issued two memos that approved every tactic the CIA had proposed. From that point forward, there was no turning back. Other OLC memos had already ruled that the Geneva Conventions did not protect al-Qaeda detainees. And as we would learn later, the OLC had secretly concluded that the Convention Against Torture's prohibition on cruel, inhuman, and degrading treatment did not apply to foreigners held in CIA custody abroad. The August 2002 memos, therefore, addressed what the OLC considered the sole remaining barrier to harsh interrogation tactics—a federal statute making torture a crime.

The initial August 2002 memo, written by John Yoo and signed by Jay Bybee, was leaked in 2004, and has already been widely discussed.[2] It defined "severe pain or suffering" by reference to an obscure and inapposite health benefits statute, concluding that in order to be "severe," pain must be "equivalent in intensity to the pain accompanying organ failure, impairment of bodily function, or even death." It interpreted "prolonged mental harm" to require proof of harm lasting "months or years." It said that the president had unchecked power to authorize torture despite a federal statute making it a crime. And it argued that an interrogator who tortured could escape liability by asserting unprecedented versions of the "self-defense" and "necessity" doctrines, advancing much broader interpretations of these concepts than most criminal defense lawyers would be willing to offer.

The same day, August 1, 2002, the OLC issued a second memo, publicly released for the first time in April 2009. It concluded that all of the CIA's proposed tactics were permissible: specifically,

(1) attention grasp, (2) walling, (3) facial hold, (4) facial slap (insult slap), (5) cramped confinement, (6) wall standing, (7) stress positions, (8) sleep deprivation, (9) insects placed in a confinement box, and (10) the waterboard.

None of these techniques, the OLC insisted, inflicted pain of a severity associated with organ failure or death. While being slammed into a wall repeatedly "may hurt. . .any pain experienced is not of the intensity associated with serious physical injury." What was the basis for these OLC conclusions? The CIA itself. With respect to waterboarding, for example, the OLC memo stated: "[the CIA has] informed us that this procedure does not inflict actual physical harm," and on that basis the memo concluded that waterboarding "inflicts no pain or actual harm whatsoever." And waterboarding cannot cause any long-term suffering, the OLC determined, because, according to the CIA, it "is simply a controlled acute episode."

The arguments of the initial August 2002 memo were so strained that the Justice Department abandoned them as soon as the memo was made public in 2004. On December 30, 2004, the department issued a replacement memo, signed by the new OLC head, Dan Levin, that pointedly departed from the August 2002 memo on several specific points. But these disagreements were purely cosmetic; behind closed doors, issuance of the ostensibly contrite replacement memo did not change *anything* with respect to the CIA's program. The memo was more an exercise in public relations than in law, since it did nothing to restrict the specific techniques that had been approved previously.

This becomes clear in three secret memos issued in May 2005, and signed by Steven Bradbury, who succeeded Levin as head of the OLC. These memos sound at first reading more reasonable than the August 2002 memos. They acknowledge more contrary arguments, and even occasionally express doubt. They were written with acute awareness of the widespread public criticism of the leaked August 2002 memo, and of the damning findings of the 2004 CIA inspector general's report. By this time, almost four years after September 11, and with substantial evidence of abuse, the OLC should have known better. Yet the May 2005 memos are in a fundamental sense the worst of the lot, and ultimately reach even more unreasonable positions than the August 2002 memos.

The May memos conclude that none of the CIA techniques, used singly or in combination, constitute either torture or cruel, inhuman, or degrading treatment. Their analysis is heavily predicated on two facts: (1) American soldiers subjected to some of these techniques in the military's counter-torture training (called Survival, Evasion, Resistance, Escape, or SERE) reportedly have not suffered severe physical pain or prolonged mental harm; and (2) doctors would be present to monitor the interrogations. Neither fact remotely supports the legality of the program.

The SERE experience is wholly inapposite. A soldier who chooses to subject himself to SERE training does so voluntarily; he knows that everything that happens to him is part of a program that he knows has clear limits. He is given a code word that he can use at any time to halt the process. By contrast, an al-Qaeda suspect finds himself an involuntary captive of his enemy in a secret prison, cut off from the outside world, unaware of any limits, and utterly powerless to make his interrogators stop.

Nor does the presence of a doctor make coercive interrogation legal. The memos stressed that medical experts with SERE experience would stop the interrogations "if deemed medically necessary to prevent severe mental or physical harm." But how is a medical expert supposed to assess whether a given technique is imposing severe rather than less-than-severe pain, or might give rise to prolonged rather than temporary psychological harm? No doctor could assess these things on the spot. Indeed, at one point the December 2004 memo seems to admit this, quoting a medical journal to the effect that "pain is a subjective experience and there is no way to objectively quantify it." And if anything, experience with SERE simulations is likely to have desensitized doctors to the potential harms presented by real coercive interrogations.

A separate memo, dated May 30, 2005, the most disingenuous of all, concluded that the CIA's techniques did not even constitute cruel, inhuman, or degrading treatment, a much lower threshold than torture. The Bush OLC had previously sidestepped the prohibition against "cruel, inhuman, or degrading treatment" altogether by maintaining, again in secret, that it did not apply to foreign nationals held outside US borders. But when that interpretation was publicly disclosed, Congress vowed to overrule it. The Bush administration vigorously resisted, but in the Detainee Treatment Act, enacted in December 2005, Congress expressly prohibited cruel, inhuman, or degrading treatment of any person in US custody.

Recognizing that this change was coming, the May 30 memo stated, once again in secret, that none of the CIA's techniques were cruel, inhuman, or degrading anyway, because they would not "shock the conscience," a test imposed by the Senate when it ratified the 1984 treaty banning torture and cruel treatment. The OLC concluded that the CIA tactics did not shock the conscience because they inflicted pain not arbitrarily but for a good end, and because the government sought to "minimize the risk of injury or any suffering that does not further the Government's interest in obtaining actionable intelligence."

The case law is clear, however, that *any* intentional infliction of pain for interrogation purposes "shocks the conscience."
And the Supreme Court has recognized no exception that would
permit the infliction of pain if the government's reason is good
enough. The Court has repeatedly held that any use or threat
of force to coerce a confession shocks the conscience—even
where employed to solve a murder.[3]

The OLC argued in its May 30 memo that this standard ought
not to apply where interrogation is used only to gather intelligence, not to convict. But in *Chavez* v. *Martinez*, the Supreme
Court in 2003 reaffirmed that any intentional infliction of pain
for interrogation would shock the conscience, even where the
statements were not used in a prosecution. In the *Chavez* case,
officers interrogated a man while he was suffering from gun-
shot wounds in a hospital, but they did not inflict any pain
themselves for the purpose of questioning. While the justices
disagreed about the specific conclusions to be drawn from the
facts alleged, and ultimately returned the case to the lower court
for resolution, all of the justices who addressed the issue agreed
that the *deliberate* infliction of pain on an individual to compel
him to talk *would* shock the conscience.

Justice Kennedy, writing for three justices, reasoned that
police "may not prolong or increase a suspect's suffering against
the suspect's will," or even give him "the impression that severe
pain will be alleviated only if [he] cooperates." Justice Thomas,
writing for another three justices, concluded that the interrogation was permissible, but only because he found "no evidence
that Chavez acted with a purpose to harm Martinez," or that
"Chavez's conduct exacerbated Martinez's injuries." Under
either approach, then, a purpose to harm is illegal. The court
of appeals on remand in the *Chavez* case unanimously held that

the alleged conduct indeed shocked the conscience, a fact not even acknowledged by the OLC memo.

The OLC memo maintained that "the CIA program is considerably less invasive or extreme than much of the conduct at issue in [*Chavez*]." In fact, the opposite is true. The officers in *Chavez* inflicted no pain for purposes of interrogation. The CIA's entire program, by contrast, was based on the deliberate infliction of pain and humiliation to compel recalcitrant suspects to talk against their will.

Tellingly, at the very end of this memo, the OLC lawyers admitted that "we cannot predict with confidence that a court would agree with our conclusion." But they then went on to reassure the CIA that the question "is unlikely to be subject to judicial inquiry." Even if the treaty prohibiting torture and cruel treatment were violated, the memo continued, "the courts have nothing to do and can give no redress." In other words, the CIA for all practical purposes was operating in a "law-free zone," or at least a zone where the law was whatever the executive said it was—in secret. And no court would ever have the opportunity to disagree.

The latest OLC memo on the CIA interrogation program to be disclosed is dated July 2007, and was publicly released on August 24, 2009.[4] By the time this memo was written, the Supreme Court had rejected the Bush administration's contention that al-Qaeda detainees were not covered by Common Article 3 of the Geneva Conventions. Common Article 3 comprehensively prohibits torture, cruelty, violence to person, and any humiliating, degrading, or inhumane treatment of wartime detainees. By 2007, the CIA had limited their interrogation tactics but were still using extended sleep deprivation, dietary manipulation, attention grasps, and slapping detainees repeatedly in the face and stomach—all of which would ordinarily violate Common Article 3.

The OLC argued that Common Article 3 permitted abuse of al-Qaeda detainees that it would not permit of any other wartime detainees, even though Common Article 3 draws no distinctions among detainees. Other courts had ruled that any deliberate infliction of pain to coerce statements from suspects is inherently degrading. The OLC rejected that view, insisting that degrading treatment was permissible as long as it was not an "outrage upon personal dignity"—but never explained why using physical pain to override a suspect's will is not inherently an outrage upon personal dignity.

Most astoundingly, the memo argued—in a footnote—that the president could avoid all of Common Article 3's requirements simply by declaring that they do not apply—even though the Supreme Court had ruled exactly the opposite one year earlier. In the OLC's view, the Military Commissions Act of 2006 gave the president the power to overrule the Supreme Court on this matter. Congress never said anything of the kind. The memo concluded with the advice that the president act somewhat less dramatically, and simply issue a regulation that "defined" Common Article 3 in a way that would allow the CIA to do what it wanted. President Bush subsequently did just that.

4.

At its best, law is about seeking justice, regulating state power, respecting human dignity, and protecting the vulnerable. Law at its worst treats legal doctrine as infinitely manipulable, capable of being twisted cynically in whatever direction serves the client's desires. Had the OLC lawyers adhered to the former standard, they could have stopped the CIA abuses in their tracks. Instead, they used law not as a check on power but to facilitate brutality, deployed against captive human beings who had absolutely no other legal recourse.

In light of these actions, it is not enough to order a cessation of such tactics, and a limited investigation of CIA agents who may have gone beyond the OLC guidelines. Official recognition that the OLC guidelines were themselves illegal is essential if we are to uphold a decent standard of law. Official repudiation is also critical if we are to regain respect around the world for the United States as a law-abiding nation, and if we hope to build meaningful safeguards against this kind of descent into cruelty happening again.

Moreover, this is not just a matter of what's right from the standpoint of morality, history, or foreign relations. The United States is *legally bound* by the Convention Against Torture to submit any case alleging torture by a person within its jurisdiction "to its competent authorities for the purpose of prosecution." President Obama and Attorney General Holder have both stated that waterboarding is torture. Accordingly, the United States is legally obligated to investigate not merely those CIA interrogators who went beyond waterboarding, but the lawyers and Cabinet officers who authorized waterboarding and other torture tactics in the first place.

The fact that such an investigation would be divisive, or might divert attention from President Obama's other priorities, is not an excuse for failing to fulfill this legal obligation, and not a justification for not prosecuting. The fact that a defendant has powerful allies does not warrant treating him more leniently. At the same time, prosecutors do have discretion not to bring charges for many reasons, and it would not be illegitimate to decline prosecution if a prosecutor concluded that it was not clear beyond a reasonable doubt that the lawyers and officials intended to violate the law.

But surely it is premature to make such judgments. All the facts are still not known. And even if prosecution were not warranted, it is still critical that there be some form of official acknowledgment of wrongdoing. The least President Obama should do, therefore, is to appoint an independent, nonpartisan commission of distinguished citizens, along the lines of the 9/11 Commission, to investigate and assess responsibility for the United States' adoption of coercive interrogation policies.

Only such a commission has the possibility of rising above the partisan wrangling that any attempt to hold accountable high-level officials of the prior administration is certain to set off. The facts that emerge should point to the appropriate response—whether a congressional resolution, disbarment proceedings against the lawyers, civil actions for money damages, or criminal prosecutions. Absent a reckoning for those responsible for making torture and cruel, inhuman, and degrading treatment official US policy, the United States' commitment to the rule of law will remain a hollow shell—a commitment to be honored only when it is not inconvenient or impolitic to do so.

ENDNOTES

1. Office of Inspector General, "Special Review: Counterterrorism Detention and Interrogation Activities (September 2001–October 2003)," May 7, 2004, available at www.aclu.org/oigreport/.

2. All of the OLC memos discussed here are reproduced in *The Torture Memos: Rationalizing the Unthinkable*, edited by David Cole and with a foreword by Philippe Sands, just published by the New Press, with

the exception of a July 2007 memo that was released only on August 24, 2009.

3. See, for example, *Rogers* v. *Richmond*, 365 US 534 (1961); *Ashcraft* v. *Tennessee*, 322 US 143 (1944).

4. "Memorandum for John A. Rizzo, Acting General Counsel, Central Intelligence Agency, Re: Application of the War Crimes Act, the Detainee Treatment Act, and Common Article 3 of the Geneva Conventions to Certain Techniques that May Be Used by the CIA in the Interrogation of High Value al Qaeda Detainees," July 20, 2007, available at www.usdoj.gov/olc/docs/memo-warcrimesact.pdf.

*David Cole teaches constitutional law, criminal justice, and national security at the Georgetown University Law Center, is the legal affairs correspondent for *The Nation*, and also contributes regularly to *The New York Review of Books*. He is the author of five books and dozens of articles on national security, civil liberties, and the rule of law.

Cole, David. 2009. The torture memos: The case against the lawyers. *The New York Review of Books*, September 10. http://www.nybooks.com/articles/archives/2009/oct/08/the-torture-memos-the-case-against-the-lawyers/.

Reprinted with permission from The New York Review of Books.

Copyright © 2009 NYREV, Inc.

Accountability for Torture: Questions and Answers

by Human Rights Watch*

Introduction

After the attacks of September 11, 2001, US officials approved various interrogation methods that were illegal under both US and international law. These included such brutal practices as painful "stress positions," prolonged exposure to cold, and "waterboarding" (near drowning), which the United States has long prosecuted as a war crime. These techniques were used on detainees in Guantánamo, Iraq, and Afghanistan and in secret CIA prisons. Yet no senior official has been held accountable for these crimes. If the United States is to restore its credibility as a nation committed to the rule of law and respect for fundamental rights, it should promptly, impartially, and thoroughly investigate and prosecute those officials, regardless of position or rank, who authorized or ordered torture and other mistreatment.

At the same time, it is crucial to understand how the United States came to employ such barbaric methods of interrogation. The American public deserves a full and public accounting of the scale of post-9/11 abuses, why and how they occurred, and who was responsible for them. An independent, nonpartisan commission should be established to examine the actions of the executive branch, the CIA, the military, and Congress, and to make recommendations to ensure that such acts are not repeated.

Some have expressed objections to the prosecution of US government officials for their role in abusive interrogation methods and to the creation of commission of inquiry. We address those objections below.

By prosecuting those who believed that they were acting in the US's best interests, aren't we "criminalizing policy differences"?

The use of torture can never be an appropriate policy option. Since the time of George Washington, the United States has rejected torture of prisoners of war. During the American Civil War, Abraham Lincoln endorsed the Lieber Code for the conduct of Union soldiers, which prohibited the use of "torture to extort confessions." In the twentieth century, the United States became party to a number of international treaties that ban torture and other ill-treatment, including the International Covenant on Civil and Political Rights and the Geneva Conventions. Under the Convention against Torture and Other Cruel, Inhuman, or Degrading Treatment or Punishment, which the United States has ratified and codified under US law, "no exceptional circumstances whatsoever, whether a state of war or a threat of war, internal political instability or any other public emergency, may be invoked as a justification of torture."

President Barack Obama has banned the use of torture, so why dig up the past and open old wounds?

Prosecuting those responsible for torture not only brings justice for past abuses, but also is the best way of ensuring that such crimes don't happen again.

President Obama took the important step of repudiating torture as an interrogation technique. On his second full day in office, he issued an executive order that closed the CIA's secret detention program, barred the agency from using coercive techniques, and required it to abide by the same interrogation standards as the US military. The order also revoked past presidential directives and other orders and regulations that authorized the abusive treatment of detainees, and repudiated previous Justice Department legal memos relating to interrogation.

But simply changing the rules without prosecuting past abuses as the crimes that they are leaves open the possibility that the rules could be changed again. Unless those responsible for authorizing and ordering torture are prosecuted, a future administration might be tempted to use such abusive practices again.

Won't prosecutions impede future counterterrorism operations by making officials fearful that their actions may later be judged illegal?

Torture is never a legitimate practice. One reason US interrogators were willing to engage in torture is that the message from the top was that it was acceptable, even expected, despite the longstanding prohibitions against such practices. Government interrogators should never again be placed in such a conflicting position. Prosecuting those responsible for the torture program will re-affirm the prohibition so that interrogators and others involved in counterterrorism operations will clearly understand what is and what is not permissible.

Why is a commission of inquiry necessary when we already know what happened?

While much is known about the interrogation methods used after 9/11, there are still many unanswered questions. The Bush administration went to great lengths to keep its actions in the "global war on terror" a state secret. The investigations conducted so far either have been limited in scope—looking at violations by military personnel at a particular place in a limited time frame, for example—or have lacked independence, with the military investigating itself. Congressional investigations have been limited to looking at a single agency or department. Individuals who planned or participated in the programs have yet to speak for the record. Many of the key documents relating to the use of abusive techniques remain secret. Many of the dots remain unconnected.

To date, there has not been a comprehensive public inquiry into the actions of the CIA, the military, Congress, and senior executive branch officials. Such an inquiry could provide a fuller picture of how the system allowed these abuses to take place, as well as the human, legal and political consequences of the policy of torture. Even prosecutions won't bring the full range of information to light. If the American public is truly to learn the lessons of this period, there needs to be a full public accounting.

Didn't the "enhanced interrogation techniques" elicit valuable information that helped keep the country safe?

There are competing, unresolved claims about whether torture yielded actionable intelligence that couldn't have been obtained any other way. Bush administration officials, including former Vice President Dick Cheney and former CIA Director Porter Goss, have contended that the CIA's interrogation program provided critical intelligence that helped thwart terrorist attacks. However, a number of former CIA interrogators have contested those claims, saying that detainees revealed actionable intelligence during "rapport building" interrogations, before they were subjected to abusive methods.

Critics also point out that torture elicits unreliable information or answers that the interrogator wants, even if untrue. The case of Ibn al-Shaykh al-Libi, one of the first top al Qaeda suspects held by the CIA, is instructive. Under "enhanced interrogation," al-Libi reportedly told interrogators that Iraq had provided chemical and biological weapons training to al Qaeda. This information—which turned out to be entirely wrong—was used in then Secretary of State Colin Powell's 2003 speech to the United Nations to justify war with Iraq. It was later revealed that al-Libi had no knowledge of training or weapons and fabricated the statements because he was terrified of further harsh treatment. Moreover, as President Obama and many others have recognized, the United States' routine mistreatment of Muslim prisoners at Guantánamo and the photographed abuse at Abu Ghraib have actually been a boon for al Qaeda, helping draw new recruits to its ranks and making the United States less safe. A commission of inquiry needs to examine all of these claims.

Won't a commission of inquiry or prosecutions divide the country and distract from President Obama's agenda to reform health care and revive the economy?

Some who say they would like to see accountability for the use of torture are opposed to both a commission of inquiry and prosecutions because they believe any kind of investigation would alienate Republicans who are needed to help President Obama implement his domestic agenda. But establishing what laws were violated and prosecuting those who violated them is not a partisan issue. Waterboarding has been prosecuted as a crime in the United States for more than 100 years. The Reagan Justice Department prosecuted a Texas sheriff and three of his deputies for waterboarding in 1983. Notably, in recent years, a group of Republican senators have been among the most persistent congressional opponents of torture.

The rule of law is undermined when government officials responsible for serious crimes are not prosecuted because it may be politically inconvenient. And the way for a commission of inquiry to avoid the taint of politics or the appearance of political motivations is to create a non-partisan body insulated from congressional or executive branch pressure, consisting of individuals of high moral standing who are not closely associated with either political party.

Why is it necessary to have both a commission of inquiry and prosecutions? Isn't one or the other enough?

A commission of inquiry and prosecutions fulfill different but complementary roles. A commission of inquiry is important for broadly establishing what happened and providing a public accounting. It should examine questions such as how widespread torture and abuse was; why and how it occurred; who was responsible for planning and implementing the interrogation program; what information or misinformation the methods uncovered; and what has become of detainees who were once in secret CIA custody. While commissions of inquiry can make beneficial use of information that would not be admissible in a court of law, rules would have to be put into place so that a commission would not inhibit future prosecutions or undermine the rights of possible criminal suspects.

Prosecutions, on the other hand, address individual accountability and uphold the rule of law. In order to repudiate torture fully, those responsible for planning and authorizing it should be held accountable. As a party to the Convention against Torture the United States is legally obligated to prosecute those responsible for torture. If there is no real accountability for these crimes, for years to come the perpetrators of atrocities around the world will point to the US's mistreatment of prisoners to deflect criticism of their own conduct. Indeed, there is no question that the credibility of the United States as a proponent of human rights has been severely damaged by its use of torture. Washington can resurrect much of that credibility through a meaningful accountability process.

Who should be prosecuted?

Human Rights Watch believes that at a minimum US officials who authorized or ordered torture or other mistreatment—regardless of rank or position—should be criminally investigated and appropriately prosecuted. This could also include Justice Department lawyers if they were part of a criminal conspiracy to protect officials from prosecution for known unlawful acts of torture and abuse. Lower level officials who participated in torture and other mistreatment should be subject to prosecution as determined by the Attorney General.

*__Human Rights Watch__ is one of the world's leading nongovernmental organizations devoted to the advancement and protection of human rights worldwide.

Human Rights Watch. 2009. Accountability for torture: Questions and answers (May). http://www.hrw.org/en/news/2009/05/13/accountability-torture. © 2009 Human Rights Watch

Used by Permission.

The Wrongheaded and Dangerous Campaign to Criminalize Good Faith Legal Advice

by Julian Ku*

[...]

I. Introduction

It is hardly unusual for a U.S. President or for a U.S. administration to be charged with committing war crimes. President Franklin Roosevelt was accused of violating the Neutrality Act in order to incite a war with Germany.[1] President Harry Truman's decision to use the atomic bomb in Japan has been called a war crime so many times it is hardly worth documenting.[2] Presidents Johnson and Nixon were pilloried over their Vietnam War and Cambodia military plans.[3] More recently, critics have brought out the "war crime" accusation against President Bush's military action in the Gulf War and Panama,[4] and President Clinton's bombings of Kosovo.[5] One only has to review the list of charges drawn up by former U.S. Attorney General Ramsey Clark over the years to get a flavor of these types of charges.[6]

The most recent wave of war crimes accusations against the George W. Bush administration is different. But the difference lies mostly in the near obsessive focus of the accusers on the legal advice of Bush Administration lawyers.[7] As the papers to this symposium demonstrate, it is likely that a majority of international lawyers and scholars reject the legal interpretations adopted by the Bush Administration in the pursuit of the war on terrorism, most especially the widely condemned "torture memos."[8] But many have gone farther than simply arguing that the legal advice was wrong. A number of scholars and advocates have argued for, indeed demanded, a criminal prosecution of such lawyers for giving their legal advice.[9]

I agree that the so-called "torture memos" drew a standard that was too loose, and I believe (with the benefit of hindsight) that I would have written an opinion more limiting of interrogation techniques than the one that was written. But to me, my disagreement with the legal analysis of the memos on interrogation policy is very different from stating that I believe the lawyers who gave that advice should be held criminally liable solely for their legal advice.

Indeed, in this short essay, I will argue that this increasingly fervent insistence on *criminal punishment* of the Bush lawyers for their legal advice is both wrong-headed and dangerous. It is wrong-headed because the insistence on criminal prosecution of attorneys based solely upon their good faith interpretation of the law is highly unlikely to succeed as a matter of both U.S. and international law. It is dangerous because, at least with respect to U.S. law, prosecuting good faith legal advice is (and should be) violations of those attorneys' constitutional rights under the U.S. Constitution's First Amendment and broader norms of free expression. Insisting on prosecuting lawyers for their good-faith legal advice, even threatening prosecution, will chill the ability of future government lawyers to give legal advice on complex and important questions implicating U.S. national security.

II. The Extremely Weak Case for Prosecuting the Bush Lawyers

It is not surprising that legal academics are generally critical of attempts to prosecute attorneys, especially for giving legal advice. In contexts other than U.S. government interrogation policies, scholars have generally criticized overzealous prosecutions of criminal defense lawyers and securities lawyers on grounds that such prosecutions chill the ability to give legal advice and legal advocacy more generally.[10]

What is surprising is the willingness of many scholars to entertain, or advocate for, criminal prosecution of the Bush lawyers. Legal scholars have relentlessly criticized the "torture memos," not to mention the legal advice undergirding the Bush Administration's policies on the war on terrorism more generally. But the attention on the legal advice is almost unprecedented.

There is only one plausible theory by which the Bush attorneys may be criminally liable for their legal advice: aiding and abetting the act of torture as defined under U.S. law and under international law.[11] There is no evidence that the Bush lawyers in any way participated in the alleged interrogations, so there can be no question of actually punishing them directly under the statute or international treaties prohibiting torture.

There are two relevant sets of laws that might be invoked to prosecute the Bush lawyers. First, under U.S. law, torture is a federal crime prohibited by 18 U.S.C. § 2430A, which itself implements U.S. obligations under the Convention Against Torture.[12] A person may then be held liable for aiding and abetting any federal crime under 18 U.S.C. § 2430A. Second, international law also directly criminalizes torture. The Rome Statute of the International Criminal Court, for instance, permits prosecution for crimes against humanity and war crimes, both of which have been understood to include torture.[13] Accomplices to a crime may be held liable for aiding, abetting or assisting in a crime "[f]or the purpose of facilitating the commission of such a crime. . ."[14] In my view, neither U.S. law nor the ICC Statute would permit criminal punishment of the Bush lawyers as accomplices in committing torture. At the very least, the case for criminal punishment under these laws is so extremely weak that initiating a prosecution of the Bush lawyers would be little more than political theater without any hope of actual success.

In order to attribute liability for aiding and abetting a crime under federal law, the government "must establish that the "'defendant associated with the criminal venture, participated in it as something he wished to bring about, and sought by his actions to make it succeed.'"[15] An aider and abettor is liable for criminal acts that are the "natural or probable consequence of the crime" that he counseled, commanded, or otherwise encouraged.[16] Similarly, under the ICC Statute, accomplices can be held liable if they aid for the "purpose of facilitating the commission of such a crime . . . ."[17] The federal law criminalizing torture punishes the infliction of "severe physical or mental pain. . . ."[18]

Therefore, in order to be held liable for aiding and abetting the torture under federal law, the Bush lawyers must have intended, through their legal advice, to purposefully bring about "severe physical or mental pain" as defined in the statute. Moreover, it is likely that the individuals would have to be found to specifically intend to inflict severe physical or mental pain for some illicit purpose in order to be liable under the federal anti-torture statute.

As the U.S. Court of Appeals for the Third Circuit recently held,[19] criminal liability for torture requires proof of the intent to inflict severe and mental pain for some illicit purpose. Infliction of severe physical or mental pain, and even knowing such pain would be inflicted, such as by housing individuals in dangerous prisons, would not be torture unless the intent by putting someone in the dangerous prison was to inflict severe mental or physical pain for some illicit purpose. Similarly, an individual could not be held liable as an accomplice unless they had knowledge and the purpose of assisting in the infliction of severe physical or mental pain for an illicit purpose.

Under these standards, I respectfully suggest that it is nearly inconceivable that a court in the U.S., or the ICC, could successfully prosecute any of the attorneys in the Bush administration for their legal advice. It is therefore not surprising to me that the Obama Justice Department has not even bothered to open a criminal inquiry into the Bush attorneys, preferring to leave it to state bar ethics reviews.[20] There has never been any evidence that the memos were given without good faith or without a sincere belief that their advice was correct. In this factual context, it is hard to imagine how the necessary intent for criminal liability could be proven.

In other words, under the view of the Bush lawyers, none of the techniques they approved qualified as "severe physical or mental pain" within the meaning of the anti-torture statute. In their now-famous formulation, the torture statute does not criminalize an act of severe pain unless the pain is significant enough to cause permanent physical damage or organ failure.[21] As subsequent memos demonstrated, the Bush attorneys faithfully hewed to this formulation by approving certain techniques (e.g., waterboarding) only after concluding that these techniques did not violate this standard. They also ruled out certain procedures as violating these standards, by for instance, limiting the number of times an individual could be waterboarded and requiring pads to be used behind an individual's neck so that any pushing would not cause injury, and requiring an insect used to frighten a detainee be clearly identified as non-deadly.[22]

This is not to say that the memos' legal analysis was correct. Rather, the point is that as long as the attorneys believed such advice was correct, they could not have the intent necessary to violate the torture statute. Similarly, the Bush attorneys would also lack the necessary "knowledge" that they were aiding and abetting a criminal act since they genuinely believed that there was no criminal act being committed. Without such intent, in my view, there is absolutely no chance of criminal liability.

Thus, critics of the Bush attorneys' advice must establish more than that their advice was wrong or even unethical. They must establish that it was unreasonable and that it was not given in good faith. This seems to be an impossible standard to meet in this case. In attacking the advice, critics have focused on three main arguments.

First, they have argued that the Bush attorneys' analysis of specific intent was incorrect and unduly narrow. Whatever one thinks of this argument, the idea that there is no specific intent requirement for the Torture Convention cannot be said to be unreasonable, especially in light of a recent Third Circuit en banc opinion adopting a similar theory.[23]

Second, critics have argued that the Commander in Chief argument is unduly broad and gives the President the right to override congressional statutes. While there are some valid criticisms of this argument, it is again hard to maintain that this argument is, in general terms, unreasonable. After all, the argument has a long pedigree and was most recently embraced by

Walter Dellinger, President Clinton's Office of Legal Counsel (OLC) chief in arguing that Congress could not restrict U.S. military cooperation with the U.N. or by President Obama himself, when he issued signing statements declaring that he would treat certain federal statutes as non-binding since they would otherwise interfere with his constitutional powers.[24]

Third, the most controversial and difficult part of the legal opinions is their definition of severe physical or mental pain. It is here that most of the critics have concentrated their fire. But given the complete lack of U.S. precedent interpreting this phrase and the uncertainty over the U.S. government's willingness to fully incorporate international definitions of "severe" pain, I cannot say that the standard drawn by the Bush lawyers is objectively unreasonable. At the very least, it is clear that the standard is not a sham standard without any actual practical limits. As later legal opinions released by President Obama demonstrated, the standard was applied in almost excruciating detail to limit the scope and nature of the interrogation techniques. For instance, a detainee who feared stinging insects could be threatened with such an insect so long as the insect was actually harmless.[25] One may still think the techniques that were authorized constitute severe pain and therefore "torture" but such a disagreement does not necessarily make the Bush lawyer opinions unreasonable.

I should, at this point, mention the only major international law precedent where attorneys were arguably punished for the content of their legal advice. In the famous Justice Case arising out of the prosecution of Nazi officials after World War II, one of the international tribunals convicted a number of high-ranking judges and legal advisors to the Nazi regime.[26]

Although superficially analogous, it is hard to see those WWII cases as providing adequate precedent for the prosecution of the Bush lawyers here. The judges convicted in the Justice Case had been part of the regime for a number of years and had participated in the formulation of legal reforms in the judicial system that resulted in discriminatory treatment and greater discretion for the Nazi regime. Such constant and longstanding participation, the tribunals found in a number of cases, was enough to establish the necessary motive and intent for criminal liability.

The most important difference is the pattern of longstanding cooperation with the Nazi regime rather than one or two legal opinions on a single issue of legal policy. Moreover, almost all of the defendants were judges, rather than executive branch attorneys, and they were chastised for violating their duties of independence in order to collaborate with the Nazi regime.[27] Their long standing cooperation on a number of issues over a series of years provides a much stronger evidence of intent. In any event, the cases did not involve any serious attempt to analyze legal opinions on a particular issue, but a pattern of conduct over a number of years of which legal advice constituted one part.

There is another legal opinion from that era that seems more analogous to the Bush legal opinions. Former U.S. President Franklin Delano Roosevelt's Attorney General, Robert Jackson (later of Nuremberg fame), wrote a legal opinion that authorized the lease of destroyers to Great Britain despite the operation of the Neutrality Act of 1917 that seemed to prohibit such leases.[28] As Yale Law School Professor Edwin Borchard pointed out at the time, the opinion relied at least in part on a serious typographical error in the Attorney General's version of the Neutrality Act that may have affected the plausibility of the legal advice.[29] Borchard, and later Daniel Patrick Moynihan, concluded that Jackson's advice was simply wrong.[30] Moynihan even hinted that Jackson may have known the advice was wrong.[31] In many ways, Jackson's advice was just as controversial and difficult as the Bush lawyers' advice. But, rightly, this advice has never been thought to constitute a crime even though it arguably had the consequence of breaking U.S. neutrality law and committing the U.S. to a war with Germany even before the attack on Pearl Harbor.

III. The Dangers of Even Unfounded Criminal Prosecution of the Bush Lawyers

Even if, as I believe, any serious attempt to prosecute the Bush lawyers would fail, there are dangerous or at least undesirable consequences to even threatened criminal prosecutions of good faith legal advice. In a number of cases, the good faith legal advice of attorneys has been held to constitute speech that is protected by the First Amendment.[32] Attorneys have invoked such free speech protections in the context of legal malpractice proceedings, challenges to ethics determinations, and criminal prosecutions.

In a recent case arising in New York, defense attorneys were prosecuted for advising their nurse-clients that it would be legal for them to resign their jobs despite the fact that they were health care workers.[33] In fact, there was a substantial dispute as to whether such mass resignations were in fact legal, but in a subsequent prosecution the New York Appellate Division held that such advice is protected by the First Amendment even if the advice was incorrect.[34]

More importantly, regardless of whether [the defendant-attorney's] legal assessment was accurate, it was objectively reasonable. We cannot conclude that an attorney who advises a client to take an action that he or she, in good faith, believes to be legal, loses the protection of the First Amendment if his or her advice is later determined to be incorrect. Indeed, it would eviscerate the right to give and receive legal counsel with respect to potential criminal liability if an attorney could be charged with conspiracy and solicitation whenever a district Attorney disagreed with that advice.[35]

Although the First Amendment argument has been invoked in a number of cases, there has been little analysis of the quality or reasonableness of the legal advice necessary to win First Amendment protection. In this case, the court required reasonable good faith legal advice and assumed the existence of such conditions for the purposes of the opinion.[36] As a practical matter, this makes sense since it is hard to see how attorneys could have an unrestricted First Amendment right to give legal advice. But the value and purposes of the First Amendment are obviously enhanced by shielding reasonable legal advice given in good faith. As I argued above, there is no evidence of such a lack of good faith regarding the Bush attorneys' legal advice.

There is one other consequence of the campaign to criminalize good faith legal advice: a chilling effect on attempts to analyze the law prohibiting torture, cruel and inhuman and degrading treatment, and other interrogation techniques. Frankly speaking, any government lawyer who offers advice allowing any sort of coercive interrogation is likely to be branded a criminal, threatened with disbarment, and sued vigorously and repeatedly in civil actions. Thus, although the initial controversial advice provided by Jay Bybee and John Yoo was withdrawn and replaced by an entirely new set of attorneys, both the old and new attorneys alike have been accused of criminal activity for reaching their controversial conclusions. It is no wonder that the Obama Justice Department has not, as far as I know, issued legal advice on the meaning of the Torture Statute or Torture Convention.

The result, of course, is that the government now operates in the assumption that any sort of deviation from the Army Field Manual is ipso facto torture. This seems implausible, as a legal matter. And even if the policy to stick with the Manual were a good one, it is a bad sign that lawyers are too afraid to even to consider alternatives. Such fears should not be limited to advice on interrogations. There are many issues over which substantial legal controversy exists, and which current government lawyers recommend at their peril. For instance, the U.S. is currently engaged in the use of Predator drone strikes in Pakistan, Afghanistan, and other areas of the world. The legality of such strikes is uncertain under international law, especially outside of states where tacit consent has been given.[37]

IV. Conclusion

In sum, I believe that there is no chance, based on the current facts, that any of the Bush attorneys could be subject to criminal liability for their good faith reasonable legal advice. The good faith nature of the advice makes it nearly impossible to establish the necessary intent for direct or accomplice liability. This appears to be true under either U.S. or international criminal law standards since both require either purposeful assistance or knowledge that their acts would assist in the commission of a crime.

But there is something larger at stake here. Government lawyers are called upon, sometimes, to give difficult and potentially controversial legal advice under situations of high stress and with enormous stakes. Prosecuting (or demanding prosecution of) government lawyers who have provided good faith legal advice can only make this difficult task nearly impossible.

ENDNOTES

1. *See, e.g.,* Elizabeth L. Hillman, *Franklin D. Roosevelt, Commander in Chief,* 29 Cardozo L. Rev. 1037, 1043 (2008) (committing U.S. resources to help the British in World War Two violated the official U.S. stance of neutrality).

2. *See, e.g.,* Matthew Lippman, *Aerial Attacks on Civilians and the Humanitarian Law of War: Technology and Terror from World War I to Afghanistan,* 33 Cal. W. Int'l L.J. 1, 29 (2002) (holding in a Japanese court that deploying the atomic bomb was a violation of international humanitarian laws of war).

3. *See, e.g.,* Edward R. Drachman & Alan Shank, Presidents and Foreign Policy Countdown to 10 Controversial Decisions 123, 151–52 (1997) (describing the war protestors and congressional backlash for both war strategies).

4. *See, e.g.,* Francis Boyle, *US War Crimes During the Gulf War,* Counterpunch, Sept. 2, 2002, http://www.counterpunch.org/boyle0902.html (last visited Nov. 16, 2009) (claiming President Bush was responsible for multiple counts of war crimes in Panama and during the Persian Gulf War including genocide).

5. *See, e.g., Hero or Villain? Bill Clinton Statue in Kosovo Angers Serbs,* Russia Today, Oct. 9, 2009, http://russiatoday.com/Top_News/2009-10-09/bill-clinton-statue-kosovo.html/print (last visited Nov. 16, 2009) (quoting the brother of Radovan Karadzic that the bombings initiated by President Clinton and NATO forces may have been the worst since World War II).

6. *See* Press Release, The Wisdom Fund, International Commission of Inquiry on Economic Sanctions, Former US Attorney General Charges US, British and UN Leaders (Nov. 20, 1996), *available at* http://www.twf.org/News/Y1997/Ramsey.html (last visited Nov. 16, 2009).

7. *See, e.g.,* PHILLIPPE SANDS, TORTURE TEAM: RUMSFELD'S MEMO AND THE BETRAYAL OF AMERICAN VALUES (2008).

8. *See, e.g., Previously Secret Torture Memo Released,* CNN, July 24, 2008, http://edition.cnn.com/2008/POLITICS/07/24/cia.torturel/?iref=hpmostpop (last visited Nov. 16, 2009) (providing links to the "torture memos"). *See also* 37 CASE W. RES. J. INT'L L. 615 (2006) (print version of the "torture memos").

9. *See, e.g.,* Milan Milanovic, *Can Lawyers Be War Criminals?,* 20 GEO. J. LEGAL ETHICS 347, 349 (2007); Joseph Lavitt, *The Crime of Conviction of John Choon Yoo: The Actuality of Criminality of OLC During the Bush Administration,* 62 MAINE L. REV. (forthcoming 2009), *available at* http://papers.ssm.com/sol3/papers.cfm?abstract_id=1474940 (last visited Nov. 16, 2009).

10. *See, e.g.*. Peter J. Henning, *Targeting Legal Avice,*54 AM. U. L. REV. 669, 675 (2005) ("Efforts to enforce criminal law, which make legal advice a target of prosecution and an indicator of guilt, are a sure sign of overcrimininalization.").

11. 18 U.S.C. § 2340A (2006).

12. *Id. See also* Convention Against Torture and Other Cruel, Inhuman or Degrading Treatment or Punishment, Dec. 10, 1984, 108 Stat. 382, 1465 U.N.T.S. 85.

13. *See* Rome Statute of the International Criminal Court art. 5, July 1, 2002, 2187 U.N.T.S. 90, *available at* http://www.un.org/law/icc/statute/romefra.htm [hereinafter ICC Statute].

14. *Id.* art. 25(3)(c).

15. United States v. Tullos, 868 F.2d 689, 694 (5th Cir. 1989), *cert. denied,* 490 U.S. 1112 (1989) (quoting United States v. Longoria, 569 F.2d 422,425 (5th Cir. 1978) (quoting United States v. Martinez, 555 F.2d 1269, 1272 (5th Cir. 1977))).

16. United States v. Fagan, 821 F.2d 1002, 1012 (5th Cir. 1987), *cert. denied,* 484 U.S. 1005 (1988) (quoting Russell v. United States, 222 F.2d 197, 199 (5th Cir. 1955)). *See also* United States v. Sellers, 483 F.2d 37, 45 (5th Cir. 1973), *cert. denied,* 417 U.S. 908 (1974).

17. ICC Statute, *supra* note 13, art. 25(3)(c).

18. 18 U.S.C. § 2340(1) (2006).

19. Pierre v. Att'y Gen., 528 F.3d 180, 189 (3d Cir. 2008).

20. *See, e.g.,* Terry Frieden, *Early Report Doesn't Recommend Charges for Torture Memos,* CNN, May. 5, 2009, http://www.cnn.com/2009/POLITICS/05/05/torture.memos/index.html (last visited Nov. 16, 2009).

21. *See* Memorandum from Jay S. Bybee, Assistant Attorney Gen., U.S. Dep't of Justice to Alberto R. Gonzales, Counsel to the President, Re: Standards of Conduct for Interrogation Under 18 U.S.C. §§ 2340–2340A, at 46 (Aug. 1, 2002), 37 CASE W. RES. J. INT'L L. 615 (2006).

22. *See* Memorandum from Jay S. Bybee, Assistant Attorney Gen., U.S. Dep't of Justice to John A. Rizzo, Acting Gen. Counsel, Central Intelligence Agency, Re: Interrogation of al Qaeda Operative (Aug. 1, 2002).

23. Pierre v. Att'y Gen., 528 F.3d 180 (3d Cir. 2008).

24. *See* Memorandum from Walter Dellinger, Assistant Attorney Gen., to the Honorable Abner J. Mikva, Counsel to the President, Re: Presidential Authority to Decline to Execute Unconstitutional Statutes (Nov. 2, 1994), *available at* http://www.justice.gov/olc/nonexcut.htm. *See also* President Barack Obama, Statement Upon Signing HR 2346 on June 24, 2009 (June 26, 2009), *available at* http://www.whitehouse.gov/the_press_office/Statement-from-the-President-upon-signing-HR-2346/.

25. *See* Memorandum for John Rizzo, Acting General Counsel of the Central Intelligence Agency from Assistant Attorney General Jay Bybee, at 3 (Aug. 1, 2002).

26. *See* 3 TRIALS OF WAR CRIMINALS BEFORE THE NUREMBERG MILITARY TRIBUNALS UNDER CONTROL COUNCIL LAW NO. 10, at 1081–82 (1951).

27. *See, e.g., id.*

28. *See generally* Acquisition of Naval and Air Bases in Exchange for Over-Age Destroyers, 39 Op. Att'y Gen. 484 (1940). *See also* Edwin Borchard, *The Attorney General's Opinion on the Exchange of Destroyers for Naval Bases,* 34 AM. J. INT'L L. 690, 690–97 (1940); DANIEL PATRICK MOYNIHAN, ON THE LAW OF NATIONS 71–72 (1990) (arguing for a return to the conventions of international behavior set out by Woodrow Wilson and the U.N.).

29. Borchard, *supra* note 28, at 693–94.

30. *Id. See also* MOYNIHAN, *supra* note 28, at 71–72.

31. *See generally* MOYNIHAN, *supra* note 28, at 71.

32. *See, e.g.,* Vinluan v. Doyle, 60 A.D.3d 237, 250–51, 873 N.Y.S.2d 72, 82–83 (A.D.2d 2009).

33. *Vinluan,* 60 A.D.3d at 239.

34. *Id.*

35. *Id.* at 252.

36. *See id.*

37. *See, e.g.,* Michelle Nichols, *U.N. Envoy Slams U.S. for Unanswered Drone Questions,* REUTERS, Oct. 27, 2009, http://in.reuters.com/article/worldNews/idININdia-43478820091028 (last visited Nov. 16, 2009).

***Julian Ku** teaches international, constitutional, and corporate law at Hofstra Law School. His main research interest is the intersection of international and domestic law. He has recently published articles on the constitutional aspects of foreign relations in the *Yale Law Journal*, the *Supreme Court Review*, and *Constitutional Commentary*.

Ku, Julian. 2009. "The wrongheaded and dangerous campaign to criminalize good faith legal advice." *Case Western Reserve Journal of International Law* 42: 440–458

Used by Permission.

Discussion Questions

1. What does the Convention Against Torture require the United States to do with respect to credible allegations of torture?

2. What would be the legal and/or political hurdles to prosecuting those who authorized the CIA to use waterboarding and other coercive tactics against al Qaeda suspects? Do those hurdles justify the Obama administration's failure even to conduct a criminal investigation?

3. What would be the costs and benefits of appointing an independent commission to investigate the decision to authorize the CIA to use waterboarding and other coercive tactics? Would such a commission satisfy our legal obligations under the Convention Against Torture? Our moral obligations? Would it help us learn from our mistakes?

4. If the lawyers who authorized waterboarding were interpreting the law in good faith, should that be a defense in a criminal prosecution?

5. What are the costs and risks associated with doing nothing to hold anyone accountable for the CIA's interrogation tactics?

PART 4:

Preventive Detention

In a country where one is presumed innocent until proven guilty, what role should preventive detention play in fighting terrorism generally, or in the fight against al Qaeda or the Taliban more specifically? Few issues have sparked more disagreement in the post-9/11 era. Shortly after the terrorist attacks of September 11, Congress authorized the president to use "all necessary and appropriate" military force against the individuals and organizations responsible for the attacks and against those who harbor them. The United States has been fighting a war, focused in Afghanistan, against al Qaeda and the Taliban ever since. In the course of that conflict, the United States has detained thousands of individuals whom the Bush administration called "enemy combatants." Some were allegedly captured on the battlefield bearing arms, but others were captured thousands of miles away in foreign lands, and still others were turned in by captors to claim generous bounties, with little evidence that they were "enemies" at all. More than 775 of such men have been held at a U.S. naval base in Guantánamo Bay, Cuba, some for nearly ten years, without criminal charges or a criminal trial.

Guantánamo has generated widespread criticism around the world, so much so that Presidents Bush and Obama, Secretary of Defense Robert Gates, and former Secretary of State Condoleezza Rice have all said that they would like to see it closed. On his second day in office, President Obama promised to close the Guantánamo detention center within one year. As of this writing, however, more than two years later, it remains open, with no closure in sight. Some argue that terrorists should either be tried on criminal charges or released. Others insist that preventive detention has a role to play even where a criminal conviction is not possible. In my essay, I argue that preventive detention during wartime is a legitimate option, but one that must be carefully limited to those fighting for al Qaeda or the Taliban in the ongoing military conflict in Afghanistan. Jack Goldsmith maintains that a national security court should be established to oversee preventive detention of terrorists, granting them greater protections than they currently enjoy. And Jules Lobel maintains that preventive detention is unnecessary, unjust, and unwise, as terrorists can and should be prosecuted as criminals.

Closing Guantánamo: The Problem of Preventive Detention

by David Cole*

Barack Obama's campaign promise to close Guantánamo hardly put him out on a limb. Republican Senator John McCain, Secretary of State Condoleezza Rice, President George W. Bush, and Defense Secretary Robert Gates have all said that they would like to close it. The facility is now a more potent symbol of the United States worldwide than the Statue of Liberty, a daily reminder of the lawless approach the outgoing administration has taken toward the so-called "war on terror." With broad support, Obama will likely close Guantánamo next year.

But closing Guantánamo will raise almost as many problems as it solves. Where, for example, will the new administration put the 250 or so men still detained there? No American city is eager to have accused al Qaeda terrorists in its backyard. And outsourcing the problem is not an option. Most of the detainees' native countries will not take them back; cannot assure us that the men won't return to battle; or may torture the detainees, thereby precluding us from repatriating them.

The difficult question of relocation, however, pales in comparison to the long-term problem of what to do with the remaining detainees. The Bush administration claims that about eighty could be criminally tried. If we cannot try the remaining 170, must we release them?

Many human rights advocates say yes. In their view, absent a war with another nation, neither the laws of war nor American laws authorize extended preventive detention. If a Guantánamo detainee is guilty of a crime, he can be tried and, if convicted, sentenced to a period of incarceration. Those who cannot be tried or convicted should be released. These advocates argue that any form of preventive detention is a dangerous departure from the existing paradigm of crime and punishment, and ought not be tolerated.

Others, such as my Georgetown University colleague Neal Katyal and Harvard Law Professor Jack Goldsmith, recommend that Congress grant the president authority to detain indefinitely anyone who can be shown to be a "suspected terrorist." They argue that the threat of terrorism warrants a sweeping new preventive detention authority and favor the creation of a specialized "national security court" to administer it.

In my view, Obama should adopt neither of these alternatives. The try-or-release approach leaves us without sufficient protection in modern-day military conflicts. At the same time, authorizing preventive detention of suspected terrorists, as Katyal and Goldsmith advocate, would be both unconstitutional and unwise. There is no justification for bypassing the criminal justice system simply because an individual is suspected of terrorism rather than drug dealing, rape, or murder. If we were to create such an exception for terrorists, what would stop its extension to other serious crimes?

There is, however, a third alternative—one that allows the United States sufficient authority to protect itself from al Qaeda fighters while avoiding the creation of an exception that threatens to swallow the rule of the criminal process. Congress should follow the example of traditional wars and give the administration the option to detain—without criminal trial—those engaged in hostilities with us for the duration of the military conflict with al Qaeda and the Taliban. Detainees should be afforded punctilious procedure to ensure that we are detaining only those who fought for al Qaeda or the Taliban and pose an ongoing threat.

Detention without trial must be a carefully circumscribed exception during peacetime, but it has long been recognized as an appropriate and necessary means of dealing with enemy fighters during wartime. If the United States could lock up German soldiers during World War II without trying them criminally, why should it not have the same option for al Qaeda fighters? The fact that the armed conflict with al Qaeda is not a war between nations ought not disable the government from holding its enemies preventively while the conflict goes on.

So the problem with Guantánamo Bay, as I have long argued, is not the detention of enemy combatants. The problem is that the Bush administration has denied fair hearings, resulting in the detention of many who were not enemy fighters; it has defined the category of "combatants" so as to sweep in grandmothers who donated unknowingly to an organization affiliated with al Qaeda; it has authorized cruelty and torture as interrogation methods; it has asserted the right to hold prisoners for the duration of the "global war on terror" (that is, forever); and, most fundamentally, it has argued that Guantánamo is a law-free zone. Guantánamo is a black mark because of this resistance to law and refusal to recognize the basic human dignity of the detainees. If we are to fix the problem, we need not abandon military detention, but we must subject it to the rule of law.

* * *

There are many reasons to be skeptical of preventive detention. They begin with experience—we have not done preventive
detention well. Consider the three most aggressive domestic
preventive detention campaigns in U.S. history (not counting
the Civil War): the Palmer Raids of 1919–20, the Japanese internment of World War II, and the widespread preventive detention
of foreign nationals in the United States after 9/11. In each
instance, the United States responded to a violent attack by
rounding up the usual suspects, based not on concrete evidence
of involvement in the violence, but on the basis of much broader
"profiles"—Communist Party membership, Japanese ancestry, or Arab or Muslim identity. None of those locked up in the
Palmer Raids was found to have engaged in the bombings that
prompted the raids. None of the Japanese or Japanese-Ameri-
can internees was a spy or saboteur. And none of the more than
5,000 foreign nationals jailed in anti-terrorism preventive detention measures in the first two years after 9/11 stands convicted
of a terrorist offense.

But the problem with preventive detention is not just that
we have managed it poorly. For three reasons, it is an inherently dangerous enterprise. First, no one can predict the future.
Preventive detention turns on predictions of future harms that
cannot ultimately be proven or disproven. In the absence of
an ability to predict, we often resort to inaccurate stereotypes
and prejudices as proxies for dangerousness. Preventing harm
is a legitimate social goal, of course, but there are many ways
to do so short of detention, such as securing borders, enhancing intelligence-gathering, safeguarding nuclear stockpiles, and
engaging in smarter foreign policy. Locking up human beings
is one of the most extreme preventive measures a state can
undertake; it should be reserved for situations in which it is

truly necessary, but uncertainty about the future makes necessity virtually impossible to establish.

Second, and relatedly, the risk of error—in particular, the error of unnecessarily detaining innocent people—is high. The detention process will undoubtedly be skewed by the fact that some kinds of errors are highly visible, while others are entirely invisible. When a judge erroneously releases an individual who poses a real danger of future harm, and the individual goes on to commit that harm, the error will be emblazoned across the front pages, there for all to see. When, by contrast, a judge detains an individual who in fact would not have committed any wrong had he been released, that error is invisible—and, indeed, unknowable. (How can one prove what someone would *not* have done had he or she been free?) Thus, human nature suggests that judges overseeing preventive detention will err on the side of custody over liberty.

Third, preventive detention is inconsistent with basic notions of human autonomy. We generally presume that individuals have a choice to conform their conduct to the law. For this reason, liberal societies do not criminalize thoughts or intentions, but actions. Dangerous activity can usually be criminally proscribed, and we ought to trust, absent some very strong showing, that individuals will obey those proscriptions. To imprison a human being on the claim that he will take dangerous and illegal action if we do not is to deny his autonomy.

Any system of preventive detention inevitably poses these problems. We can mitigate them, but they cannot be eliminated. Accordingly, any consideration of preventive detention should begin with a strong constitutional presumption that our society deals with dangerous people through criminal prosecution and punishment, not preventive detention. We should depart from the criminal justice model only where the criminal process *cannot* adequately address a particularly serious danger.

And, indeed, U.S. law has long recognized the propriety of preventive detention where the criminal justice system is demonstrably inadequate. We permit civil commitment of persons who, because of a mental disability, literally cannot be held responsible by the criminal justice system—they lack the requisite intent to be held culpable. We authorize detention without bail of persons facing criminal trial or deportation when they pose a danger to the community or a risk of flight. We cannot instantaneously adjudicate criminal liability or immigration status, and so while the system proceeds, preventive detention is allowed. Quarantines similarly fit this model. We cannot make it a crime to have a disease, so quarantines rely on preventive detention to protect the community from a danger that the criminal justice system cannot address.

Absent similar showings that the criminal process is inadequate, preventive detention is an unconstitutional infringement on liberty. Thus, there is no justification for creating a preventive detention regime aimed at suspected terrorists, as Katyal and Goldsmith advocate. A recent report by former prosecutors Richard Zabel and James Benjamin, Jr., prepared for Human Rights First, analyzed 107 terrorism cases prosecuted in American courts since the 9/11 attacks. The report shows that the criminal justice system has proven capable of incapacitating, trying, and convicting terrorists before and after 9/11. Terrorism is a serious crime, but just like other serious crimes, it can and should be addressed through the criminal justice system.

* * *

We need to find a way to address serious and legitimate security concerns without the overkill of a general system of preventive detention for suspected terrorists. An alternative approach, sensitive to both security and liberty, would permit preventive detention, but only for detainees identified as fighters in an ongoing military conflict.

Preventive detention has long been accepted in wartime, precisely because the criminal justice system cannot address the problem of incapacitating enemy soldiers. In a traditional war, enemy soldiers are generally "privileged" to fight, and therefore we cannot make it a crime for the soldier to fight for the other side. In addition, we cannot presume that enemy soldiers will conform their actions to our laws by avoiding combat if we release them, because they are compelled by their own countries' laws to fight. Finally, problems of proof regarding battlefield captures and the need to maintain military secrets during an armed conflict mean that criminal prosecution will often be practically foreclosed even where it is a legal possibility. No one disputes, then, that a nation fighting a traditional war against another nation has the right to capture and detain enemy soldiers for as long as the conflict lasts.

But the conflict with al Qaeda is not a traditional armed conflict. Al Qaeda is not a state, has not signed the Geneva Conventions, is difficult to identify, and targets civilians. Nevertheless, we are in an armed conflict with al Qaeda. The "global war on terror" is an ill-conceived metaphor or slogan, but the military conflict with al Qaeda is real. Al Qaeda declared war on the United States, and has attacked it both at home and abroad. The attacks of 9/11 were of such a scale that both NATO and the United Nations General Assembly recognized that a military response in self-defense was justified. Approximately 120 nations signed on to the United States' invasion of Afghanistan after the Taliban refused to turn over Osama bin Laden, al Qaeda's leader. The conflict continues to this day and, if anything, appears to be growing worse.

Unlike an opponent in a traditional armed conflict, however, al Qaeda is an "unprivileged belligerent"; it has no right to wage war against the United States. Its actions can be, and for the most part have been, criminalized. Because the criminal option remains available, the case for preventive detention here is less clear-cut.

Still, there are many reasons why the criminal process is insufficient to incapacitate the enemy in an armed conflict—even an enemy such as al Qaeda, which is subject to criminal prosecution under the laws of war. These include the difficulty of collecting and maintaining evidence in wartime settings, the heightened need for secrecy in an ongoing military conflict, and the possibility that enemies might use the criminal process to pass information to their compatriots.

In addition, the burden of proof in criminal cases, including war crimes cases, is very high—the government must prove culpability beyond a reasonable doubt. Suppose that the government has "clear and convincing evidence" that an individual was captured while actively engaged in armed conflict on behalf of al Qaeda, and that, furthermore, the individual has boasted that he would return to the struggle if released. Now suppose also that the government is unable to convince a jury—civilian or military—that the individual is guilty beyond a reasonable doubt of a specific crime. Must he be released? An Italian soldier who prevailed in a war crimes trial during World War II would not be entitled to release upon acquittal but only upon the cessation of hostilities. Why should an unprivileged belligerent fighting for an entity that has no right to fight receive better treatment than an Italian soldier fighting for Italy during World War II?

Put simply, the fact that al Qaeda is engaged in criminal warfare should not restrict the United States' options in defending itself. We certainly have the right to try al Qaeda fighters for war crimes, and we also have the right to try them for ordinary crimes. But should we be *required* to try them in either forum, particularly while the conflict is ongoing? In a traditional international armed conflict, the fact that a given detainee may be tried as a war criminal does not mean that he *must* either be tried or released. War crimes trials typically occur at the conclusion of a war because a nation at war has a strong interest in focusing its resources on the conflict itself and in not revealing what it knows about the enemy. In the meantime, the suspected war criminal may be held as a combatant for the duration of the conflict, whether or not he is ever criminally tried.

Thus, traditional concepts of justice during wartime do allow for preventive detention to forestall a combatant's return to the field of battle. Suspicion of terrorism is no basis on which to hold detainees preventively, but active engagement in an ongoing armed conflict is.

* * *

The most important issue in devising an acceptable, limited preventive detention regime is the definition of who may be detained. We need to distinguish those who are actively engaged as belligerents, albeit in an unconventional war, from those who are not.

In *Hamdi v. Rumsfeld*, the Supreme Court ruled that the executive could hold persons captured on the battlefield in Afghanistan fighting for the Taliban or al Qaeda against the

United States. This is surely the core case, and few would deny that such fighters are subject to military detention. But how far should the detention power extend beyond that? What about people captured far from the battlefield? What about members of the Taliban who have never fought against the United States? What about those who sympathize with al Qaeda, and may even be inspired by it to engage in terrorism, but remain independent actors? What about someone who provides financial support to al Qaeda or the Taliban, but is not a member of either? What about a doctor who has provided medical attention to a Taliban fighter?

The Bush administration took an extraordinarily sweeping view of who may be detained as an enemy combatant. It defined the category as containing not only members of al Qaeda or the Taliban, but also those "associated" with these groups; those who have merely "supported" these groups; and those who are members, associates, or supporters of other groups "affiliated" with al Qaeda or the Taliban.

This goes too far. If one analogizes to World War II, for example, we were entitled to detain as enemy combatants anyone who fought for the German armed forces, but not anyone who paid taxes in Germany, treated a German soldier in a hospital, or was a member of a "Friends of Germany" association.

In a case the Supreme Court has agreed to hear, the U.S. Court of Appeals for the Fourth Circuit recently addressed the question of who may be detained as an enemy combatant. While residing in the United States, Ali Saleh Kahlah al-Marri, a citizen of Qatar, was transferred from civilian to military custody shortly before he was to go on trial for criminal charges relating to identity fraud and lying to FBI agents. Al-Marri is the only enemy combatant currently in military custody in the United

States. The United States alleged that al-Marri trained in an al Qaeda training camp, worked closely with and took orders from the al Qaeda leadership, and came to the United States as an al Qaeda agent for the purpose of engaging in terrorist activities in the United States. In a splintered opinion, the court held that if the allegations against him were true, he could be detained as an enemy combatant. But it also found that he had not been afforded a fair hearing.

Four dissenting judges maintained that only those captured on a foreign battlefield or foreign soil could be detained as enemy combatants. This seems too restrictive. If an enemy fighter is captured outside the field of battle, but the capturing nation has reason to believe that if left free the fighter would resume hostilities against it, why should it be compelled to release him? In World War II, the Supreme Court upheld the detention and military trial of several members of the German armed forces, including an American citizen, who were captured in various U.S. cities, far from any battlefield. Moreover, where the enemy does not recognize any limits on whom it may target or where it may attack, restricting military detention to those found on traditional battlefields would unreasonably hamstring U.S. defenses.

The judges in the majority agreed that the dissenters' definition was too narrow, but could not agree on an alternative. Judge J. Harvey Wilkinson's opinion is the most convincing. He would require the government to establish that an individual is (1) a member of (2) an organization against which Congress has authorized the use of military force (3) who "knowingly plans or engages in conduct that harms or aims to harm persons or property for the purpose of furthering the military goals of an enemy nation or organization." The first two criteria, Wilkinson explains, establish whether the individual is an "enemy"—a term that encompasses only those formally members of an entity against which Congress has authorized the use of military force. The third criterion determines whether the individual is a "combatant," and serves to distinguish "mere members" from those actually engaged in hostilities on behalf of the enemy.

These criteria would be an excellent guide for legislation; what is less clear, and what the U.S. Supreme Court will now consider, is where the authority to detain such individuals comes from in the absence of express congressional authorization.

The Israeli Supreme Court has also recently addressed the issue of who may be detained in an armed conflict with a terrorist organization—in this case, Hezbollah. It authorized detention where the government proves that an individual either (1) took a non-negligible part in hostilities against Israel, or (2) was a member of an organization engaged in such hostilities and "made a contribution to the cycle of hostilities in its broad sense."

The approaches of Judge Wilkinson and the Israeli Supreme Court differ in important ways, but they share certain features that should be at the core of any conception of enemy combatants. First, both treat detention as justified only by a military conflict, a requirement that significantly checks the power to detain preventively. The United States has suffered numerous terrorist attacks over the course of its history but has authorized the use of military force in response only once. Furthermore, armed conflicts, even where they are extended, come to an end someday. Thus, a military detention power is a temporary authority with a defined end point, even if one cannot predict precisely when it will come. A preventive detention statute for suspected terrorists, by contrast, would be a permanent feature of the law.

Second, neither Judge Wilkinson nor the Israeli Supreme Court would permit detention of mere supporters of the enemy organization, much less supporters of affiliated groups. And, equally significantly, neither would permit detention based on membership alone. Why? Because unlike a military force, a terrorist organization is a political organization, and one cannot presume that all of its members are involved in hostilities.

Finally, neither the Israeli Supreme Court nor Judge Wilkinson would restrict military detention to battlefield captures, for the reasons I noted above.

In short, were Congress to so provide, a limited group of individuals could constitutionally be subject to detention in the ongoing military conflict with al Qaeda and the Taliban. That category of enemy combatants should be confined to (1) persons involved in actual hostilities with the United States on the part of al Qaeda or the Taliban; or (2) members of al Qaeda or the Taliban who can be shown, by their activities or their positions in the organization, to have played a direct role in furthering its military ends through training fighters or planning, directing, or engaging in hostile military activities.

* * *

Defining the category of enemy combatants is difficult and important. Almost as difficult and important is ascertaining whether an individual is in fact a combatant. What kind of process should we follow in determining who is legitimately detained?

The Bush administration initially insisted that the Guantánamo detainees were entitled to no process whatsoever. After the Supreme Court held in *Hamdi* that citizens were entitled to due process, the administration hastily created "Combatant

Status Review Tribunals." In these CSRTs, detainees were not allowed the assistance of a lawyer, the tribunals heard no live testimony, and much of the evidence was confidential and hidden from the detainee, making a meaningful rebuttal impossible. Moreover, the hearing officers were subordinates of commanders who had already determined—without a hearing—that the detainees were enemy combatants.

The CSRT process is insufficient, particularly given the lengths of the detentions and the challenge of distinguishing genuine enemy combatants from innocents turned in by bounty hunters. According to the *Hamdi* decision, due process requires that the detainee be afforded notice of the factual basis for his detention, a meaningful opportunity to rebut that argument, and a neutral decision-maker. Even this, however, is only a starting point, which leaves at least four basic questions unresolved: Do the same due process rights apply to foreign nationals? What is the burden of proof? Are detainees entitled to lawyers? And how should confidential information be handled?

First, there ought be no double standards in the treatment of citizens and foreign nationals. The due process inquiry balances the individual's interest in liberty against the government's interest in security. On both sides of the scale, these interests are the same whether the suspected enemy is a foreign national or a U.S. citizen. Therefore, the procedural guarantees ought not differ.

Second, the government should be required to establish the need for detention by "clear and convincing evidence"—a standard that falls between the standards for criminal and civil cases. Periodic reviews of the detainee's legal status should be required, and, as the Israeli Supreme Court ruled, the longer a detention continues, the stronger the government's showing should have to be.

Military detention is always indefinite because one cannot know whether the war will last months, years, or decades, but at least we know what the end of a traditional war looks like. It is difficult to predict what form the end of the conflict with al Qaeda will take. This difference ought not eliminate the possibility of preventive detention altogether, but it should require more careful and regular procedures for assessing and reassessing whether continued detention is necessary.

Third, detainees must be afforded a truly independent assessment of the facts, as well as the assistance of a lawyer. Leaving detention decisions to military subordinates is deeply problematic, as two recent federal court decisions ordering the release of Guantánamo detainees for lack of sufficient evidence vividly demonstrate. In both cases, CSRTs rubberstamped the military's detention decisions, but when independent judges reviewed the evidence in an adversarial setting with legal representation for the detainees, they found it wanting.

Finally, one of the most difficult procedural issues lies in reconciling the individual's right to a fair hearing with the state's interest in maintaining secrecy. While the military often has a legitimate interest in maintaining the confidentiality of relevant information in an ongoing conflict, it should be allowed to use confidential information only if (1) it has exhausted all options that might protect both its interest and the interest of the detainee; and (2) its use does not defeat the individual's meaningful opportunity to respond. There are numerous options available to reduce the unfairness of secret evidence, including declassification review, the use of unclassified summaries, and provision of security clearances for defense attorneys so they may have access to the classified evidence. The bottom line must be that indefinite detention cannot be imposed unless the detainee has a meaningful chance to defend himself. In the case of an irreconcilable conflict, liberty must prevail.

Congress has thus far left the regulation of enemy combatant detentions to executive innovation. Considering the hazards involved—both for the detainees, who have already spent years in detention, and for the United States, whose reputation has been severely damaged worldwide by its failure to accord the detainees a fair process—a statute setting forth carefully crafted and fair rules for enemy combatant hearings is critical. And as court decisions have shown, if Congress does not act, the courts will.

* * *

Some will object that establishing such a preventive detention regime may open the door to the use of preventive detention against organized crime, drug gangs, and terrorists generally. This slippery slope would be a genuine concern were we to adopt a statute focused on suspected terrorists, because such a statute would not be limited to wartime. There is little doubt that there is an ongoing military conflict in Afghanistan. The same has never been true with respect to drugs, organized crime, or indeed, most acts of terrorism. Even if we occasionally deploy the military to interdict drug dealers abroad, Congress has never "declared war" against drug dealers in the non-metaphorical way it has declared war against al Qaeda. The situations in which war will be a legitimate response are likely to be exceptional, and thus the requirement of an ongoing military conflict should reserve preventive detention to where it is truly necessary.

Any preventive detention regime undeniably presents substantial risks that individuals will be detained unnecessarily. One might reasonably conclude that we ought not go down this path in the first place. But then one would need to show why all the forms of preventive detention that the United States and other liberal democracies already tolerate are not equally illegitimate. The real question is why military detention of enemy fighters in an ongoing armed conflict ought not be as appropriate a basis for preventive detention as civil commitment of the dangerous and mentally incompetent, or a quarantine of those who may spread disease. No society of which I am aware rejects all preventive detention. We would do best to control the risk of expanding this inherently dangerous tool by adopting a regime justified only as *military* detention, a concept with narrow and well-established parameters.

There is no doubt that Guantánamo needs to be closed. But closing Guantánamo will do little to resurrect our reputation worldwide unless we simultaneously institute an acceptable way of dealing with the detainees after that lone prison is shuttered. Releasing all who cannot be convicted criminally is not a realistic option as long as the war is ongoing and they pose a real threat. Creating an entirely new concept of detaining suspected terrorists invites a slippery slope and fails to satisfy the threshold requirement of showing that the criminal justice system is not up to the task. Resting our policy on accepted tools of military conflict seems far more likely to achieve the security—and the legitimacy—we need.

*David Cole teaches constitutional law, criminal justice, and national security at the Georgetown University Law Center, is the legal affairs correspondent for *The Nation*, and also contributes regularly to *The New York Review of Books*. He is the author of five books and dozens of articles on national security, civil liberties, and the rule of law.

Cole, David. 2009. Closing Guantánamo: The problem of preventive detention, *Boston Review* (December/January 2009). http://bostonreview.net/BR34.1/cole.php.

Used by Permission.

Long-Term Terrorist Detention and a U.S. National Security Court

by Jack Goldsmith*

For years there has been a debate about whether to create a national security court to supervise the noncriminal military detention of dangerous terrorists. The debate has many dimensions, and it often is confusing. Some opponents of a national security court are really opposed to the noncriminal military detention system that such a court would supervise; they insist that terrorists be tried in criminal court or released. Other opponents of a national security court accept the need for noncriminal military detention but do not favor institutionalizing a new, "secret" court to oversee detentions. Proponents of a national security court come in many stripes as well. They advocate different versions of the court, to which they assign different tasks, ranging from various forms of detention supervision to the conduct of criminal trials.

This chapter attempts to simplify the issues, at least a bit. It argues that the national security court debate—a debate in which I have participated[1]—is largely a canard. The fundamental issue is whether the United States should have a system of noncriminal military detention for enemy terrorists who, for many reasons, are difficult to convict in a criminal trial. If the Obama administration chooses to maintain a system of noncriminal military detention—and for reasons set forth below, I think that it should—it will also necessarily choose to have a national security court. That is because the federal courts that would constitute a "national security court" must supervise noncriminal detention under the constitutional writ of habeas corpus and a likely statutory jurisdiction conferred by Congress. Viewed that way, the United States has had a centralized and thinly institutionalized national security court for years in the federal courts of the District of Columbia, which have been supervising military detentions at Guantánamo Bay. The hard question about a national security court, once the need for noncriminal military detention is accepted, is not whether it should exist. The hard question concerns what its rules should be and, just as important, who should make those rules. In my view, Congress and the president, rather than the courts, must play the predominant role in crafting the rules. After explaining these points, I outline some of the issues and legal policy trade-offs that the political branches should address in doing so, including whether such a court should be an independent institution akin to the Foreign Intelligence Surveillance Court and whether it should conduct criminal trials in addition to supervising detention.

The Necessity and Legality of Long-Term Detention

The principle that a nation at war has the power to hold members of the enemy's armed forces until the cessation of hostilities is as old as warfare itself and should be uncontroversial.[2] The purpose of military detention, former Justice Sandra Day O'Connor explained in 2004, "is to prevent captured individuals from returning to the field of battle and taking up arms once again."[3] As the Nuremberg Tribunal noted, the capture and detention of enemy soldiers is "neither revenge, nor punishment, but solely protective custody, the only purpose of which is to prevent the prisoners of war from further participation in the war."[4] Military detention of enemy soldiers is the military equivalent of the long-standing practice of noncriminal administrative or preventive detention of dangerous persons such as the mentally ill, those infected with contagious diseases, or sexual predators.[5]

The wisdom of the rule of detention becomes clear as more is learned about what has happened to some of the Guantánamo detainees who have been released. Although reports about the severity of the problem differ, it is clear that a good number of the detainees released on the grounds that they were "non-dangerous" have ended up back on the battlefield, shooting at Americans or non-American civilians abroad.[6] One such person, Said Ali al-Shihri, became the deputy leader of al Qaeda's Yemeni branch and is suspected of involvement in the 2008 bombing of the U.S. embassy in Yemen.[7]

Yet if the detention rule is so clear, why is the use of detention so controversial in the war against al Qaeda and its affiliates? One reason is that many observers believe that the nation is not, or cannot be, at war with nonstate actors. That is simply wrong. The United States has fought congressionally authorized wars against nonstate actors such as slave traders and pirates.[8] During the Mexican-American War, the Civil War, and the Spanish-American war, U.S. military forces engaged military opponents who had no formal connection to the state enemy.[9] Presidents also have used force against nonstate actors outside of congressionally authorized conflicts. President McKinley's use of military force to put down the Chinese Boxer Rebellion was directed primarily at nonstate actors.[10] President Wilson sent more than 7,000 U.S. troops into Mexico to pursue Pancho Villa, the leader of a band of rebels opposed to the recognized

Mexican government.[11] And President Clinton authorized cruise missile strikes against al Qaeda targets in Sudan and Afghanistan.[12] In all of those instances, presidents, acting in their role as commander-in-chief, exercised full military powers against nonstate actors—sometimes with congressional authorization and sometimes without.

Consistent with those precedents, every branch of the U.S. government today agrees that the nation is in an "armed conflict" (the modern legal term for "war") with al Qaeda, its affiliates, and other Islamist militants in Afghanistan, Iraq, and elsewhere. Former president Bush took that view in September 2001, and President Obama shows no sign of adopting a different stance. Congress embraced the same view in the September 2001 Authorization for Use of Military Force (AUMF) and reaffirmed it in the Military Commissions Act of 2006 (MCA).[13] And the Supreme Court has stated or assumed that the country is at war many times.[14]

Why, then, has there been so much controversy about holding enemy soldiers at Guántanamo? Part of the reason is the suspicion of abuse of prisoners there. But even if there were no such suspicions, the war on terror has three characteristics that, taken together, make a military detention authority problematic:

—First, in most prior wars, it was easy to determine who was a member of the enemy armed forces because those people wore uniforms and usually fought for a nation-state. In this war, the enemy wears no uniforms and blends with civilians. That unfortunate fact dramatically increases the possibility erroneous detention.

—Second, this war, unlike any other in U.S. history, seems likely to continue indefinitely; indeed, no one knows what the end of the war will look like. That means, among other things, that mistaken detentions might result in the long-term or even indefinite detention of an innocent person.

—Third, even if mistakes are not made, indefinite detention without charge or trial strikes many as an excessive remedy for "mere" membership in enemy terrorist organization, especially since a detainee may, after some period, no longer pose a threat to the United States.

These three concerns do nothing to eliminate the need for detention to prevent detainees from returning to the battlefield, but they do challenge the traditional detention paradigm. And while many observers believe that the country can meet that need by giving trials to everyone that it wants to detain and then incarcerating those individuals under a theory of conviction rather than of military detention, I disagree. For many reasons, it is too risky for the U.S. government to deny itself the traditional military detention power altogether and commit itself instead to trying or releasing *every* suspected terrorist.

For one thing, military detention will be necessary in Iraq and Afghanistan for the foreseeable future. For another, the country likely cannot secure convictions of all of the dangerous terrorists at Guantánamo, much less all future dangerous terrorists, who legitimately qualify for noncriminal military detention. The evidentiary and procedural standards of trials, civilian and military alike, are much higher than the analogous standards for detention. With some terrorists too menacing to set free, the standards will prove difficult to satisfy. Key evidence in a given case may come from overseas, and verifying it, understanding its provenance, or establishing its chain of custody in the manner typically required in criminal trials maybe difficult. That problem is exacerbated when evidence is gathered on a battlefield or during an armed skirmish, and it only grows larger when the evidence is old and stale. And perhaps most important, the use of such evidence in a criminal process may compromise intelligence sources and methods, requiring the disclosure of the identities of confidential sources or the nature of intelligence-gathering techniques.

Opponents of noncriminal detention observe that despite these considerations, the government has successfully prosecuted some al Qaeda terrorists—in particular, Zacharias Moussaoui and Jose Padilla. That is true, but it does not follow that prosecutions are achievable in every case in which disabling a terrorist suspect is a surpassing government interest. Moreover, the Moussaoui and Padilla prosecutions highlight an underappreciated cost of trials, at least in civilian courts. Those trials were messy affairs that stretched, and some observers believe broke, ordinary U.S. criminal trial conceptions of conspiracy and the rights of the accused, among other things. The Moussaoui trial, for example, watered down the important constitutional right of the defendant to confront witnesses against him in court, and the Padilla trial rested on an unprecedentedly broad conception of conspiracy law.[15] An important cost of trying all cases is that the prosecution will invariably bend the law in ways that are unfavorable to civil liberties and due process, and those changes, in turn, will invariably spill over into nonterrorist prosecutions, thus skewing the larger criminal justice process.[16]

A final problem with using any trial system, civilian or military, as the sole lawful basis for terrorist detention is that the trials can result in short sentences (the first military commission trial did) or even acquittal of a dangerous terrorist.[17] In criminal trials, defendants often go free because of legal technicalities, government inability to introduce probative evidence, and other factors besides the defendant's innocence. These factors are all exacerbated in terrorist trials by the difficulty of getting information from the place of capture, by restrictions on access to classified information, and by stale or tainted evidence. One way to get around the problem is to assert the authority, as the Bush administration did, to use noncriminal military detention for persons acquitted or given sentences too short to neutralize the danger that they pose. But such authority would undermine the whole purpose of trials and render them a sham. As a result, putting a suspect on trial can make it hard to detain terrorists that the government deems dangerous. For example, the government would have had little trouble defending the indefinite detention of Salim Hamdan, Osama bin Laden's driver, under a military detention rationale. Having put him on trial before a military commission, however, it was stuck in the light sentence that Hamdan has now completed at home in Yemen.

As a result of these problems, insistence on the exclusive use of criminal trials and the elimination of noncriminal detention would significantly raise the chances of releasing dangerous terrorists who would return to kill Americans or others. Since noncriminal military detention is clearly a legally available option—at least if it is expressly authorized by Congress and includes adequate procedural guarantees—that risk should be unacceptable. In past military conflicts, the release of an enemy soldier posed risks. But they were not dramatic risks, for there was only so much damage a lone actor or small group of individuals could do.[18] Today, however, that lone actor can cause far more destruction and mayhem, because technological advances are creating ever-smaller and ever-deadlier weapons. It would be astounding if the pre–9/11 U.S. legal system had struck the balance between security and liberty in a manner that precisely and adequately addressed the modern threats posed by asymmetric warfare. Today the country faces threats from individuals that are of a different magnitude than the threats posed by individuals in the past; government authorities should reflect that change.

Nonetheless, in supplementing its trial system with a detention system, the United States must design the detention system with careful attention to the three problems with detentions identified above: the possibility of detaining an innocent person, the indefinite duration of the war, and the possibility that terrorists will become less dangerous over time. While those problems do not argue for eliminating military detention, they do not argue for simply abiding by the Geneva Conventions either. A dirty little secret is that the United States already provides the Guantánamo detainees with rights that far exceed the requirements of the Geneva Conventions. That said, it does not offer enough process to overcome the anxieties that the three problems generate. The problems with indefinite detention for modern terrorists argue for a more rigorous process and for higher standards than were available for noncriminal military detention in past wars with nation-states. They argue as well for individualizing both the detention assessment and the determination of which detainees are ready for release. They argue, in short, for updating the traditional military detention model to address the novel problems presented by terrorism and to ensure that it is consistent with modern notions of due process. What the updates should look like is the subject of the remainder of this chapter.

A National Security Court Already Exists

Once one accepts the need for some system of noncriminal military detention, suddenly much less is at stake in the debate over a national security court than the heat generated by that debate would suggest. That is because any system of long-term noncriminal detention of terrorists must and will be supervised by federal judges. At a minimum, federal judges will exercise constitutional habeas corpus jurisdiction over the incarceration of suspected terrorists, thereby having the final legal say over any detention system. In addition, Congress will likely establish statutory federal court review over any detention program that it establishes, as it has already attempted to do once. So one way or another, Article III judges will be in the detention game, helping to regularize, legalize, and legitimize the detention process while reviewing the adequacy of the factual basis for each detention judgment.

In other words, once one accepts that there will be a system of long-term, noncriminal, military detention of alleged terrorists and that federal judges will supervise the process, the debate about a national security court becomes a debate about what form federal judicial supervision should take. Those favoring a national security court prefer a relatively centralized and institutionalized form of federal court supervision. Those disfavoring it prefer relatively decentralized and non-institutionalized federal court supervision.

At one extreme is the wholly decentralized and non-institutionalized system of habeas review that prevailed before the Supreme Court's initial assertion in 2004 of habeas jurisdiction in *Rasul* v. *Bush*.[19] Before then, terrorist suspects at Guantánamo could bring habeas suits in any federal district court in the country in which they could obtain jurisdiction. No special statute governed the substance of or procedure in those cases. Under this regime, the "national security court" consisted of all federal district courts in the country acting with practically no guidance from Congress, subject to appellate review in the courts of appeals and finally in the Supreme Court.

Very few people thought that this system was a good idea, and since the summer of 2004 the de facto "national security court" supervising detention has become centralized and institutionalized in two ways. First, after *Rasul* federal courts spontaneously determined that all habeas cases from Guantánamo should be brought to the federal district court of the District of Columbia, subject to appellate review in the D.C. Circuit Court.[20] Justice Anthony Kennedy confirmed the appropriateness of this judicial centralization of habeas review in 2008 in his opinion in *Boumediene* v. *Bush.*[21] Following *Boumediene,* the federal court of the District of Columbia placed Judge Thomas F. Hogan in charge of coordinating and managing most of the Guantánamo Bay cases; of ruling on procedural issues common to these cases; and of identifying substantive issues that are common to all.[22] The second centralizing and institutionalizing move came from Congress, which in 2006 required all appeals of Combatant Status Review Tribunal decisions to go to the U.S. Court of Appeals for the District of Columbia Circuit, providing minimal statutory guidance on either the substance or procedure for review. (Those appeals became a moot point after *Boumediene,* when the D.C. Circuit stopped hearing them in light of the Court's decision.)

In effect, then, the United States already has a thinly institutionalized "national security court" in the federal courts of the District of Columbia. This national security court possesses—and is further developing—some of the virtues that national security court proponents have long argued for. It is relatively centralized, it contains a limited number of judges under the procedural supervision of a single judge, it has seen many different terrorism detention cases already, and it deals with them much more efficiently than the decentralized system. The court has been developing and will continue to develop specialized expertise in the issues brought before it. It also has been developing and will continue to develop relatively coherent substantive and procedural doctrines and rules to deal with detention cases—coherent, that is, in terms of learning from the run of cases and in treating like cases alike, especially in comparison with a system in which potentially every district judge and circuit court in the country is involved.

The main problem with the national security court as it now exists is that it is almost entirely a creature of the federal courts. With respect to judicial supervision of terrorist detainees, Congress has done little more than authorize the use of force against al Qaeda and its affiliates in September 2001 and provide for undefined judicial review of Combatant Status Review Tribunal decisions in 2006, a power of review whose existence is now entirely redundant given the habeas jurisdiction being exercised by the courts and that has lapsed as a consequence. Every other question about the current national security court—involving novel issues of institutional design as well as the substantive and procedural rights of terrorist detainees—are being answered by the courts on an ad hoc basis with little guidance from precedent and even less guidance from Congress.

The real question about the national security court, therefore, is not whether the nation will have one but whether it will be designed by judges or by the political branches. The answer to that question must be the political branches. Judges should find facts and enforce basic constitutional, statutory, and treaty norms, but they should not design the national security court system from scratch and should not write the details of the law for that system. For one thing, no single branch of government should determine the entire content of the law and then apply the law, least of all the judicial branch in the area of national security and terrorism. Every single decision about the national security court will affect both the nation's security and the liberty of those in the government's custody. Any rule has the potential to push the country in the direction of excessive security or excessive liberty, with many costs in both directions. Courts lack expertise about the nature and goals of terrorism and the optimal policy responses to terrorist threats needed to make these trade-offs.[23] And they lack accountability to the people if they get it wrong, either way.

Justice O'Connor summed up those points well in a 2005 speech at West Point, responding to the criticism that the Supreme Court had done too little in making its war-on-terrorism decisions:

> The Court is only one branch of government, and it cannot, and should not, give broad answers to the difficult [war-on-terror] policy questions that face our nation today. . . . We guard the ground rules, so that the people, through their elected representatives, can run the country. . . . I think it is not too much to say that I believe some clarity from Congress and the President would be welcomed by our armed forces.[24]

Unfortunately, Justice O'Connor's words remain as relevant and true today as when she spoke them.

How to Improve the National Security Court

The United States already has a national security court, but Congress must—if it wishes to maintain noncriminal military detention generally—get involved to provide the court with the rules and institutional structures that it needs to improve its organization and ensure greater legitimacy and effectiveness for the long haul. Sensible legislation would address the following distinct issues.

CITIZENSHIP

The first and most important challenge for Congress is to define the universe of people subject to detention. I will discuss that issue presently, but whatever the definition that Congress adopts, the definition should extend to U.S. citizens as well as to aliens. Detention policy to date has drawn sharp distinctions between the treatment of U.S. citizens and the treatment of aliens. That distinction should be eliminated, for two reasons.

The first was captured by Justice Robert Jackson, who wrote that "there is no more effective practical guaranty against arbitrary and unreasonable government than to require that the principles of law which officials would impose upon a minority must be imposed generally."[25] Designing detention procedures that are appropriate and legitimate in detaining dangerous U.S. citizen terrorists will ensure—and will credibly demonstrate to both domestic courts and the world in general—that the unusual detentions and the unusual procedures associated with them are legitimate and fair.

Second, there is no reason to think that the threat of terrorism is limited to noncitizens. Intelligence officials have made clear that al Qaeda and its associates are trying to recruit Westerners, including U.S. citizens, for attacks within the United States.[26] And as former attorney general Alberto Gonzales warned, "the threat of homegrown terrorist cells . . . may be as dangerous as groups like al Qaeda, if not more so."[27] The law cannot presume that the next attacker will be an alien. The system must be designed not just for the last attack, but for likely future attacks as well.

DEFINITION OF THE ENEMY

I turn now to the hardest question in detention policy: the definition of the enemy that will determine the universe of people subject to detention. The standard articulated by the Bush administration, based on the Authorization for Use of Military Force, is too vague and malleable. It extends the government's detention power to include

> an individual who was part of or supporting Taliban or Al Qaida forces, or associated forces that are engaged in hostilities against the United States or its coalition partners. This includes any person who has committed a belligerent act or has directly supported hostilities in aid of enemy armed forces.[28]

In its early court filings, the Obama administration adjusted this standard only trivially, restricting it to someone who was "part of, or *substantially* supported [emphasis added]" Taliban, al Qaeda, or associated forces.[29] The problem is that the phrase "associated forces" is indeterminate, and without further elaboration—perhaps by reference to a concept of co-belligerency[30]—it might justify sweeping up persons who lack the dangerousness that would warrant indefinite noncriminal detention. The phrase "directly supported" also is potentially quite broad.

But crafting a narrower standard that ensures detention of very dangerous terrorists is tricky. The main problem is that the group of people dangerous enough for the government reasonably to want to detain does not fit within traditional criteria for enemy combatancy. They do not fit because the terrorists blend in with civilians and do not organize themselves into traditional hierarchical commands and because the threat of terrorism is increasingly dispersed into decentralized copycat cells.

Two definitions promise more discipline than the current enemy combatant definition: terrorists who are in the command structure of al Qaeda and its co-belligerent terrorist organizations; and terrorists who directly participate in armed conflict against the United States.

Membership in the Command Structure of a Covered Terrorist Organization

Terrorist organizations have leadership and command structures, however diffuse, and persons who receive and execute orders within the command structure of an enemy terrorist group are analogous to traditional combatants. The most promising and least controversial detention criterion, therefore, is *membership in the command structure of al Qaeda and its co-belligerent terrorist organizations.*[31] This criterion would include the leadership of al Qaeda (people such as Osama bin Laden and Khalid Sheik Mohammad), subordinate al Qaeda personnel who occupy an operational role (such as Mohammed Atta) and people like Ali Saleh Kahlah al-Marri, an alleged al Qaeda operative who, in Judge Wilkinson's formulation, "knowingly plans or engages in conduct that harms or aims to harm persons or property for the purpose of furthering the military goals of an enemy nation or organization."[32]

The command structure criterion is consistent with Congress's authorization to the president for the use of force "against those . . . organizations" responsible for "the terrorist attacks that occurred on September 11, 2001," a descriptor that expressly includes members of al Qaeda and under traditional principles of co-belligerency includes al Qaeda's affiliated terrorist organizations."[33] Independent of the Authorization for Use of Military Force, the command structure criterion is consistent with the traditional understanding of detention in non-international armed conflicts, which the Supreme Court has deemed the conflict with al Qaeda to be.[34] And the command structure criterion makes intuitive sense. If there is a group of people who are highly likely to be dangerous to the United States, it is the group formed by those who voluntarily associate themselves with the command structure of a terrorist organization whose aim is to kill Americans.

Direct Participation in Hostilities

The command structure criterion is useful as far as it goes. But it leaves out two important classes of terrorists that Congress might want to include. The list consists of those who fall outside the al Qaeda and co-belligerent chain of command but who nonetheless associate with terrorist organizations in ways that indicate individual dangerousness or that promote terrorists' dangerous goals. For example, individuals outside of the al Qaeda command structure might receive weapons training in an al Qaeda camp, give logistical support related to a particular act of violence (for example, by creating an improvised explosive device to be used by someone else), or provide more generalized logistical support (for example. by raising funds to be used for violent activity). The second class consists of members of terrorist organizations inspired by al Qaeda or its jihadist principles but that are not al Qaeda co-belligerents. In other words, they do not act as agents of al Qaeda, participate with al Qaeda in acts of war against the United States, systematically provide military resources to al Qaeda, serve as fundamental communication links in the war against the United States, or systematically permit their buildings and safe houses to be used by al Qaeda in the war against the United States.

Congress could address the second class of terrorists simply by adding their organization to the list of organizations against which the United States is at war, but such organizations are so diffuse and can morph so quickly into other forms that adding them is not a stable solution. In any event, that solution does not address the problem of the first class of terrorists, who provide logistical and other non-operational support for covered terrorist organizations but who are not in the command structure. If Congress chooses to detain either class of terrorists, a status-based detention criterion like "membership in command structure" will not do. Congress will need to craft a conduct-based criterion that gets at the class of dangerous terrorists not already included in the "membership" test but that is not over-inclusive.

The best candidate for such a conduct-based criterion—best in terms of both its legal pedigree and its intuitive appeal—is the "direct participation in hostilities" standard.[35] This standard originated as a rule identifying circumstances in which a civilian—ordinarily immune from being made the object of an attack—may be targeted with lethal force.[36] But it has evolved into a more general test to distinguish those against whom military force (including detention) can be used legitimately from those against whom it cannot. The idea of detaining those who "directly participate" in hostilities captures many people's intuition about the class of terrorists who should be detained. Unfortunately, however, "direct participation" is contested in application in at least two ways.[37] First, experts disagree concerning the substance of direct participation itself. Everyone agrees that the concept applies to persons who literally engage in violence, such as by firing a rifle or setting off an explosive. But uncertainty arises as the concept moves beyond those paradigm cases to persons whose connections to violence are less direct. Does one directly participate in hostilities by ferrying ammunition to persons who are firing weapons or by constructing improvised explosive devices to be used by others? Second, experts also disagree with respect to the temporal boundaries of direct participation. When can a person be said to have ceased being a direct participant in hostilities?[38] Some have expressed concern about a revolving-door interpretation that enables civilians to contribute to violence but then immediately reacquire their protected status before facing any military consequences.[39]

There is little clear legal guidance in the laws of war—and even less clear state practice—to help Congress and the president resolve these issues and decide how to define the contours of "direct participation" as a detention criterion in a war against nonstate actors. Simply embracing the direct participation standard without more operational guidance would leave too much discretion to courts, which might interpret or apply the standard in radically over-inclusive or under-inclusive ways. In the final analysis, the proper calibration of the direct participation standard turns on how much and what kind of risk—to security and to liberty—the nation's leaders want to assume. The direct participation test provides a legitimate legal hook and general guidance, but the political branches must make the tough call about where and how to draw the line. Their choice will also, of course, be informed by the procedural safeguards associated with each substantive determination. Tighter safeguards may warrant broader detention criteria, and vice versa.

Procedural Issues

Courts have been developing procedural rules for the review of terrorist detentions on their own under the guise of some combination of due process and pragmatic justice. The following are the most important procedural questions that Congress should address:

Evidentiary and Informational Issues

There are a variety of different approaches to deciding what evidence the national security court should consider in reviewing terrorist detentions. The best approach is hard to state in the abstract—the devil is in the details. But it is clear that some deviation from ordinary criminal trial rules is necessary, especially so in four areas.

First, it will be necessary to permit introduction of hearsay and related evidence. The best approach here would be to follow the rule in international criminal courts, which have permitted evidence so long as it is relevant and "necessary for the determination of the truth."[40] The International Criminal Tribunal for the Former Yugoslavia, for example, permits the admission of hearsay and related evidence that "is relevant and has probative value, focusing on its reliability."[41]

Second, a decision will need to be made about evidence that is tainted because it was extracted in illegal or morally problematic ways. Here again international criminal tribunals might provide guidance. The International Criminal Court, for example, permits the introduction of evidence "obtained by means of a violation of this Statute or internationally recognized human rights" unless "(a) The violation casts substantial doubt on the reliability of the evidence; or (b) The admission of the evidence would be antithetical to and would seriously damage the integrity of the proceedings."[42]

Third is the question of classified information—in particular the question of whether the government should be able to establish the factual predicate for detention by presenting evidence on an ex parte basis. The ex parte approach serves the compelling government interest in preserving the secrecy of sensitive intelligence information, but it seems illegitimate to detain someone without letting him or at least his representative know about and contest the evidence. If Congress provides counsel to a detainee (as I suggest it should below), it can mediate these conflicting principles by allowing the counsel to remain during presentation of classified evidence.

The fourth and final issue concerns the government's disclosure obligations. The issue has both a substantive component (which agencies have an obligation to disclose information and what should the nature of that obligation be?) and a procedural component (who should have responsibility for enforcing disclosure obligations and what mechanism should there be, if any, for seeking to compel disclosure when necessary?). It is possible that, as with classified information, creative approaches to the use of counsel may help to finesse the tensions inherent in this issue. At a substantive minimum, however, the government should have a duty to disclose all exculpatory information and perhaps all material information reasonably within its possession.[43]

Publicity

The national security court should operate with the strong presumption that its processes and decisions will receive maximum public disclosure. Particularly with a novel procedure, public knowledge of how the system operates in practice will be essential to building both domestic and international credibility. The system will need to close its proceedings when considering classified material, just as Article III courts and courts martial do. But the default option should be openness, and the government should face a burden of proof if it wishes to change that option in a given case.

Regularized Review

One could argue that there should be no outside limit on the time available for detention orders. England limits noncriminal detention to twenty-eight days,[44] and France limits it to six days unless someone is charged with a crime, but those limited detention periods assume that war powers are not in effect.[45] Moreover, if someone poses a very serious threat to the United States and cannot practically be tried, a single period of detention is unlikely to mitigate the threat. So there exists a legitimate need for a long-term period of detention.

At the same time, Congress should not countenance indefinite detention lightly, especially under some of the looser standards articulated above. The appropriate compromise is to limit a detention order to some period of time, say six months, subject to extension using the same processes governing the initial order. In each instance, the government will have to convince the national security court that the individual remains a threat and satisfies other detention criteria. The fact that the government will have to come back to court repeatedly to justify a detention decision will also act as a natural constraint on the expansion of preventative detention. Many government officials will dislike the continued need to justify detention and where possible will favor prosecution instead.

At some point, moreover, the periods of semiannual detention may come to look more like punishment than does detention based on dangerousness. As detention continues for years, it may be appropriate to put an escalating burden of proof on the government—perhaps from a "preponderance of the evidence" standard to something more akin to "clear and convincing evidence" or "beyond a reasonable doubt." As an alternative, it may be appropriate to insist on specialized procedures that are triggered when an individual is detained for more than a certain number of years.

Lawyers

The government should be represented in the national security court by lawyers in the Justice Department. Potential detainees should be represented by a standing pool of government-paid defense lawyers. The defense lawyers would possess security clearances, thus avoiding the problem of not providing lawyers to detainees for years. Detainees could supplement their representation by government attorneys with counsel of their own choice as long as the lawyers that they choose receive appropriate security clearances. (In chapter 5, Robert Litt and Wells Bennett propose a similar arrangement for criminal proceedings in federal court.)

GREATER INSTITUTIONALIZATION

Perhaps the most controversial issue about a national security court is whether and how it should become more institutionalized. I used to believe that this issue was more important than I now believe it to be. Once one realizes that the federal courts of the District of Columbia are a de facto national security court for detention review and that Congress can build on this court structure as it deems appropriate, the institutionalization questions become somewhat less salient. Nonetheless, three issues still dominate the debate.

Should the National Security Court Be a Stand-alone Institution?

The national security court could continue to be staffed by the federal judges of the District of Columbia, but it could also become a new, stand-alone institution modeled on the Foreign Intelligence Surveillance Court. The arguments for such an institution arc diminished by the fact that a national security court already is in operation and that Congress can simply amplify or tweak the current system. Possible benefits of a stand-alone institution are, first, that the judges of the national security court could be drawn from the hundreds of existing judges around the country rather than from the relatively homogenous federal district court in the District of Columbia; second, that such a court, having special and discrete jurisdiction, could more readily receive novel and specialized evidentiary, procedural, and classified information rules; and third, that such a court would minimize the problem of precedential spillover into the civilian justice system.

If Congress were to create such a stand-alone institution, it should not simply expand the current Foreign Intelligence Surveillance Court's jurisdiction to cover detention. The Foreign Intelligence Surveillance Act (FISA) established a court to operate in secret. By contrast, many of the issues that a national security court would deal with could appropriately be taken up in open court, as the proceedings in the current national security court of the District of Columbia have shown. To bring the FISA court into the open, even in limited settings, might hamper the work and safety of FISA jurists. And because FISA's strong default mode is to operate in secrecy, vesting that court with jurisdiction over detentions may lead to greater secrecy than is optimal in the context of detention. In addition, expanding the FISA court's duties may very well interfere with that court's ability to carry out its current functions.

First-order Detention Determinations

The current national security court reviews the legality of detentions made by a military Combatant Status Review Tribunal (CSRT), which makes the first-order judgments of the propriety of a given detention. The CSRTs could continue to serve that function, subject to review in the national security court. As an alternative, Congress could transfer the first-order determinations to a nonmilitary or judicial body under the supervision of the national security court or to the federal judges on the national security court itself.

Trials

The national security court might also replace criminal trials by military commission, courts martial, or even ordinary criminal trials in civilian courts. It could serve either as a trial body or as an appellate body or conceivably as both. The argument here is that a national security court might be able to achieve some of the benefits of legitimacy of an Article III criminal trial while at the same time avoiding the costs of such trials. So, for example, Congress might be able to give a national security court somewhat more procedural flexibility in protecting classified information than it can an ordinary civilian criminal court. It might also be able to better protect judges and jurors in such a court. Congress also might be able to limit the court's precedents to ensure that any adjustments to substantive and procedural criminal law—as in *Moussaui* and *Padilla*—do not spill over into the ordinary criminal trial process, under which the government should bear ordinary burdens of proof.[46]

The question of whether the jurisdiction of the new court should expand beyond detention to trials is a large and complicated one that is beyond the scope of this analysis. But at a minimum, Congress must consider the design of a national security court in conjunction with the design of the trial system, for each would have profound effects on the other's effectiveness.[47]

Sunset

Any legislation related to a national security court should include a sunset provision. The United States still lacks information about its enemies and the precise threats that they pose; the nation also possesses relatively little information on how any particular national security court design would work in practice and what effect it would have on liberty and security. Those points suggest that Congress would be wise to revisit the design and operations of the national security court in a few years, after more information becomes available. Forcing Congress to reconsider a legislative scheme typically is difficult and politically costly. The ordinary problems of inertia are exacerbated by the president's veto power, which means that modifying or eliminating a poorly functioning national security court might take a supermajority rather than a simple majority.[48] Even when a majority of Congress's members want to change a law that is already on the books, it can require substantial effort, energy, and political capital to translate that wish into successful legislation. Often such efforts fail.

A good example of how sunset provisions can respond to such structural, political, and human error variables can be found in the experience with the independent counsel law.[49] The institution of independent counsel was unfamiliar to the U.S. constitutional system, and because the policy implications were so severe, Congress decided to impose a sunset. That was a wise decision. It would have been extraordinarily difficult, given the political repercussions, for members of Congress to stand up and say that they were "against independent investigations" and "against ethics in government." Yet the independent counsel law produced a constitutional monster, accountable to no one. Because of the sunset mechanism, no independent counsel law is on the books today. It was simply too difficult, in the wake of the Iran–Contra and the Whitewater–Lewinsky investigations, for members of Congress to stand up and affirmatively persuade their colleagues to vote for reauthorization of the act. But it might have been very difficult to affirmatively abrogate, had the default setting mandated its continued existence.

Similar considerations led to the sunset provision in the USA Patriot Act.[50] President Bush signed the act into law on October 26, 2001.[51] The act included December 31, 2005, sunset provisions for its most expansive and potentially controversial components.[52] Attempts to reauthorize the act began in late 2004, but Congress and the president could not agree on a single version for reauthorization, so Congress twice enacted short extensions of the soon-to-expire provisions.[53] Congress ultimately adopted two pieces of legislation that, together, increased judicial review for surveillance activities, required additional reporting by the executive branch to Congress, enhanced mandatory procedures for employing some of the Patriot Act's more controversial tools, and included further sunsets for two controversial provisions.[54] While the reauthorization made most of the provisions that were scheduled to expire permanent, it only extended the sunset for two provisions, requiring that reauthorization for them be sought again in 2009.

Advocates on both sides of the aisle praised the original Patriot Act's sunset provisions. Senator Patrick Leahy attributed both improved congressional oversight and the opportunity to improve the act to the sunset provisions.[55] Representative Martin Meehan stated that "[f]ortunately, the bill included sunset provisions, allowing Congress to revisit the law, reflect on its implementation, and fix those parts of the law that have dearly become overreaching."[56] Following reauthorization, Viet Dinh—who had authored large sections of the Patriot Act while at the Department of Justice—wrote that "[t]he reauthorization process provided a chance to fine tune, clarify, and improve upon the original provisions of the Act. It also provided an opportunity for debate about what tools law enforcement and intelligence officials need in the war on terror."[57]

Amplifications to the national security court would be appropriate candidates for a legislative sunset. Time will tell whether any such court meets the fate of the Patriot Act (renewal with some changes) or the independent counsel law (complete nonrenewal). But in the interim, the inclusion of a sunset would help forestall government abuse of detention power, because the government would know that the entire system is up for renewal and must therefore operate responsibly and with the possibility of abrogation.

Conclusion

Almost five years ago, the 9/11 Commission stated that "Americans should not settle for incremental, ad hoc adjustments to a system designed generations ago for a world that no longer exists."[58] And yet that is precisely what the country has done since the commission published those words. It is time for the president and Congress to work together to address the terrorist detention problem in a comprehensive way. If a detention system becomes part of the solution, as I believe it should, then a national security court will be part of the solution as well. It is far better to have a well-designed national security court—a court designed in a systematic way by political leaders—than to have courts making ad hoc decisions in the rough-and-tumble of high-stakes litigation.

ENDNOTES

†I thank Will Levi, Hagan Scotten, J. B. Tarter, and J. B. Ward for excellent research assistance and Robert Chesney and Benjamin Wittes for very helpful comments and for past collaborations on related topics.

1. See Jack Goldsmith and Neal Katyal, "The Terrorists' Court," *New York Times,* July 11, 2007, opinion section.

2. See, for example, Geneva Convention (III) Relative to the Treatment of Prisoners of War, August 12, 1949 [1955], 6 U.S.T. 3316, 3406, T.I.A.S. No. 3364, 75 U.N.T.S. 135, art. 118, stating that "[p]risoners of war shall be released and repatriated without delay after the cessation of active hostilities"; Hague Convention (II) with Respect to the Laws and Customs of War on Land, July 29,1899, 32 Stat. 1803, art. 20 (www.icrc.org/ihl.nsf/FULL/150?opendocument), as soon as possible after "conclusion of peace."

3. *Hamdi* v. *Rumsfeld,* 542 U.S. 507, 518 (2004), plurality opinion.

4. "International Military Tribunal (Nuremberg), Judgment and Sentences," reprinted in *American Journal of International Law* 41 (1947), pp. 172, 229.

5. For critical treatments, see Paul H. Robinson, "Punishing Dangerousness: Cloaking Preventive Detention as Criminal Justice," *Harvard Law*

Review 114 (2001), pp. 1429–32; Carol S. Steiker, "Foreword: The Limits of the Preventive State," *Journal of Criminal Law and Criminology* 88 (1998), pp. 771, 777–81.

6. Geoff Morell, "Department of Defense News Briefing," January 13, 2009 (www.defenselink.mil/transcripts/transcript.aspx?transcriptid=4340); Associated Press, "Report: Guantánamo Detainees Return to Battlefield," *International Herald Tribune,* January 13, 2009 (www.iht.com/articles/ap/2009/01/13/america/NA-US-Guantánamo-Detainees.php),

7. Robert F. Worth, "Freed by the U.S., Saudi Becomes al Qaeda Chief," *New York Times,* January 23, 2009 (www.nytimes.com/2009/01/23/world/middleeast/23yemen.html).

8. Curtis A. Bradley and Jack L. Goldsmith, "Congressional Authorization and the War on Terrorism," *Harvard Law Review* 118 (2005), pp. 2047, 2073–74.

9. See William E. Birkhimer, *Military Government and Martial Law,* 3rd ed., rev. (Kansas City: Franklin Hudson, 1914), pp. 123–24, 354–55; William Winthrop, *Military Law and Precedents,* 2nd ed., rev. (Boston: Little, Brown, and Co., 1896), pp. 783–84; ibid. at 832–34.

10. See, generally, Diana Preston, *Besieged in Peking: The Story of the 1900 Boxer Rising* (London: Constable, 1999), pp. 25–30; Chester C. Tan, *The Boxer Catastrophe* (New York: Columbia University Press, 1955), pp. 35–36.

11. John S.D. Eisenhower, *Intervention! The United States and the Mexican Revolution 1913–1917* (New York: W.W. Norton, 1993), pp. 231–60.

12. See National Commission on Terrorist Attacks upon the United States, *The 9/11 Commission Report* (2004) (www.9-11commission.gov/report/911Report.pdf.), p. 117.

13. See Authorization for Use of Military Force. Public Law No. 107-40, 115 Stat. 224 (2001); Military Commission Act of 2006, Pub. L. No. 109-366, 120 Stat. 2600 (codified as amended at 10 U.S.C. § 948a).

14. *Hamdi* v. *Rumsfeld.* 542 U.S. 507, 518 (2004); *Hamdan* v. *Rumsfeld,* 548 U.S. 557, 568 (2006); *Boumediene* v. *Bush,* 128 S.Ct. 2229, 2240-41 (2008).

15. Robert Chesney and Jack Goldsmith, "Terrorism and the Convergence of Criminal and Military Detention Models," *Stanford Law Review* 60 (2008), pp. 1079, 1104–08.

16. See, generally, Charles Weisselberg, "Terror in the Courts: Beginning to Assess the Impact of Terrorism-Related Prosecutions on Domestic

Criminal Law and Procedure in the USA," *Crime, Law, and Social Change* 50 (2008), p. 25.

17. This paragraph is drawn from Jack Goldsmith and Benjamin Wittes, "A Blueprint for the Closure of Guantánamo Bay," *Slate,* December 8, 2008 (www.slate.com/id/2206229/).

18. The exception was political assassination, which could produce substantial turmoil. Today, assassination is just one of several modern threats that can be inflicted by small groups of individuals.

19. *Rasul* v. *Bush,* 542 U.S. 466 (2004).

20. After *Padilla* and *Rasul* were decided in summer of 2004, the Supreme Court remanded *Gherebi* (a habeas petition filed in California) to the Ninth Circuit Court, which then cited *Padilla* and *Rasul* en route to concluding that it would be appropriate to transfer that petition to D.C. See *Gherebi* v. *Bush,* 374 F.3d 727, 739 (9th Cir. 2004). The court did not elaborate on why transfer was appropriate except to say that "[i]t appears to us that the proper venue for this proceeding is in the District of Columbia." Ibid. Since then all Guantánamo-related habeas petitions have been transferred to the federal district courts in Washington, D.C.

21. *Boumediene* v. *Bush,* 128 S.Ct. at 2276, concluding that "[i]f, in a future case, a detainee files a habeas petition in another judicial district in which a proper respondent can be served, the Government can move for change of venue to the court that will hear these petitioners' cases, the United States District Court for the District of Columbia." Citations eliminated.

22. See Resolution of the Executive Session of the United States District Court for the District of Columbia, July 1, 2008 (www.dcd.uscourts. gov/public-docs/system/files/Guantánamo-Resolution070108.pdf).

23. Cf. 128 S. Ct. at 2276-77, stating that "[u]nlike the President and some designated members of Congress, neither the members of this Court nor most federal judges begin the day with briefings that may describe new and serious threats to our Nation and its people."

24. Sandra Day O'Connor, "Remarks upon Receiving the Sylvanus Thayer Award," speech, United States Military Academy, West Point, N.Y., October 20, 2005 (www.westpointaog.org/NetCommunity/Page. aspx?pid=514).

25. *Railway Express Agency* v. *New York,* 336 U.S. 106, 112 (1949), J. Jackson, concurring.

26. Mark Mazetti, "Intelligence Chief Says Al Qaeda Improves Ability to Strike in U.S.," *New York Times*, February 6, 2008, world news section.

27. Alberto Gonzales, "Remarks on Stopping Terrorists before They Strike: The Justice Department's Power of Prevention," speech, World Affairs Council of Pittsburgh, Pittsburgh, August 16, 2006.

28. Deputy Secretary of Defense, "Implementation of Combat Status Review Tribunal Procedures for Enemy Combatants Detained at U.S. Naval Base Guantánamo Bay, Cuba," memorandum, July 14, 2006 (www. defenselink.mil/news/Aug2006/d20060809CSRTProcedures.pdf).

29. Respondents' Memorandum Regarding the Government's Detention Authority Relative to Detainees Held at Guantánamo Bay, Misc. No. 08-442 (TFH), U.S. District Court for the District of Columbia, March 13, 2009 (www.scotusblog.com/wp/wp-content/uploads/2009/03/ doj-detain-authority-3-13-09.pdf).

30. Cf. Bradley and Goldsmith, *supra,* note 8, at 2112–13.

31. In the laws of war, a co-belligerent state is a "fully fledged belligerent fighting in association with one or more belligerent powers." Morris Greenspan, *The Modern Law of Land Warfare* (University of California Press, 1959), p. 531. As applied to nonstate actor terrorist organizations, co-belligerents would include terrorist organizations that act as agents of al Qaeda, participate with al Qaeda in acts of war against the United States, systematically provide military resources to al Qaeda, or serve as fundamental communication links in the war against the United States; it would perhaps also include those that systematically permit their buildings and safe houses to be used by al Qaeda in the war against the United States. These organizations are analogous to co-belligerents in a traditional war.

32. See *al-Marri* v. *Pucciarelli,* 534 F.3d 213, 325 (4th Cir. 2008), Wilkinson, J., concurring and dissenting in part.

33. See Bradley and Goldsmith, *supra,* note 8, at 2112–13. *Hamdi* held that the authorization to use force entails authorization to detain in an international armed conflict, and the plurality's uncertainty about extending that rationale to the war against al Qaeda concerned the indefiniteness of detention and not whether "force" entailed detention authority in that context. See *Hamdi,* 542 U.S. at 521, stating that "we understand Congress' grant of authority for the use of 'necessary and appropriate force' to include the authority to detain for the duration of the relevant conflict, and our understanding is based on longstanding law-of-war principles. If the practical circumstances of a given conflict are entirely

unlike those of the conflicts that informed the development of the law of war, that understanding may unravel."

34. See Chesney and Goldsmith, *supra*, note 15, at 1121–23; *Hamdan* v. *Rumsfeld,* 548 U.S. 557, 629–31 (2006).

35. The discussion in this paragraph and in the next is drawn from Chesney and Goldsmith, *supra*, note 15, at 1123–26.

36. For a thorough overview of the direct participation concept, see the trio of reports following from expert meetings on the subject jointly convened by the International Committee of the Red Cross (ICRC) and the TMC Asser Institute: Third Expert Meeting on the Notion of Direct Participation in Hostilities (2005) (www.icrc.org/Web/eng/siteeng0.nsf/htmlall/participation-hostilities-ihl-311205/$File/Direct_participation_in_hostilities_2005_eng.pdf); Second Expert Meeting: Direct Participation in Hostilities under International Humanitarian Law (2004) (www.icrc.org/Web/eng/siteeng0.nsf/htmlall/participation-hostilities-ihl-311205/$File/Direct_participation_in_hostilities_2004_eng.pdf); Direct Participation in Hostilities under International Humanitarian Law (2003) (www.icrc.org/Web/eng/siteeng0.nsf/htmlall/participation-hostilities-ihl-311205/$File/Direct%20participation%20in%20hostilities-Sept%202003.pdf).

37. See ICRC Direct Participation studies, *supra,* note 36.

38. See, for example, Third Expert Meeting, *supra,* note 36, at 59–68, discussing the temporal component of the direct participation inquiry; HCJ 769/02 *Pub. Comm. against Torture in Israel* v. *Gov't of Israel,* para 35 [Dec. 11, 2005], broadly construing the temporal element of direct participation in the context of members of terrorist organizations (http://elyonl.court.gov.il/Files_ENG/02/690/007/a34/02007690.a34.pdf).

39. See, for example, W. Hays Parks, "Air War and the Law of War," *Air Force Law Review* 32 (1990), pp.119–20.

40. Michael A. Newton, "The Iraqi Special Tribunal: A Human Rights Perspective," *Cornell International Law Journal* 35 (2005), pp. 863, 885.

41. *Prosecutor* v. *Tadic,* Case No. IT-94-1, Decision on the Defense Motion on Hearsay, August 5, 1996; see also Rome Statute of the International Criminal Court, art. 69(4), 2187 U.N.T.S. 90, stating that "[t]he Court may rule on the relevance or admissibility of any evidence, taking into account, inter alia, the probative value of the evidence and any prejudice that such evidence may cause to a fair trial or to a fair evaluation of the testimony of a witness."

42. Rome Statute, *supra,* note 41, art. 69(7).

43. Cf. *Parhat* v. *Gates,* 532 F. 3d 834 (D.C. Cir. 2008).

44. The Counter-Terrorism Bill of 2008 would increase the limit to forty-two days. As of October 22, 2008, it was still under debate.

45. In France, as well as in Spain, pretrial detention can last for many years without a trial. But an indictment must be made within six days of detention, and the detention process is supervised by an independent judge of liberty. The French model thus offers a different alternative worth examining—pretrial detention in which formal charges have been filed (as opposed to a preventive detention model without charge).

46. Others might want a national security court to examine other areas of law, such as those civil cases in which the "state secrets" privilege is invoked to block litigation.

47. See Goldsmith and Wittes, *supra,* note 17.

48. See U.S. Const. art. I, § 7.

49. Independent Counsel Reauthorization Act of 1994, Public Law No. 103-270, § 2, 108 Stat. 732,732.

50. Uniting and Strengthening America by Providing Appropriate Tools Required to Intercept and Obstruct Terrorism Act of 2001, Public Law No. 107-56, 115 Stat. 272 (2001), codified as amended in scattered sections of 18, 47 and 50 U.S.C.

51. Robert E. Pierre, "Wisconsin Senator Emerges as a Maverick; Feingold, Who Did Not Back Anti-Terrorism Bill, Says He Just Votes His Conscience," *Washington Post,* October 27, 2001, p. A08.

52. American Civil Liberties Union, "The Sun Also Sets: Understanding the Patriot Act 'Sunsets'" (http://action.aclu.org/reformthepatriotact/sunsets.html).

53. Brian T. Yeh and Charles Doyle, *CRS Report for Congress, USA Patriot Improvement and Reauthorization Act of 2005: A Legal Analysis* (Congressional Research Service, 2006) (www.fas.org/sgp/crs/intel/RL33332.pdf), p. 2.

54. USA Patriot Improvement and Reauthorization Act of 2005, Public Law 109-177, 120 Stat. 177 (2006); USA Patriot Act Additional Reauthorizing Amendments Act of 2006, Public Law 109-178, 120 Stat. 278 (2006). See generally Viet D. Dinh and Wendy J. Keefer, "FISA and the Patriot Act: A Look Back and a Look Forward," *Georgetown Law Journal Annual Review of Criminal Procedure* 35 (2006), pp. iii, xxxii-iii (2006). On the two new

sunsets, see Yeh and Doyle, *supra,* note 53, at 3. The two provisions are "roving wiretaps"—those that follow a given targeted individual even as he changes his communications platform—and access to certain business records under FISA. Ibid.

55. Patrick Leahy, "Patriot Bill: A Missed Opportunity to Protect Americans' Security And Civil Liberties," press release, December 8, 2005 (http:leahy.senate.gov/press/2OO512/120805.html).

56. 151 Cong. Rec. H11,509-10 (daily ed., December 14, 2005), remarks of Martin Meehan on reauthorization of Patriot Act, United States House of Representatives, Washington, D.C.

57. Dinh and Keefer, *supra,* note 54, at xxx.

58. National Commission on Terrorist Attacks upon the United States, *supra,* note 12, at 399.

*Jack Goldsmith teaches international law, foreign relations law, and national security at Harvard Law School. He served as assistant attorney general for the Office of Legal Counsel at the Department of Justice from October 2003 through July 2004 and as special counsel to the general counsel of the Department of Defense from September 2002 through June 2003.

Goldsmith, Jack. 2009. Long-term terrorist detention and a U.S. national security court. In *Legislating the War on Terror*, ed. Ben Wittes, 75–97. Washington, D.C.: Brookings Institution.

Used by permission.

Preventive Detention: A National Security Policy Obama Should Abandon

*by Jules Lobel**

[...]

III. Guantánamo and Preventive Detention

[Pres. Barack Obama] stated during the [2008] election campaign that he would close Guantánamo, and one of his first actions upon taking office was to sign an Executive Order committing the government to close Guantánamo within a year.[52] Yet the question remains about what to do with the approximately 220 prisoners currently detained at Guantánamo.[53] President Obama recently stated in a major national security speech that there may be a number of detainees at Guantánamo who cannot be prosecuted for past crimes "yet who pose a clear danger to the American people" and therefore must be subject to some preventive detention legal regime.[54]

Various proposals for a preventive detention statute have been articulated by scholars. Jack Goldsmith, former head of the Justice Department's Office of Legal Counsel in the Bush administration, and Neal Katyal, who is currently Deputy Solicitor General for the Obama administration, proposed in 2008 that a new national security court be established by Congress to detain "suspected terrorists" after a hearing that provided substantial procedural safeguards.[55] Other scholars have also argued for a preventive detention law that would give a national security court jurisdiction "over citizens and non-citizens who operate in a loose network for terrorist purposes—whether here or abroad."[56] Professor David Cole, however, rejects any broad preventive detention authority to detain suspected terrorists, as well as the creation of a special national security court, but would nonetheless permit the government to preventively detain those who are found to be fighters for al Qaeda—whether they are captured on battlefields in Afghanistan or in the United States—after a fair hearing before a military tribunal.[57]

All of these proposals are premised on the rationale that the normal criminal process is insufficient to address the problem of detaining captured terrorists. Some argue that most of the evidence available against suspected terrorists is predicated on intelligence information or other classified information and that the government should not be forced to choose between disclosing this information to the terrorist suspect in order to try him criminally, or releasing the detainee to avoid compromising such confidential, national security sensitive material.[58] In addition, some argue that the standards of proof required for evidence to be admitted in a federal criminal trial might not be met for evidence collected on battlefields abroad.[59] Another argument for some form of preventive detention is that the burden of proof in criminal cases requiring the government to prove culpability beyond a reasonable doubt is prohibitively high.[60]

There are several reasons that the Obama administration should reject a system of preventive detention and the establishment of a separate national security court. First, a long-term, indefinite preventive detention scheme for suspected terrorists poses grave dangers for the rule of law and constitutional governance. To deprive someone of their liberty for what could very well be their entire lifetime without charging them with any crime and without having the evidence necessary to convict them in a regular court strikes at the heart of our core constitutional values. Second, such a system has not been shown to be necessary as either a legal or a practical matter.

To adopt a preventive detention scheme generally requires the government to show a necessity for one. All preventive detention policies hitherto recognized in the United States provide for the detention of individuals who cannot be tried by the normal judicial system because they have committed no crime. Thus, the Supreme Court has allowed the civil commitment of persons who are mentally ill and dangerous, but have committed no crime and therefore cannot be prosecuted.[61] Similarly, U.S. law allows preventive detention in the form of quarantine to isolate a person with a dangerous disease who could not be prosecuted criminally.[62] The Court has allowed detention without bail of persons who have been charged criminally and are deemed to pose a danger to the community or a risk of flight.[63] Again, we permit preventive detention in that circumstance because the criminal justice system cannot instantaneously adjudicate criminal liability, so preventive detention is viewed as a necessary measure imposed until the criminal process can reach a conclusion. Finally, the laws of war permit the detention of captured enemy soldiers for the duration of the war. Those soldiers, such as the hundreds of thousands of German soldiers held during World War II, have committed no crime. They are detained not because they are criminals, nor because they are generally dangerous, but to prevent them from returning to the battle on behalf of the enemy during the course of war.

In the current conflict with al Qaeda, in contrast to the typical wars that the United States has fought in the past, anyone who can be detained as an al Qaeda fighter will also, almost by definition, have committed a crime under U.S. law.[64] Therefore, unlike preventive detention permitted either domestically or pursuant to the laws of war authorizing the detention of enemy prisoners of war, the criminal justice system is theoretically available to prosecute and detain individuals found fighting for al Qaeda.[65] The fact that al Qaeda terrorists can be prosecuted by the criminal justice system thus removes the linchpin characteristic of all the current examples of preventive detention—that the criminal justice system cannot adequately provide for these individuals' detentions because they have committed no crimes, or because they need to be detained for a relatively short period of time while the criminal justice process determines whether they have committed crimes.

The argument for preventive detention of al Qaeda suspects, therefore, is not that it is theoretically impossible to criminally prosecute al Qaeda terrorists, but rather that it is impractical or difficult to do so. Yet there is virtually no evidence beyond pure speculation that it is impractical to prosecute terrorists in criminal courts.[66] Indeed, the evidence is to the contrary. A recent lengthy, well-documented report for Human Rights First, written by two former federal prosecutors, examined the actual experience of more than 100 international terrorism cases that have been prosecuted in federal courts over the past fifteen years.[67] The authors conclude that, "contrary to the views of some critics, the court system is generally well equipped to handle most terrorism cases."[68]

More particularly, the two prosecutors conclude that the often asserted problem involving the government's need to introduce classified evidence is adequately addressed by the Classified Information Procedures Act (CIPA), [69] which allows for detailed procedures when classified evidence is at issue to ensure that such evidence is protected from disclosures.[70] The CIPA procedures have allowed the government to offer relevant classified evidence while protecting national security. Based on their review of the case law the authors concluded, "we are not aware of a single terrorism case in which CIPA procedures have failed and a serious security breach has occurred."[71] They discount the difficulty of introducing evidence into federal criminal trials pursuant to the Federal Rules of Evidence, arguing that they are not aware of any terrorism case in which an important piece of evidence has been excluded on authentication or other grounds.[72]

The Human Rights First report's conclusions are echoed by jurists with considerable experience in trying terrorism cases.[73] For example, Judge John C. Coughenour testified before the Senate Judiciary Committee that the federal courts "are not only competent, but also uniquely situated to conduct terrorism trials."[74] Judge Coughenour's twenty-seven years of experience on the federal bench, which includes presiding over the trial of the so-called "Millennium Bomber" Ahmed Ressam in 2001, led him to conclude that the CIPA contains "extensive precautions" that were "more than adequate in that case," and that any shortcomings in the law can and should be addressed by further revision, rather than by a separate, parallel scheme of preventive detention.[75] While the federal courts may be stretching the bounds of what is constitutionally permissible by permitting the admission of evidence without sufficient safeguards[76] or by allowing prosecutions for "material support" crimes that are broadly and vaguely defined,[77] the answer is not to create a separate judicial or military process to preventively detain suspected terrorists for whom prosecution is difficult even under these flexible criminal procedures.

Moreover, neither the Bush or Obama administrations nor academic supporters of a preventive detention scheme have ever made any factual showing that there are a significant number of alleged terrorists detained who could not be tried on criminal charges in federal court, but nonetheless could be detained after a fair hearing in which evidence that they were indeed al Qaeda members or fighters was subjected to rigorous scrutiny. Indeed, the evidence adduced thus far is to the contrary; virtually all of the habeas cases that federal courts have decided to date of Guantánamo detainees have held that the government has no objective evidence justifying the detentions.[78] Most of these cases have been decided by conservative judges in the D.C. Circuit.[79] As one D.C. Circuit panel stated "Lewis Carroll notwithstanding, the fact that the government has 'said it thrice' does not make an allegation true."[80]

Nor does it make much logical sense that there would be a significant number of detainees who could not be tried criminally but nonetheless could be detained preventively after a fair hearing. It seems unlikely that there would be many cases where the government has clear and convincing evidence that a detainee is an al Qaeda fighter or is plotting a terrorist crime and could convince a neutral judge that the person was a terrorist after a fair hearing which afforded the detainee a meaningful opportunity to respond to the government's evidence, but where the government nonetheless could not have convicted that person of a crime after a trial in federal court.

As is now widely recognized, the government should not be able to detain someone based on mere speculation or suspicion of what they might do in the future, but must have concrete evidence that they fought for al Qaeda, participated in al Qaeda attacks or were at least conspiring to engage in such attacks. Moreover, it also seems to be widely acknowledged that the Bush administration's system of military detainee review by the Combatant Status Review Tribunals contained woefully inadequate procedural mechanisms to review detainees' status, and that more robust procedural safeguards are required.[81] Reasonable procedural safeguards would ensure that detainees be provided a lawyer, that evidence procured by torture be deemed unreliable and inadmissible, that the military tribunal be constituted in a manner that is truly independent, that the detainee or his lawyer have access to and an opportunity to contest the factual information—whether classified or not—that forms the basis of the government's allegations, and that the government should have to make a substantial showing under "clear and convincing evidence" or some similar test.[82]

However, once clear and meaningful detention standards are set forth and robust procedural safeguards applied, it seems at best uncertain that any significant number of alleged enemy terrorists would be able to be detained who could not be prosecuted. Once we assume that the government has clear and convincing evidence that someone is an enemy terrorist and combatant and that it must accord the detainee or his lawyer sufficient access to that evidence that would afford him a meaningful right to respond and thus comport with due process—which is all that CIPA requires in a criminal trial—why would it be so difficult to prosecute that person criminally? It may well be that there are a few detainees who could be detained under an independent and rigorous system of military review that would comport with due process, yet would be acquitted in criminal trials, but it makes little sense for Congress to design an entire system of preventive detention with either military tribunals or a new national security court to deal with the hypothetical few cases. For Congress to do so there must, at minimum, be a strong factual showing that there are a considerable number of detainees for whom a criminal trial is impractical but who nonetheless could be detained under a system requiring robust review. Such a showing has certainly not been made until now, and it seems unlikely that it can be made. In any event, that some suspected terrorists might be acquitted if prosecuted is no argument for a preventive detention scheme, for no fair criminal procedure system can or ought to guarantee the government a conviction in every case.

President Obama has suggested that it might be impossible to prosecute some detainees "because the evidence may be tainted."[83] But if the evidence against a detainee has been obtained by torture and is therefore "tainted," it is not only inadmissible, but also unreliable and ought to be inadmissible in either a military court or any fair proceeding. It would be contrary to our constitutional values and due process to detain someone preventively based on evidence procured by torture.

Finally, not only is a preventive detention scheme unnecessary, but it is also dangerous for two reasons. First, to detain persons who are dangerous because they are al Qaeda fighters for the duration of the conflict in all likelihood means to detain them for the rest of their lives, or at minimum for a very long time. The military conflict with al Qaeda has been ongoing now for over seven years and shows no signs of ending any time soon. In virtually all other modern warfare—even civil conflicts between insurgents and governments—there is some prospect of a negotiated settlement ending the conflict. Here there is none. Moreover, since al Qaeda has morphed into a loose network of affiliated groups in far-flung nations, there seems little possibility of a definitive military victory over al Qaeda, even if the United States were to achieve military success in Afghanistan and Pakistan. Preventive detention in this circumstance, therefore, means the virtually permanent incarceration in harsh conditions of people who often are not captured in any visible battleground, but in civilian areas.

The Supreme Court has recognized this danger. In *Boumediene*, the Court continually emphasized the lengthy duration of the conflict with al Qaeda and of the detentions of the Guantánamo prisoners, noting that "the cases before us lack any historical parallel. They involve individuals detained by executive order for the duration of a conflict that, if measured, from September 11, 2001 to the present, is already among the longest wars in American history."[84] That Court recognized that where the consequence of error may be detention of persons for the duration of hostilities that may last a generation or more, "the risk of error is too significant to ignore."[85]

The Court ended its *Boumediene* opinion by again emphasizing the potentially indefinite and permanent nature of the conflict against terrorism: "Because our Nation's military conflicts have been of limited duration, it has been possible to leave the outer boundaries of war powers undefined. If, as some fear, terrorism continues to pose dangerous threats to us for years to come, the Court might not have this luxury."[86]

In *Boumediene*, the Court seemed to harken back to a point that the *Hamdi* plurality foreshadowed when it suggested that the virtually permanent and ambiguous nature of the war against terrorism could undermine the applicability of the preventive detention war model to alleged al Qaeda or Taliban detainees: "[i]f the practical circumstances of a given conflict are entirely unlike those of the conflicts that informed the development of the law of war, that understanding [that the President has detention authority under the law of war] may unravel."[87] While the Court did not reach that question in *Boumediene*, the Court did seem to recognize that the practical circumstances in this conflict are sufficiently unlike prior military conflicts to render preventive detention for the duration of this conflict far more dangerous to liberty than in traditional wars. The danger of a virtually life imprisonment preventive detention scheme[88] suggests that, at minimum, it should not be adopted unless the criminal justice system has been demonstrably unavailable in a significant number of cases. That showing has simply not been made.

The experience of democracies with preventive detention against alleged terrorists illustrates its grave dangers. The United Kingdom experimented with preventive detention in the 1970s when it interned hundreds of suspected Irish Republican Army (IRA) members without trial. But the British later realized that this policy generated sympathy for the IRA and aided recruitment efforts, and changed its policy. The British Ministry of Defense later acknowledged, "With the benefit of hindsight, it was a major mistake."[89] Indeed, while there have been terrorist attacks in a number of countries in Europe before and after the September 11 attacks, and many European nations have combat troops fighting alongside U.S. armed forces in Afghanistan, no European country has adopted a long-term preventive detention scheme to detain al Qaeda operatives as enemy combatants. Instead, they all utilize their criminal justice systems to try alleged terrorists. Indeed, most European states do not have any preventive detention or coercive measures—apart from immigration regulations linked to the expulsion of foreign nationals—to address a situation where a person who is suspected of terrorist activities is considered a threat to national security but is not prosecuted.[90] Even the few who do have preventive coercive measures, such as Great Britain, generally restrict a person's liberty by placing them under special police supervision or imposing restrictions such as a curfew, but do not deprive a person of their liberty by detaining them.[91] No European country has thus far implemented a long-term preventive detention scheme of the sort Obama now suggests.

[…]

ENDNOTES

[†]I wish to thank my research assistant, Emily Town, for her excellent research help with this article and the staff of the Document Technology Center at the University of Pittsburgh for their invaluable assistance in preparing it for publication. I also want to thank Kim Scheppele for her extremely helpful comments on a draft.

[…]

52. Exec. Order No. 13,492, 74 Fed. Reg. 4897 (Jan. 22, 2009).

53. Peter Finn, *Guantánamo Closure Called Obama Priority*, WASH. POST, Nov. 12, 2008, at A1; William Glaberson, *Post-Guantánamo: A New Detention Law?*, N.Y. TIMES, Nov. 15, 2008, at 13; Benjamin Wittes, *Wrenching Choices on Guantánamo*, WASH. POST, Nov. 21, 2008, at A23.

54. Remarks by the President on National Security (May 21, 2009), *supra* note 3.

55. Jack L. Goldsmith & Neal Katyal, *The Terrorists' Court*, N.Y. TIMES, July 11, 2007, at A19.

56. Harvey Rishikof, *Is it Time for a Federal Terrorist Court?*, 8 SUFFOLK J. TRIAL & APP. ADV. 1, 5 (2003); *See also* Glenn M. Sulmasy, *The Legal Landscape After Hamdan: The Creation of Homeland Security Courts*, 13 NEW ENG. J. INT'L & COMP. L. 1 (2006) (calling for homeland security courts to detain and try terrorists in the "Global War on Terror"); Robert Chesney & Jack Goldsmith, *Terrorism and the Convergence of Criminal and Military Detention Models*, 60 STAN. L. REV. 1079, 1120–23 (2008) (discussing various possible criteria for detention of individuals "in al Qaeda and its co-belligerent terrorist organizations").

57. David Cole, *Closing Guantánamo: The Problem of Preventive Detention,* BOSTON REVIEW (Jan./Feb. 2009), internet-only publication *available at* http://www.bostonreview.net/BR34.1/cole.php.

58. *Improving Detainee Policy: Handling Terrorism Detainees within the American Justice System: Hearing Before the Senate Comm. on the Judiciary,* 110th Cong. (2008) (statement of Prof. Amos N. Guiora).

59. Goldsmith & Katyal, *supra* note 55; James Jay Carafano & Paul Rosenzweig, *Time to Rethink Preventive Detention,* HERITAGE FOUNDATION (Oct. 4, 2004), *available at* http://www.heritage.org/press/commentary/ed100504a.cfm.

60. Cole, *supra* note 57, at 4; Matthew Waxman, *Detention as Targeting: Standards of Certainty and Detention of Suspected Terrorists,* 108 COLUM. L. REV. 1365 (2008) (arguing that the laws of war, particularly targeting decisions, can supply a level of certainty for detention decisions that is less than that required for criminal trial and that appropriately fits the conflict with al Qaeda).

61. *See* Addington v. Texas, 441 U.S. 418 (1979).

62. *See* O'Connor v. Donaldson, 422 U.S. 563, 586 (1975) (Burger, C.J., concurring).

63. *See* United States v. Salerno, 481 U.S. 739 (1987).

64. In addition, it is not even clear whether al Qaeda fighters fall into the category of individuals who can be detained pursuant to the laws of war as enemy combatants. The International Red Cross and a number of international law scholars have argued that in non-international wars, such as that between a non-state actor like al Qaeda and the United States, there is no recognized legal category of enemy combatant. INT'L COMM. OF THE RED CROSS, OFFICIAL STATEMENT: THE RELEVANCE OF IHL IN THE CONTEXT OF TERRORISM, at 1, 3 (Feb. 21, 2005), *available at* http://www.icrc.org/Web/Eng/siteeng0.nsf/htmlall/terrorism-ihl-210705. That view was adopted by a majority of the Fourth Circuit panel in *Al Marri v. Wright,* 487 F.3d 160 (4th Cir. 2007), and by four judges who participated in the *en banc* review of that ruling, Al Marri v. Pucciarelli, 534 F.3d 213, 233 (4th Cir. 2008) (*en banc*) (Motz, J., concurring). The case was later ordered dismissed as moot after the detainee was transferred from military custody to the criminal system. Al-Marri v. Spagone, 129 S. Ct. 1545 (2009).

65. The USA PATRIOT Act of 2001 amended the statute of limitations provisions of federal criminal law to provide for an eight-year statute of

limitations (instead of the general five-year limitations period) for terrorism offenses, and also provided that there would be no limitation for any terrorism offense that resulted in, or created, a foreseeable risk of death or serious bodily injury to another person. Pub. L. No. 107–56, §809, 115 Stat. 272, 379–380 (codified at 18 U.S.C. §3386 (2006)).

66. David Cole has argued that "the fact that Al Qaeda is engaged in criminal warfare should not restrict the United States' options in defending itself." For him, the right of the United States to try al Qaeda fighters for either war crimes or ordinary crimes "does not mean that we should be *required* to try them in either forum, particularly while the conflict is ongoing Cole, *supra* note 57, at 4 (emphasis in original). But, as he recognizes, "we should depart from the criminal justice model only where the criminal process *cannot* adequately address a particularly serious danger." *Id.* at 3. Therefore, it is incumbent on those arguing for either a narrow war model preventive detention system tied to Congress' authorization of force against the September 11 terrorists, or a broader preventive detention scheme to detain terrorists generally, to demonstrate that the criminal courts cannot, as a practical matter, prosecute some significant number of terrorists.

67. Richard B. Zahel & James J. Benjamin, Jr., *In Pursuit of Justice: Prosecuting Terrorism Cases in the Federal Courts*, HUMAN RIGHTS FIRST (May 2008).

68. *Id.* at 5.

69. Classified Information Procedures Act, Pub. L. No. 96-456, 94 Stat. 2025, 2025-31 (1980) (codified at 18 U.S.C. app. 3)

70. Zahel & Benjamin, *supra* note 67, at 9.

71. *Id.* at 9.

72. *Id.* at 11.

73. *See* Judge Leonie M. Brinkema, Terrorism Cases in Civilian Courts: Balancing the Powers of Government, Address at Princeton University Woodrow Wilson School of Public and International Affairs (Apr. 28, 2008), event information available at http://lapa.princeton.edu/eventdetail.php?!D=160; *Improving Detainee Policy: Handling Terrorism Detainees within the American Justice System: Hearing Before the Senate Comm. on the Judiciary*, 110th Cong. (2008) (statement of Judge John C. Coughenour) [hereinafter Coughenour statement].

74. Coughenour statement, *supra* note 73.

75. *Id.*

76. *See,* e.g., United States v. Moussaoui, 382 F.3d 453 (2004).

77. *See* COLE & LOBEL, *supra* note 6, at 49-50.

78. *See* Parhat v. Gates, 532 F.3d 834 (D.C. Cir. 2008) (ordering either the release of the detainee or a new CSRT with new evidence supporting his detention); Boumediene v. Bush, 579 F. Supp. 2d 191 (D.D.C. 2008) (granting the release of five of six detainees who petitioned for writ of habeas corpus).

79. *See* cases cited, *supra* note 78.

80. *Parhat,* 532 F.3d at 848-849 (citing LEWIS CARROLL, THE HUNTING OF THE SNARK 3 (1876) ("I have said it thrice: what I tell you three times is true.")).

81. *See,* e.g., Boumediene v. Bush, 128 S. Ct. 2229 (2008).

82. *See,* e.g., Cole, *supra* note 57, at 7-8.

83. Remarks by the President on National Security, *supra* note 3.

84. *Boumediene,* 128 S. Ct., at 2275.

85. *Id.* at 2270.

86. *Id.* at 2277.

87. Hamdi v. Rumsfeld, 542 U.S. 507, 521 (2004) (plurality opinion).

88. The suggestion that an inclusion of periodic reviews of a detainee's dangerousness might ameliorate the long-term nature of indefinite preventive detention for al Qaeda detainees would not seem to be useful for many detainees, for the dangerousness of a captured al Qaeda fighter or supporter would not diminish over time unless the individual renounced his or her affiliation with al Qaeda, or al Qaeda was destroyed.

89. *See* Kenneth Roth, *After Guantánamo,* FOREIGN AFF., May/June 2008, at 2, 2.

90. Commission of the European Communities Document SEC (2009) 225, Final Synthesis of the Replies From the Member States to the Questionnaire on Criminal Law, Administrative Law/Procedural Law and Fundamental Rights in the Fight Against Terrorism, at 21.

91. *Id.* at 19-21 (describing German, Italian and British law). Great Britain's 2005 Prevention of Terrorism Act provided for the government to place restrictions in the form of control orders on persons who the government has reasonable grounds for suspecting is or has been involved in terrorism-related activity. Control orders issued pursuant to the Act have been subject to a considerable amount of litigation with the House of Lords imposing procedural restraints on the government's powers.

See, e.g., Sec'y of State v. AF, 2009 UKHL 28 (HL). The British statute provides for two kinds of control orders: non-derogating orders which only restrict a person's liberty and a derogating order which would deprive a person of their liberty and therefore would require the government to derogate from Article 5 of the European Convention on Human Rights. To date, Britain has never utilized a derogatory order which would deprive a suspect of his liberty. Commission of the European Communities Document SEC (2009) 225, *supra* note 90, at 20.

[. . .]

*Jules Lobel teaches constitutional law, international law, and foreign affairs at the University of Pittsburgh Law School. He is a vice president of the Center for Constitutional Rights, with which he has litigated several cases involving national security and civil liberties. He is the author of three books and many articles on national security, civil liberties, international law, and progressive lawyering.

Lobel, Jules. 2009. Adapted from: Preventive detention and preventive warfare: U.S. national security policies Obama should abandon, *Journal of National Security Law and Policy* 3: 351–359.

Used by Permission.

Discussion Questions

1. Should the United States engage in preventive detention of suspected terrorists or should it limit detention to those whom it can convict for crimes in civilian courts? What should be done with individuals we consider dangerous but for whom we have insufficient evidence to convict in a criminal trial?

2. In a traditional war between nations, it has long been permissible to detain preventively members of the opposition's armed forces as prisoners of war. Should that authority be applicable to the ongoing conflict with al Qaeda and the Taliban, neither of which is a state, or is the conflict sufficiently different that traditional military detention authority is inapplicable?

3. Should Guantánamo remain open or should it be closed? If it is to be closed, what should be done with the individuals detained there?

4. Should Congress create a special "national security court" to hear detention cases or does such an establishment risk institutionalizing preventive detention?

PART 5

The Terrorist Surveillance Program and Inherent Executive Power

Does the president as commander in chief have the authority to ignore or violate federal criminal law, or would that make him impermissibly "above the law?" Shortly after the attacks of September 11, 2001, President Bush authorized the National Security Agency (NSA) to conduct warrantless electronic surveillance of international communications between persons in the United States and persons outside the country where the government suspected that at least one of the parties to the communication was a member of al Qaeda or what it called "affiliated terrorist organizations." This surveillance was conducted outside the strictures of any of the surveillance statutes Congress has enacted, including the Foreign Intelligence Surveillance Act of 1978 (FISA), which was designed to regulate electronic surveillance for national security intelligence-gathering purposes. It was also conducted without the approval of any court. And, the program was instituted and carried out in secret; its existence did not become public until the *New York Times* disclosed it in 2005.

The legality of the program raises fundamental issues about the scope of executive power in our constitutional democracy. Congress provided in FISA that its statutes were the exclusive basis for conducting wiretapping in the United States, and further provided that conducting wiretapping without statutory authorization was a felony. Yet President Bush claimed that his constitutional powers to "engage the enemy" as commander in chief trumped that provision, allowing him to undertake the kind of spying that Congress had declared a crime. Accordingly, perhaps more than any other issue since 9/11, the NSA's warrantless wiretapping program presents core issues of executive vs. legislative power in wartime. The two selections included here, both initially presented as testimony to Congress, set forth the competing arguments. Then-attorney general Alberto Gonzales defends the program based on a robust vision of presidential power during wartime. Louis Fisher, a longtime constitutional scholar for the Congressional Research Service, maintains that the program was unconstitutional because the president lacks the power to contravene express congressional statutes in this context.

Statement of Alberto Gonzales

STATEMENT OF ALBERTO GONZALES*
BEFORE THE SENATE SELECT COMMITTEE ON INTELLIGENCE

"Concerning the Terrorist Surveillance Program Authorized by the President"

FEBRUARY 9, 2006

We cannot forget the threat that the al Qaeda terrorist network poses to our Nation. Long before September 11th, al Qaeda promised to attack the United States. In 1998, Osama bin Laden declared a jihad against our country, and incited "every Muslim who can do it" "[t]o kill the Americans and their allies—civilians and military" "in any country in which it is possible to do it." Statement of Osama bin Laden, Ayman al-Zawahiri, et al., *Fatwah Urging Jihad Against Americans,* published in Al-Quds al-'Arabi (Feb. 23, 1998). Al Qaeda members and agents have carried out bin Laden's orders with a vengeance; al Qaeda attacked the U.S.S. Cole in Yemen, the United States Embassies in Kenya and Tanzania, and then, of course, the United States itself on September 11, 2001.

On September 11th, the al Qaeda terrorist network executed the most deadly foreign attacks on this Nation's soil in history. Al Qaeda planners and operatives carefully selected and hijacked four commercial jetliners, each fully loaded with fuel for a transcontinental flight. Within hours, the Twin Towers of the World Trade Center lay in ruin. The terrorists also managed to strike the headquarters of the Nation's Armed Forces, the Pentagon. And it is believed that the target of the fourth plane, United Flight 93, was either the White House or the Capitol Building, suggesting that al Qaeda had sought to decapitate the federal Government. The attacks of September 11th resulted in approximately 3,000 deaths—the highest single-day death toll from a foreign attack on the United States in the Nation's history. These attacks shut down air travel in the United States, disrupted the Nation's financial markets and government operations, and caused billions of dollars in damage.

Our Nation responded by taking up arms against al Qaeda, affiliated terrorist networks, and the governments that sheltered them. A coalition of our allies has supported the United States in this war. Indeed, shortly after the attacks, NATO—for the first time in its 46-year history—invoked article 5 of the North Atlantic Treaty, which provides that an "armed attack against one or more of [the parties] shall be considered an attack against them all." North Atlantic Treaty, Apr. 4, 1949, art. 5, 63 Stat. 2241, 2244, 34 U.N.T.S. 243, 246.

It has become more clear in the days, weeks, and years since September 11th that our enemy in this war is no ordinary terrorist organization. Al Qaeda demonstrated on September 11th that it could execute a highly sophisticated operation, one that required al Qaeda operatives to live in our midst for years, to transfer money into the country, to arrange training, and to communicate with planners overseas. And it has promised similar attacks in the future.

Al Qaeda is not content with the damage it inflicted on September 11th. Since that day, al Qaeda leaders have repeatedly promised to deliver another, even more devastating attack on America. *See, e.g.,* Osama bin Laden, videotape released on

Al-Jazeera television network (Oct. 24,2004) (warning United States citizens of further attacks and asserting that "your security is in your own hands"); Osama bin Laden, videotape released on Al-Jazeera television network (Oct. 18, 2003) ("God willing, we will continue to fight you and will continue martyrdom operations inside and outside the United States . . . ."); Ayman Al-Zawahiri, videotape released on the Al-Jazeera television network (Oct. 9, 2002) ("I promise you [addressing the 'citizens of the United States'] that the Islamic youth are preparing for you what will fill your hearts with horror.").

As recently as December 7, 2005, Ayman al-Zawahiri professed that al Qaeda "is spreading, growing, and becoming stronger," and that al Qaeda is "waging a great historic battle in Iraq, Afghanistan, Palestine, and even in the Crusaders' own homes." Ayman al-Zawahiri, videotape released on Al-Jazeera television network (Dec. 7, 2005). And less than three weeks ago, we heard Osama bin Laden warn that the United States could not prevent attacks on the homeland. He continued:

> The proof of that is the explosions you have seen in the capitals of European nations. . . . The delay in similar operations happening in America has not been because of failure to break through your security measures. The operations are under preparation and you will see them in your homes the minute they are through (with preparations), with God's permission.
> Quoted at http://www.breitbart.com/news/2006/01/19/D8F7SMRH5. html (Jan. 19, 2006).

Al Qaeda poses as much of a threat as a traditional nation state, and in many ways, a greater threat. Indeed, in the time since September 11th, al Qaeda and its allies have staged several large-scale attacks around the world, including in Indonesia, Madrid, and London, killing hundreds of innocent people. Al Qaeda's leaders have repeatedly made good on their threats, and al Qaeda has demonstrated its ability to insert foreign agents into the United States to execute attacks.

In confronting this new and deadly enemy, President Bush promised that "[w]e will direct every resource at our command—every means of diplomacy, every tool of intelligence, every tool of law enforcement, every financial influence, and every weapon of war—to the disruption of and to the defeat of the global terror network." President Bush Address to a Joint Session of Congress (Sept. 20, 2001). The terrorist surveillance program described by the President is one such tool and one indispensable aspect of this defense of our Nation.

The terrorist surveillance program targets communications where one party to the communication is outside the U.S. and the government has "reasonable grounds to believe" that at least one party to the communication is a member or agent of al Qaeda, or an affiliated terrorist organization. This program is reviewed and reauthorized by the President approximately every 45 days. The Congressional leadership, including the leaders of the Intelligence Committees of both Houses of Congress, has been briefed about this program more than a dozen times since 2001. The program provides the United States with the early warning system we so desperately needed on September 10th.

The terrorist surveillance program remains highly classified, as it should be. We must protect this tool, which has proven so important to protecting America. An open discussion of the operational details of this program would put the lives of Americans at risk. The need to protect national security also means that I must confine my discussion of the legal analysis to those activities confirmed publicly by the President; I cannot and will not address operational aspects of the program or other purported activities described in press reports. These press accounts are in almost every case, in one way or another, mis-informed, confused, or wrong.

Congress and the American people are interested in two fundamental questions: is this program necessary and is it lawful. The answer to both questions is yes.

The question of necessity rightly falls to our Nation's military leaders, because the terrorist surveillance program is an essential element of our military campaign against al Qaeda. I therefore address it only briefly. The attacks of September 11th placed the Nation in a state of armed conflict. In this armed conflict, our military employs a wide variety of tools and weapons to defeat the enemy. General Michael Hayden, Principal Deputy Director of National Intelligence and former Director of the NSA, recently explained why a terrorist surveillance program that allows us quickly to collect important information about our enemy is so vital and necessary to the War on Terror.

The conflict against al Qaeda is, in fundamental respects, a war of information. We cannot build walls thick enough, fences high enough, or systems strong enough to keep our enemies out of our open and welcoming country. Instead, as the bipartisan 9/11 and WMD Commissions have urged, we must understand better who the enemy is and what he is doing. We have to collect the right dots before we can "connect the dots." The terrorist surveillance program allows us to collect more information regarding al Qaeda's plans, and, critically, it allows us to locate al Qaeda operatives, especially those already in the United States and poised to attack. We cannot defend the Nation without such information, as we painfully learned on September 11th.

As Attorney General, I am primarily concerned with the legal basis for these necessary military activities. The Attorney

General of the United States is the chief legal adviser for the President and the Executive Branch. Accordingly, the Department of Justice has thoroughly examined this program and concluded that the President is acting within his power in authorizing it. The Department of Justice is not alone in concluding that the program is lawful. Career lawyers at NSA and its Inspector General office have been intimately involved in the oversight of the program. The lawyers have found the program to be lawful and reviewed its conduct. The Inspector General's office has exercised vigorous reviews of the program to provide assurance that it is carried out within the terms of the President's authorization.

The terrorist surveillance program is firmly grounded in the President's constitutional authorities. The Constitution charges the President with the primary responsibility for protecting the safety of all Americans, and the Constitution gives the President the authority necessary to fulfill this solemn duty. *See, e.g., The Prize Cases*, 67 U.S. (2 Black) 635, 668 (1863). It has long been recognized that the President's constitutional powers include the authority to conduct warrantless surveillance aimed at detecting and preventing armed attacks on the United States. Presidents have repeatedly relied on their inherent power to gather foreign intelligence for reasons both diplomatic and military, and the federal courts have consistently upheld this longstanding practice. *See In re Sealed Case,* 310 F.3d 717, 742 (Foreign Intel. Surv. Ct. of Rev. 2002).

If this authority is available in ordinary times, it is even more vital in the present circumstances of our armed conflict with al Qaeda. The President authorized the terrorist surveillance program in response to the deadliest foreign attack on American soil, and it is designed solely to prevent the next al Qaeda attack. After all, the goal of our enemy is to blend in with our civilian population in order to plan and carry out future attacks within America. We cannot forget that the September 11th hijackers were in our country, living in our communities.

The President's authority to take military action—including the use of communications intelligence targeted at the enemy—does not come merely from his constitutional powers. It comes directly from Congress as well. Just a few days after the attacks of September 11th, Congress enacted a joint resolution to support and authorize the military response to the attacks on American soil. Authorization for Use of Military Force, Pub. L. No. 107-40, 115 Stat. 224 (Sept. 18, 2001) ("AUMF"). In the AUMF, Congress did two important things. First, it expressly recognized the President's "authority under the Constitution to take action to deter and prevent acts of international terrorism against the United States." Second, it supplemented that authority by authorizing the President to "use all necessary and appropriate force against those nations, organizations, or persons he determines planned, authorized, committed, or aided the terrorist attacks" in order to prevent further attacks on the United States.

Accordingly, the President's authority to use military force against those terrorist groups is at its maximum because he is acting with the express authorization of Congress. Thus, under the three-part framework of Justice Jackson's concurring opinion in *Youngstown Sheet & Tube Co. v. Sawyer*, 343 U.S. 579, 635-38 (1952) (Jackson, J., concurring), the President's authority falls within Category I, and is at its highest. He is acting "pursuant to an express or implied authorization of Congress," and the President's authority "includes all that he possesses in his own right [under the Constitution] plus all that Congress can" confer on him.

In 2004, the Supreme Court considered the scope of the AUMF in *Hamdi v. Rumsfeld*, 542 U.S. 507 (2004). There, the question was whether the President had the authority to detain an American citizen as an enemy combatant for the duration of the hostilities. The Supreme Court confirmed that the expansive language of the AUMF—"*all* necessary and appropriate force"—ensures that the congressional authorization extends to traditional incidents of waging war. *See also* Curtis A. Bradley & Jack L. Goldsmith, *Congressional Authorization and the War on Terrorism*, 118 Harv. L. Rev. 2048, 2092 (2005). And, just like the detention of enemy combatants approved in *Hamdi*, the use of communications intelligence to prevent enemy attacks is a fundamental and accepted incident of military force.

This fact is amply borne out by history. This Nation has a long tradition of wartime enemy surveillance—a tradition that can be traced to George Washington, who made frequent and effective use of secret intelligence. One source of Washington's intelligence was intercepted British mail. *See* Central Intelligence Agency, *Intelligence in the War of Independence* 31, 32 (1997). In fact, Washington himself proposed that one of his Generals "contrive a means of opening [British letters] without breaking the seals, take copies of the contents, and then let them go on." *Id*. at 32 ("From that point on, Washington was privy to British intelligence pouches between New York and Canada."). And for as long as electronic communications have existed, the United States has intercepted those communications during wartime, and done so, not surprisingly, without judicial warrants. In the Civil War, for example, telegraph wiretapping was common and provided important intelligence for both sides. In World War I, President Wilson authorized the military to intercept all telegraph, telephone, and cable communications into and out of the United States; he inferred the authority to do so from the

Constitution and from a general congressional authorization to use military force that did not mention anything about such surveillance. *See* Exec. Order No. 2604 (Apr. 28, 1917). So too in World War II; the day after the attack on Pearl Harbor, President Roosevelt authorized the interception of *all* communications traffic into and out of the United States. The terrorist surveillance program, of course, is far more focused, since it involves the interception only of international communications that are linked to al Qaeda.

Some have suggested that the AUMF did not authorize intelligence collection inside the United States. That contention cannot be squared with the reality of the September 11th attacks on our soil, launched from within the country, and carried out by sleeper agents who had lived amongst us. Given this background, Congress certainly intended to support the President's use of force to repel an unfolding attack within the United States. Congress also must be understood to have authorized the traditional means by which the military detects and responds to such attacks. Nor can this contention be squared with the language of the AUMF itself, which calls on the President to protect Americans both "*at home* and abroad," to take action to prevent further terrorist attacks "against the United States," and directs him to determine who was responsible for the attacks. Such a contention is also contrary to the long history of wartime surveillance, which has often involved the interception of enemy communications into and out of the United States.

Against this backdrop, the NSA's focused terrorist surveillance program falls squarely within the broad authorization of the AUMF even though, as some have argued, the AUMF does not expressly mention surveillance. The AUMF also does not mention detention of enemy combatants. But we know from the Supreme Court's decision in *Hamdi* that such detention is authorized even for U.S. citizens. Justice O'Connor reasoned: "Because detention to prevent a combatant's return to the battle-field is a fundamental incident of waging war, in permitting the use of 'necessary and appropriate force,' Congress has clearly and unmistakably authorized detention in the narrow circumstances considered here." 542 U.S. at 519 (plurality opinion).

As Justice O'Connor recognized, "it is of no moment that the AUMF does not use specific language of detention" or even refer to the detention of U.S. citizens as enemy combatants at all. *Id.* Nor does it matter that individual Members of Congress may not have specifically intended to authorize such detention. The same is true of electronic surveillance. It is a traditional incident of war, and, thus, as Justice O'Connor said, it is "of no moment" that the AUMF does not explicitly mention this activity. Congress has "clearly and unmistakably authorized" it.

These omissions are not at all surprising. In enacting the AUMF, Congress made no attempt to catalog every aspect of the use of force it was authorizing. Instead, following the model of past military force authorizations, Congress—in general, but broad, terms—confirmed the President's authority to use traditional and accepted incidents of military force to identify and defeat the enemy. In doing so, Congress must be understood to have endorsed the use of so fundamental an aspect of the use of military force as electronic surveillance.

Some contend that even if the President has constitutional authority to engage in the surveillance of our enemy during an armed conflict, that authority has been constrained by Congress with the passage in 1978 of the Foreign Intelligence Surveillance Act ("FISA"). Generally, FISA requires the Government to obtain an order from a special FISA court before conducting "electronic surveillance." 50 U.S.C. §§ 1803-1805 (2000 and Supp. II 2002). FISA defines "electronic surveillance" carefully and precisely. *Id.* § 1801(f). And, as confirmed by another provision, 18 U.S.C. § 2511(2)(f) (Supp. II 2002) (carving out from statutory regulation the acquisition of intelligence information from "international or foreign communications" and "foreign intelligence activities . . . involving a foreign electronic communications system" as long as they are accomplished "utilizing a means other than electronic surveillance as defined" by FISA), and by FISA's legislative history, Congress did *not* intend FISA to regulate certain communications intelligence activities of the NSA, including certain communications involving persons in the United States. *See, e.g.,* S. Rep. No. 95-604, at 64 (1978). Because I cannot discuss operational details, for purposes of this discussion, I will assume that intercepts of international al Qaeda communications under the terrorist surveillance program fall within the definition of "electronic surveillance" in FISA.

Even with FISA's careful carve out for certain NSA signals intelligence activities as they existed in 1978, the legislative history makes clear that there were concerns among Members of Congress about the constitutionality of FISA itself if construed to be an exclusive means for electronic surveillance. *See, e.g.,* H.R. Conf. Rep. No. 95-1720, at 35 ("The conferees agree that the establishment by this act of exclusive means by which the President may conduct electronic surveillance does not foreclose a different decision by the Supreme Court."). The FISA Court of Review, the special court of appeals charged with hearing appeals of decisions by the FISA court, stated in 2002 that "[w]e take for granted that the President does have that [inherent] authority" and, "assuming that is so, FISA could not encroach on the President's constitutional power." *In re Sealed Case,* 310 F.3d at 742.

It is a serious question whether, consistent with the Constitution, FISA may encroach upon the President's Article II powers during the current armed conflict with al Qaeda by prohibiting the terrorist surveillance program. Fortunately, for the reasons that follow, we need not address that difficult question.

FISA allows Congress to respond to new threats through separate legislation. FISA prohibits persons from intentionally "engag[ing]. . . in electronic surveillance under color of law *except as authorized by statute*." 50 U.S.C. § 1809(a)(1) (2000) (emphasis added). For the reasons I have already discussed, the AUMF provides the relevant statutory authorization for the terrorist surveillance program. *Hamdi* makes clear that the broad language in the AUMF can satisfy a requirement for specific statutory authorization set forth in another law.

Hamdi involved a statutory prohibition on all detention of U.S. citizens except as authorized "pursuant to an Act of Congress." 18 U.S.C. § 4001(a) (2000). Even though the detention of a U.S. citizen involves a deprivation of liberty, and even though the AUMF says nothing on its face about detention of U.S. citizens, a majority of the members of the Supreme Court nevertheless concluded that the AUMF satisfied the statutory requirement. *See Hamdi*, 542 U.S. at 519 (plurality opinion); *id.* at 587 (Thomas, J., dissenting). The same is true for the prohibition on warrantless electronic surveillance in FISA.

FISA also expressly allows the President to conduct warrantless surveillance for 15 days following a congressional declaration of war. 50 U.S.C. § 1811 (2000). That provision shows that Congress understood that warrantless surveillance would be essential in wartime. But no one could reasonably suggest that all such critical military surveillance in a time of war would end after only 15 days. Instead, the legislative history of this provision makes clear that Congress elected *not to decide* how surveillance might need to be conducted in the event of a particular armed conflict. Congress expected that it would revisit the issue in light of events and likely would enact a special authorization during that 15-day period. H.R. Conf. Rep. No. 95-1720, at 34. That is exactly what happened three days after the attacks of September 11th, when Congress passed the AUMF, authorizing the President to employ "all necessary and appropriate" incidents of military force—including the use of communications intelligence activities targeted at the enemy.

Some have argued that Title III (the domestic law-enforcement wiretap provisions) and FISA are the "exclusive means" for conducting electronic surveillance as defined by FISA. It is true that section 2511 (2)(f) of title 18, U.S. Code, provides that the "procedures in [Title III]. . . and [FISA] shall be the exclusive means by which electronic surveillance . . . may be conducted." But, as I have said before, FISA itself prohibits the Government from engaging in electronic surveillance "except as authorized by statute." 50 U.S.C. § 1809(a)(1). It is noteworthy that FISA does not say that "the Government cannot engage in electronic surveillance 'except as authorized by FISA and Title III.'" Instead, FISA allows electronic surveillance that is authorized by statute—any statute. And, in this case, that other statute is the AUMF.

Even if some might think this is not the only possible reading of FISA and the AUMF, in accordance with long recognized canons of construction, FISA must be interpreted in harmony with the AUMF to allow the President, as Commander in Chief during a congressionally authorized armed conflict, to take the actions necessary to protect the country from another catastrophic attack. So long as such an interpretation is "fairly possible," the Supreme Court has made clear that it must be adopted in order to avoid the serious constitutional issues that would otherwise be raised. *See, e.g., INS v. St. Cyr*, 533 U.S. 289, 299-300 (2001). Application of the canon of constitutional avoidance is particularly appropriate here. As noted, Congress recognized in 1978 that FISA might approach or exceed its constitutional authority. Since FISA's enactment, the means of transmitting communications has undergone extensive transformation. This technological change substantially altered the effects of FISA's careful definition of "electronic surveillance" and has resulted in increased and unintended interference with some of the activities Congress decided to exclude from regulation in 1978.

Many people ask why the President elected not to use FISA's procedures for securing court orders for the terrorist surveillance program. We have to remember that what is at issue is a wartime intelligence program designed to protect our Nation from another attack in the middle of an armed conflict. It is an "early warning system" with only one purpose: to detect and prevent the next attack on the United States from foreign agents hiding in our midst. It is imperative for national security that we can detect reliably, immediately, and without delay whenever communications associated with al Qaeda enter or leave the United States. That may be the only way to alert us to the presence of an al Qaeda agent in our country and to the existence of an unfolding plot.

The optimal way to achieve the speed and agility necessary to this military intelligence program during the present armed conflict with al Qaeda is to leave the decisions about particular intercepts to the judgment of professional intelligence officers, based on the best available intelligence information. These officers are best situated to make decisions quickly and accurately. If, however, those same intelligence officers had to navigate through the FISA process for each of these intercepts, that would necessarily introduce a significant factor of delay, and there would be critical holes in our early warning system. Importantly, as explained below, these intelligence officers apply a probable cause standard. The critical advantage offered by the terrorist surveillance program compared to FISA is *who* makes the probable cause determination and how many layers of review must occur *before* surveillance begins.

Some have pointed to the provision in FISA that allows for so-called "emergency authorizations" of surveillance for 72 hours without a court order. There is a serious misconception about these emergency authorizations. We do not and cannot approve emergency surveillance under FISA without knowing that we meet FISA's normal requirements. In order to authorize emergency surveillance under FISA, the Attorney General must personally "determine[] that . . . the factual basis for issuance of an order under [FISA] to approve such surveillance exists." 50 U.S.C. § 1805(f). FISA requires the Attorney General to determine *in advance* that this condition is satisfied. That review process can, of necessity, take precious time. And that same process takes the decision away from the officers best situated to make it during an armed conflict.

Thus, to initiate surveillance under a FISA emergency authorization, it is not enough to rely on the best judgment of our intelligence officers. Those intelligence officers would have to get the sign-off of lawyers at the NSA, and then lawyers in the Department of Justice would have to be satisfied that the statutory requirements for emergency authorization are met, and finally as Attorney General, I would have to be satisfied that the proposed surveillance meets the requirements of FISA. Finally, the emergency application must be filed "as soon as practicable," but within 72 hours.

A typical FISA application involves a substantial process in its own right: The work of several lawyers; the preparation of an application and related legal papers; the approval of a designated Cabinet-level officer; a certification from a designated Senate-confirmed officer; and, finally, of course, the approval of an Article III judge who sits on the FISA Court. *See* 50 U.S.C. § 1804. Needless to say, even under the very best of circumstances, this process consumes valuable resources and results in significant delay. We all agree that there should be appropriate checks and balances on the Branches of our Government. The FISA process makes perfect sense in almost all cases of foreign intelligence monitoring in the United States. Although technology has changed dramatically since FISA was enacted, FISA remains a vital tool in the War on Terror, and one that we are using to its fullest and will continue to use against al Qaeda and other foreign threats. But as the President has explained, the terrorist surveillance program operated by the NSA requires the maximum in speed and agility, since even a very short delay may make the difference between success and failure in preventing the next attack. And we cannot afford to fail.

Finally, the NSA's terrorist surveillance program fully complies with the Fourth Amendment, which prohibits unreasonable searches and seizures. The Fourth Amendment has never been understood to require warrants in all circumstances. The Supreme Court has upheld warrantless searches at the border and has allowed warrantless sobriety checkpoints. *See, e.g., Michigan v. Dept. of State Police v. Sitz*, 496 U.S. 444 (1990); *see also Indianapolis v. Edmond*, 531 U.S. 32, 44 (2000) (stating that "the Fourth Amendment would almost certainly permit an appropriately tailored roadblock set up to thwart an imminent terrorist attack"). Those searches do not violate the Fourth Amendment because they involve "special needs" beyond routine law enforcement. *Vernonia Sch. Dist. v. Acton*, 515 U.S. 646, 653 (1995). To fall within the "special needs" exception to the warrant requirement, the purpose of the search must be distinguishable from ordinary general crime control. *See, e.g., Ferguson v. Charleston*, 532 U.S. 67 (2001); *City of Indianapolis v. Edmond*, 531 U.S. 32, 41 (2000).

The terrorist surveillance program fits within this "special needs" category. This conclusion is by no means novel. During the Clinton Administration, Deputy Attorney General Jamie Gorelick testified before Congress in 1994 that the President has inherent authority under the Constitution to conduct foreign intelligence searches of the private homes of U.S citizens in the United States without a warrant, and that such warrantless searches are permissible under the Fourth Amendment. *See Amending the Foreign Intelligence Surveillance Act: Hearings Before the House Permanent Select Comm. on Intelligence*, 103d Cong. 2d Sess. 61, 64 (1994) (statement of Deputy Attorney General Jamie S. Gorelick). *See also In re Sealed Case*, 310 F.3d at 745-46.

The key question under the Fourth Amendment is not whether there was a warrant, but whether the search was *reasonable*. Determining the reasonableness of a search for Fourth Amendment purposes requires balancing privacy interests with the Government's interests and ensuring that we maintain appropriate safeguards. *United States v. Knights*, 534 U.S. 112, 118-19 (2001). Although the terrorist surveillance program may implicate substantial privacy interests, the Government's interest in protecting our Nation is compelling. Because the need for the program is reevaluated every 45 days and because of the safeguards and oversight, the al Qaeda intercepts are reasonable.

No one takes lightly the concerns that have been raised about the interception of domestic communications inside the United States. But this terrorist surveillance program involves intercepting the *international* communications of persons reasonably believed to be members or agents of al Qaeda or affiliated terrorist organizations. This surveillance is narrowly focused and fully consistent with the traditional forms of enemy surveillance found to be necessary in all previous armed conflicts. The need for the program is reviewed at the highest levels of government approximately every 45 days to ensure that the al Qaeda threat to the national security of this Nation continues to exist. Moreover, although the Fourth Amendment does not require application of a probable cause standard in this context, the "reasonable grounds to believe" standard employed in this program is the traditional Fourth Amendment probable cause standard. As the Supreme Court has stated, "The substance of all the definitions of probable cause is a *reasonable ground for belief* of guilt." *Maryland v. Pringle*, 540 U.S. 366, 371 (2003) (internal quotation marks omitted) (emphasis added).

This Administration has chosen to act now to prevent the next attack with every lawful tool at its disposal, rather than wait until it is too late. It is hard to imagine a President who would not elect to use these tools in defense of the American people—in fact, it would be irresponsible to do otherwise. The terrorist surveillance program is both necessary and lawful. Accordingly, as the President has explained, he intends to continue to exercise this authority as long as al Qaeda poses such a grave threat to the national security. If we conduct this reasonable surveillance—while taking special care to preserve civil liberties as we have—we can all continue to enjoy our rights and freedoms for generations to come.

*Alberto Gonzales served as White House counsel from 2001 to 2005 and attorney general from 2005 to 2007. Prior to his service in the federal government, he served as a justice on the Texas Supreme Court and as counsel to then-governor George W. Bush. He resigned as attorney general in 2007.

Prepared Statement of the Hon. Alberto R. Gonzales, attorney general of the United States, before the Senate Select Committee on Intelligence. February 9, 2006. Concerning the terrorist surveillance program authorized by the president. 109th Cong.

Statement of Louis Fisher

STATEMENT OF LOUIS FISHER* SPECIALIST IN
CONSTITUTIONAL LAW

APPEARING BEFORE THE HOUSE COMMITTEE ON THE
JUDICIARY

"Constitutional Limitations on Domestic Surveillance"

JUNE 7, 2007

Mr. Chairman, thank you for inviting me to testify on the constitutional limitations that apply to domestic surveillance. The committee provides an important public service in exploring the issues raised by the "Terrorist Surveillance Program" (TSP), authorized by the administration after 9/11 and conducted by the National Security Agency (NSA). I begin by summarizing what happened in the 1960s and 1970s with domestic surveillance. Two basic points. First: intelligence agencies were willing to violate the Constitution, including the First and Fourth Amendments. Second: federal courts rejected the theory that the President has "inherent" constitutional authority to engage in warrantless domestic surveillance.

I. Lessons of Domestic Surveillance

Illegal eavesdropping by the executive branch surfaced as a prominent issue in the 1960s and 1970s, after it was publicly disclosed that U.S. intelligence agencies had been monitoring the domestic activities of Americans. In 1967, when the U.S. Army wanted the NSA to eavesdrop on American citizens and domestic groups, the agency agreed to carry out the assignment.[1] NSA began to put together a list of names of opponents of the Vietnam War. Adding names to a domestic "watch list" led to the creation of MINARET: a tracking system that allowed the agency to follow individuals and organizations involved in the antiwar movement.[2] NSA thus began using its surveillance powers to violate the First and Fourth Amendments. From mid-1969 to early 1970, the White House directed the FBI to install without warrants 17 wiretaps to eavesdrop on government officials and reporters.[3] Newspaper stories in 1974 revealed that CIA had been extensively involved in illegal domestic surveillance, infiltrating dissident groups in the country and collecting close to 10,000 files on American citizens. CIA Director William Colby later acknowledged the existence of this program while testifying before a Senate committee.[4]

THE HUSTON PLAN

On June 5, 1970, President Richard M. Nixon met with the heads of several intelligence agencies, including the NSA, to initiate a program designed to monitor what the administration considered to be radical individuals and groups in the United States. Joining others at the meeting was Tom Charles Huston, a young aide working in the White House. He drafted a 43-page, top secret memorandum that became known as the Huston Plan. Huston put the matter bluntly to President Nixon: "Use of this technique is clearly illegal; it amounts to burglary."[5] His plan, which Nixon approved, directed the NSA to use its technological capacity to intercept—without judicial warrant—the domestic communication of U.S. citizens using international phone calls or telegrams.[6]

Under pressure from FBI Director J. Edgar Hoover and Attorney General John Mitchell, Nixon withdrew the Huston Plan.[7] Placed in a White House safe, Huston's blueprint became public in 1973 after Congress investigated the Watergate affair and uncovered documentary evidence that Nixon had ordered the NSA to illegally monitor American citizens.[8] To conduct its surveillance operations under such programs as SHAMROCK (in operation from August 1945 to May 1975), NSA entered into agreements with U.S. companies, including Western Union and RCA Global. U.S. citizens, expecting that their telegrams would be handled with the utmost privacy, learned that American companies had been turning over the telegrams to the NSA.[9]

JUDICIAL REACTION

A 1972 decision by the Supreme Court involved the government's use of warrantless electronic surveillance to prevent what the government feared was an attempt by domestic organizations to attack and subvert the existing structure of government. As the Court framed the issue, it needed to balance both to "the Government's right to protect itself from unlawful subversion and attack" and "the citizen's right to be secure in his privacy against unreasonable Government intrusion."[10]

In district court, defendants prosecuted by the government requested all records of warrantless surveillance directed at them and asked for a hearing to determine whether any of the evidence used to indict them was tainted by illegal actions. The district court held that the warrantless electronic surveillance was not justified on the ground that certain domestic organizations were engaged in subverting the government, and that the government had to make full disclosure to the defendants of illegally monitored conversations. It ordered an evidentiary hearing to determine taint.[11] The court did not accept the government's argument that the Attorney General, "as agent of the President, has the constitutional power to authorize electronic surveillance without a court warrant in the interest of national security."[12] The court expressly rejected the claim of "inherent" presidential power.[13] The President was "still subject to the constitutional limitations imposed upon him by the Fourth Amendment."[14]

The district court's decision was affirmed by the Sixth Circuit, which examined the government's claim that the power at issue in the case "is the inherent power of the President to safeguard the security of the nation."[15] The Sixth Circuit found that argument unpersuasive, in part because the Fourth Amendment "was adopted in the immediate aftermath of abusive searches and seizures directed against American colonists under the sovereign and inherent powers of King George III."[16] The Constitution was adopted "to provide a check upon 'sovereign' power," relying on three coordinate branches of government "to require sharing in the administration of that awesome power."[17] The Sixth Circuit further noted: "It is strange, indeed, that in this case the traditional power of sovereigns like King George III should be invoked on behalf of an American President to defeat one of the fundamental freedoms for which the founders of this country overthrew King George's reign."[18]

A unanimous ruling by the Supreme Court affirmed the Sixth Circuit. Inherent in the concept of a warrant issued under the Fourth Amendment "is its issuance by a 'neutral and detached magistrate.'"[19] Fourth Amendment freedoms "cannot properly be guaranteed if domestic security surveillances may be conducted solely within the discretion of the Executive Branch. The Fourth Amendment does not contemplate the executive officers of Government as neutral and disinterested magistrates."[20] Executive officers charged with investigative and prosecutorial duties "should not be sole judges of when to utilize constitutionally sensitive means in pursuing their tasks."[21]

The government advised the Court that the domestic surveillances at issue in this case were directed primarily at collecting and maintaining intelligence about subversive forces, rather than an effort to gather evidence for criminal prosecution. Moreover, the government insisted that courts lacked the knowledge and expertise to determine whether domestic surveillance was needed to protect national security.[22] To the Court, those arguments did not justify departure from Fourth Amendment standards.[23]

Finally, the Court held that Section 2511(3), enacted as part of the Omnibus Crime Control Act of 1968, merely disclaimed congressional intent to define presidential powers in matters affecting national security and did not grant authority to conduct warrantless national security surveillance.[24] The Fourth Amendment required prior judicial approval for the type of domestic security surveillance involved in this case. The Court carefully avoided the question of surveillance over foreign powers, whether within or outside the country.[25]

CONGRESSIONAL ACTION

The Court's decision in 1972 put pressure on Congress to develop statutory guidelines. In part, Congress responded by setting up the Church and Pike Committees to study the scope of executive branch illegality and propose a system of effective legislative and judicial checks. From those hearings and reports came the creation of new intelligence committees in the House and the Senate to closely monitor the agencies, followed by the landmark Foreign Intelligence Surveillance Act (FISA) of 1978. In congressional hearings, Attorney General Edward H. Levi testified in support of legislation that would require "independent review at a critical point by a detached and neutral magistrate."[26] FISA established a special court, the Foreign Intelligence Surveillance Court (FISC), to assure a judicial check on executive activities and established a Court of Review to hear appeals by the government from FISC denials of applications to engage in electronic surveillance. Moreover, it clearly stated that the procedures of FISA for electronic surveillance within the United States for foreign intelligence purposes "shall be the exclusive means" of conducting such surveillance.

At today's hearing we face issues that were studied extensively and carefully in the 1970s and supposedly remedied by legislation. Once again Congress is in the position of insisting that federal agencies adhere to the rule of law, respect constitutional and statutory limits, and protect fundamental rights of individual privacy and civil liberties.

The balance of my statement focuses on three points: (1) the legal justifications offered by the administration for the TSP; (2) the lack of access by the Judiciary Committees to briefings on the TSP conducted by the executive branch and to records and documents withheld from them; and (3) observations about the implications of the TSP for congressional control, the rule of law, and individual rights and liberties.

II. The Administration's Legal Defense

On January 19, 2006, the Office of Legal Counsel (OLC) in the Justice Department released a 42-page white paper justifying the legality of the TSP.[27] It offered two principal arguments, one statutory, the other constitutional. The first interpreted the Authorization for Use of Military Force (AUMF), enacted after 9/11. The second explored the President's authorities under Article II of the Constitution, with special emphasis on the availability of "inherent" powers.

THE AUMF

OLC argued that in passing the AUMF "Congress by statute has confirmed and supplemented the President's recognized authority under Article II of the Constitution to conduct such warrantless surveillance to prevent further catastrophic attacks on the homeland."[28] The statute authorized the President to "use all necessary and appropriate force against those nations, organizations, or persons he determines planned, authorized, committed, or aided the terrorists attacks" of September 11 in order to prevent "any future acts of international terrorism against the United States."[29] To OLC, history "conclusively demonstrates that warrantless communications targeted at the enemy in time of armed conflict is a traditional and fundamental incident of the use of military force authorized by the AUMF."[30]

"All necessary and appropriate force" does not mean whatever the President decides to do, particularly when a selected instrument of force conflicts with statutory law. In FISA, Congress established a set of procedures to be "exclusive" for domestic surveillance. If Congress after 9/11 wanted to modify those procedures and permit the President to engage in national security surveillance without a judicial check, it knows how to amend a statute. Either it brings up the bill in whole to debate changes, with all Members of Congress aware of what they are doing, or adopts a free-standing amendment with FISA clearly and specifically in mind, such as debating language that states: "notwithstanding the provision in Title II, Section 201(b), Subsection (f), of the Foreign Intelligence Surveillance Act, the President is hereafter authorized to engage in the following warrantless surveillance." In floor debate, lawmakers must expressly know that the bill language under consideration covers warrantless surveillance and that the judicial check in FISA is to be waived.

Amendments to statutory law must be explicit and evident, with clear understanding by all lawmakers as to what is at stake. Amendments are not made by implication, with Members unaware of what they are voting on. There is no basis for finding in the debate of the AUMF that Members of Congress understood that they were setting FISA to the side to allow the President warrantless surveillance over domestic matters. It is quite true, as OLC said, that FISA "also contemplates that Congress may authorize such surveillance by a statute other than FISA."[31] Congress is always at liberty to adopt a future statute that modifies an earlier statute. But when it acts it does so expressly and consciously, in full light of the changes made and their significance, not by vague implications. OLC would have Congress legislate in the dark. It is my impression that the administration no longer seriously argues that the AUMF is legal justification for the TSP, and that it relies essentially on some form of "inherent" powers under Article II (or perhaps even outside the Constitution).

INHERENT POWERS

OLC argued that NSA's activities under what became known as the TSP "are supported by the President's well-recognized inherent constitutional authority as Commander in Chief and sole organ for the Nation in foreign affairs to conduct warrantless surveillance of enemy forces for intelligence purposes to detect and disrupt armed attacks on the United States."[32] Let me unpack each of these key words: well-recognized, inherent, Commander in Chief, and "sole organ."

1. Well-recognized? Federal courts have made many observations about the President's powers in foreign affairs and his duty to gather intelligence for national security. Language appears at times in the decisions; just as frequently remarks are made in dicta that is extraneous to the issue before the court. Some rulings encourage a broad reading of presidential power; others are much more restrictive. The record is quite mixed and does not reflect the existence of any settled, "well-recognized" position in the federal judiciary.

The same indefinite position applies to Members of Congress. Some are persuaded of independent and inherent presidential power in foreign affairs; others flatly reject legal doctrines that assert such a sweep of executive authority. There is no "well-recognized" view in Congress regarding the claim that OLC makes. In FISA, in fact, Congress expressly left no room for inherent and independent power by the President to conduct warrantless surveillance.

Similarly, the academic community has never developed a "well-recognized" position on the President's inherent constitutional authority as Commander in Chief to conduct warrantless surveillance. Existing studies demonstrate a wide variety of opinions and judgments.[33]

2. Inherent? Any claim of "inherent" power for the President must be approached with extreme caution and wariness. First, it is only a claim or an assertion, not fact. Second, it has a self-serving motivation, for it comes from the branch claiming the authority. Third, the word has an indefinite and indefinable quality that leaves the door open to illegal, unconstitutional, and extra-constitutional powers. Fourth, there should be heightened concern because the claim of "inherent" authority has been used in recent years to justify military commissions, torture memos, indefinite detention of U.S. citizens designated as "enemy combatants," extraordinary rendition, and the TSP. To appreciate the dangers of "inherent" power, compare three words we use to determine the source of constitution power: *express, implied,* and *inherent.*

The first two words preserve and protect constitutional government. Express powers are there in black and white. They can be seen in print and analyzed, usually accompanied by extensive meaning from history and framers' intent. Implied also has a definite quality, because an implied power must be reasonably drawn from an existing express power. For example, the President has an express power to see that the laws are faithfully executed. If a Cabinet official prevents the discharge of a law, the President has an implied power to remove the individual pursuant to his constitutional duty to assure compliance with the law. From the express power to legislate, Congress has an implied power to investigate, issue subpoenas, and hold executive officials in contempt. Express and implied powers are consistent with a constitutional system of limited government.

The same cannot be said of "inherent." The word is defined in some dictionaries as an "authority possessed without its being derived from another. . . . Powers over and beyond those explicitly granted in the Constitution or reasonably to be implied from express powers."[34] If not in the Constitution, either by express or implied powers, what is the source of authority? In other definitions, "inherent" may be a power that "inheres" in an office or position, or something that is "intrinsic" or "belonging by nature."[35] Those concepts are highly ambiguous. The purpose of a constitution is to specify and confine government powers to protect rights and liberties reserved to individuals. That objective is undermined by claims of open-ended authorities (such as "inherent") that are not easily defined or circumscribed. Vague words invite political abuse and endanger individual liberties. In the context of this hearing, claims of "inherent" presidential power directly threaten the prerogatives of Congress. Anything that weakens congressional power weakens democracy and popular sovereignty. The claim of inherent presidential power moves the nation from one of limited powers to boundless and ill-defined executive authority. Such assertions do substantial damage to the doctrine of separation of powers and the crucial system of checks and balances.

3. Commander in Chief? It is analytically meaningless to merely cite three words from Article II as though the case for presidential power is self-evident and needs no further argument. One has to explain what those words mean. Closer scrutiny eliminates any notion of plenary power for the President as Commander in Chief. First, the President is Commander in Chief "of the Militia of the several States, when called into the actual Service of the United States." As is clear from Article I, Congress does the calling. Second, the President is Commander in Chief of the Army and Navy of the United States, but as Article I again demonstrates, Congress has ample authorities to raise and support armies and navies, to make rules for the regulation of the land and naval forces, and to provide for organizing, arming, and disciplining the militia. The appropriations power of Congress is broadly available to direct and limit military operations.[36]

Third, the Constitution does not empower the President as Commander in Chief to initiate and continue wars. Those powers existed for English kings and in the writings of William Blackstone, but the framers deliberately rejected that form of government.[37] Fourth, the President is Commander in Chief for unity of command, but the President's authority to bring unity of purpose in military command does not deprive Congress of its own independent constitutional duty to monitor war and decide whether to restrict or terminate military operations. Fifth, the President is Commander in Chief to preserve civilian supremacy over the military. As explained by Attorney General Edward Bates in 1861, whatever soldier leads U.S. armies "he is subject to the orders of the *civil magistrate*, and he and his army are always 'subordinate to the civil power.'"[38] Congress is an essential part of that civil power. Just as military officers are subject to the direction and command of the President, so is the President subject to the direction and command of Members of Congress as representatives of the sovereign people.

4. "Sole Organ"? In the history of American constitutional doctrines, there is probably nothing as shallow, empty, and misleading as the OLC claim that the President as "sole organ" in foreign affairs is granted some type of exclusive, plenary power. The phrase comes from a speech by Cong. John Marshall in 1800, when he said that the President "is the sole organ of the nation in its external relations, and its sole representative with foreign nations."[39] In his decades of distinguished federal service, as

Secretary of State, Member of the House, and Chief Justice of the Supreme Court, Marshall at no time advocated an independent, inherent, or exclusive power of the President over external affairs. The purpose of his speech in 1800 was merely to state that President John Adams had a constitutional duty under the Take Care Clause to see that an extradition treaty with Britain was faithfully carried out. That was all. The context of his speech makes it clear that he was speaking of presidential power to execute *the policy of Congress*, whether expressed in statute or treaty. Marshall never implied any authority of the President to act independent of statutes or treaties, much less in opposition to them. For example, Chief Justice Marshall ruled in 1804 that when a presidential proclamation in time of war conflicts with a statute passed by Congress, the statute prevails.[40]

What OLC does is to take Marshall's speech not as it was given, and not as it was meant, but as it was misinterpreted and distorted by Justice Sutherland in *United States* v. *Curtiss-Wright* (1936).[41] How did Sutherland misuse the speech? First, the case *had nothing to do with presidential power*. It had to do with the *power of Congress* to delegate certain discretionary authority in the field of international affairs. In exercising authority given to him in 1934 to impose an arms embargo in South America, President Franklin D. Roosevelt relied solely on statutory—not inherent—authority.[42] Second, Sutherland's misuse of Marshall's speech appears in dicta, not in the decision. Third, the dicta is bad dicta, as has been pointed out repeatedly in scholarly studies. Sutherland promoted misconceptions not only about Marshall's speech but also about the concept of sovereignty, inherent presidential power, extra-constitutional powers, the distinction between internal and external affairs, and the competing powers of Congress.[43] To the extent that *Curtiss-Wright* suggests that foreign affairs are outside the Constitution and not subject to congressional control, the Supreme Court has not followed it.

III. Briefings and Consultation

After 9/11 and the initiation of the TSP, the administration gave regular briefings about the surveillance program to the "Gang of Eight" and to the chief judge of the FISA court. The Gang of Eight includes the leadership of each house and the chair and ranking member of each Intelligence Committee. Lawmakers who were briefed were directed by executive officials not to take notes or share what they heard with colleagues or with their staff. Not being part of the Gang of Eight, the Judiciary Committee chairmen and ranking members were not briefed as part of this process. Several issues emerge.

First, it is constructive for the executive branch to brief and consult Members of Congress *provided that the program is legal, constitutional, and in harmony with statutory law.* Briefing Members about an illegal program does not make it legal. It would be as though executive officials briefed the chair and ranking member of the two Appropriations Committees that funds had been withdrawn from the Treasury without an appropriation. With or without the briefing, the action would be unconstitutional.

Second, was the Gang of Eight the proper procedure to follow? My understanding of the Gang of Eight is that it was established as a means of informing the congressional leadership and the top levels of the Intelligence Committees about a pending *covert action* (50 U.S.C. Section 413b(c)(2)), which is an activity "to influence political, economic, or military conditions abroad" (50 U.S.C. Section 413b(e)). In my judgment, the Gang of Eight was not the right procedure to brief members about the TSP, which has nothing to do with destabilizing or altering a foreign country.

Third, what duty falls on a member of the Gang of Eight in being briefed about a program that waives FISA and dispenses with independent judicial checks? Are they bound by some vow of secrecy insisted on by the executive officials doing the briefing? No. Members of Congress who receive confidential briefings from executive officials belong to a separate branch with separate institutional responsibilities, including the duty to assure that the executive branch complies with the law. After being briefed, lawmakers may reach out to colleagues, top staff, and to the leadership of the Judiciary Committees to receive their legal and constitutional analysis. Members of Congress take an oath to the Constitution, not to the President. They have a special obligation to protect the powers of their institution.

Fourth, what duty falls on a chief judge of the FISA Court after being briefed about a program that waives FISA and dispenses with independent judicial checks? The primary duty of the chief judge is not to remain silent but to inform the other ten judges on the Court. They must then decide what to do, because it is their duty to see that the law is obeyed, including the judicial check that Congress placed in FISA.

Fifth, the Judiciary Committees (at least the chairmen and ranking members) needed to be informed about the TSP because of their jurisdiction over FISA. Generally speaking, the Intelligence Committees will focus more on policy and programmatic issues, while the Judiciary Committees will place greater emphasis on legal and constitutional issues and the integrity of FISA.

IV. What Does "Legal" Mean Today?

NSA's surveillance program raises elementary questions about the constitutional duty of Congress to make law. In the Steel Seizure Case of 1952, Justice Robert Jackson eloquently summarized our constitutional principles: "With all its defects, delays and inconveniences, men have discovered no technique for long preserving free government except that the Executive be under the law, and that the law be made by parliamentary deliberations."[44] Simple words but so profound. The Executive is under the law, not above it. The law is made by Congress.

The TSP represents a direct challenge to our system and form of government. Under the guise of "inherent" power, the executive branch claims the right to ignore statutory law in order to give preference to executive-made law, all done in secret. Other countries have adopted this approach, at great cost to democratic institutions and individual rights.

INDEPENDENT EXECUTIVE LAW?

On December 17, 2005, after the *New York Times* published the story about the NSA eavesdropping program, President Bush in a radio address acknowledged that he had authorized the agency to conduct the surveillance, "consistent with U.S. law and the Constitution."[45] In subsequent statements, as President Bush continued to refer to "U.S. law" or "authority," it appeared that he meant law created solely within the executive branch, even if contrary to a law passed by Congress. He underscored his independent Article II constitutional powers: "The authorization I gave the National Security Agency after Sept. 11 helped address that problem [of combating terrorism] in a way that is fully consistent with my constitutional responsibilities and authorities."[46]

He said he had "reauthorized this program more than 30 times since the Sept. 11 attacks."[47] Similarly, on December 19 Attorney General Alberto Gonzales stated that "the President has the inherent authority under the Constitution, as Commander-in-Chief, to engage in this kind of activity."[48]

Michael V. Hayden appeared before the Senate Intelligence Committee on May 18, 2006, to testify on his nomination to be CIA Director. Previously he had served as NSA Director at the time the TSP was initiated. At the hearing, he defended the legality of the program on constitutional, not statutory, grounds. In recalling his service at NSA after 9/11, he told the committee that when he talked to NSA lawyers "they were very comfortable with the Article II arguments and the president's inherent authorities."[49] When they came to him and discussed the lawfulness of the program, "our discussion anchored itself on Article II."[50] The attorneys "came back with a real comfort level that this was within the president's authority [under Article II]."[51]

This legal advice was not put in writing and Hayden "did not ask for it." Instead, "they talked to me about Article II."[52] What could the talk have been about? The President as Commander in Chief? What other words in Article II would have clarified the legal analysis and produced a comfort level? Apparently the NSA General Counsel was not asked to prepare a legal memo defending the TSP. No paper trail. No accountability. Just informal talks. We all know that hallway discussions about legal and constitutional issues are not likely to look as persuasive or as sound when put on paper and submitted to peers for their independent assessment.

During the hearing, Hayden repeatedly claimed that the NSA program was legal and that in taking charge of the CIA the agency "will obey the laws of the United States and will respond to our treaty obligations."[53] Given what he said throughout the hearing, what did he mean by "law"? A policy drawn solely from within the executive branch, depending on someone's interpretation of Article II? That appears to be what he meant. After 9/11, while at NSA, he said he "had two lawful programs in front of me, one authorized by the president [the TSP], the other one would have been conducted under FISA as currently crafted and implemented."[54] In other words, he had two choices: one authorized by the President, the second authorized by Congress. He selected the former. He told one Senator: "I did not believe—still don't believe—that I was acting unlawfully. I was acting under a lawful authorization."[55] He meant a presidential directive issued under Article II, even if in violation of the exclusive policy set forth in FISA.

Hearing him insist that he was acting legally in implementing the NSA program, a Senator said: "I assume that the basis for that was the Article II powers, the inherent powers of the president to protect the country in time of danger and war." Hayden replied: "Yes, sir, commander in chief powers."[56] Hayden seemed to clearly imply that he was willing to overstep statutory law in order to carry out presidential law. After 9/11, CIA Director George Tenet asked whether NSA could "do more" to combat terrorism with surveillance. Hayden answered: "not within current law."[57] In short, it appears that the administration knowingly and consciously decided to act against statutory policy. It knew that the NSA eavesdropping program it decided to conduct was illegal under FISA but decided to go ahead, banking on Article II powers.

At one point in the hearings, Hayden referred to the legal and political embarrassments of NSA during the Nixon administration, when it conducted warrantless eavesdropping against domestic groups. In discussing what should be done after 9/11, he told one group: "Look, I've got a workforce out there that remembers the mid-1970s." He asked the Senate committee to forgive him for using "a poor sports metaphor," but he advised the group in this manner: "since about 1975, this agency's had a permanent one-ball, two-strike count against it, and we don't take many close pitches."[58] TSP was a close pitch. If Congress learns more about the program, we may learn if NSA hit or missed.

CONTINUED RELIANCE ON ARTICLE II

In January 2007, after several setbacks in the federal district courts on the TSP, the administration announced it would no longer skirt the FISA Court but would instead seek approval from it, as required by statute. Exactly what "orders" the FISA Court issued is unclear, because they have not yet been released to Congress. The announcement seemed to promise compliance with FISA, but there is insufficient information to know what the new policy is or how permanent it is.

Was the administration now relying solely on statutory authority or had it kept in reserve its Article II, inherent power arguments? Had the administration merely offered a temporary accommodation while keeping the door open to Article II claims? At oral argument on January 31, 2007 before the Sixth Circuit, regarding one of the TSP cases, one of the judges asked the government: "You could opt out at any time, couldn't you?" The Deputy Solicitor General acknowledged the possibility.[59]

At a May 1, 2007 hearing before the Senate Intelligence Committee, the administration seemed to promote Article II. Michael McConnell, the Director of National Intelligence, signaled that the administration might not be able to keep its pledge to seek approval from the FISA Court. When asked by Senator Russ Feingold whether the administration would no longer sidestep the FISA Court, McConnell replied: "Sir, the president's authority under Article II is in the Constitution. So if the president chose to exercise Article II authority, that would be the president's choice." McConnell wanted to highlight that "Article II is Article II, so in a different circumstance, I can't speak for the president what he might decide."[60]

We're back to basics: Who makes law in the national government? If Congress passes a law through the procedures specified in Article I, is the President obliged under Article II to "take Care that the Laws be faithfully executed"? Alternatively, is the President at liberty to craft—in secret—an executive-made law that supplants and overrides statutory law? These hearings will help Congress and the public take part in an all important debate on what constitutes "the rule of law" in America. It has been our foreign policy to support and encourage the rule of law abroad. Shall we also have it here at home?

ENDNOTES

1. James Bamford, Body of Secrets: Anatomy of the Ultra-Secret National Security Agency 428 (2002 ed.).
2. Id. at 428-29; James Bamford, The Puzzle Palace 323-24 (1983 ed.).
3. Richard E. Morgan, Domestic Intelligence: Monitoring Dissent in America 6 (1980).
4. Kathryn S. Olmsted, Challenging the Secret Government: The Post-Watergate Investigations of the CIA and FBI 11-12, 35 (1996).
5. Keith W. Olson, Watergate: The Presidential Scandal That Shook America 16 (2003); Fred Emery, Watergate 25 (1995 ed.); Loch K. Johnson, America's Secret Power: The CIA in a Democratic Society 133-56 (1989).
6. Bamford, Body of Secrets, at 430.

7. Emery, Watergate, at 26-27.

8. Bamford, Body of Secrets, at 431-32.

9. Id. at 438-39; Morgan, Domestic Intelligence, at 75-76. For further details on domestic surveillance during the 1960s and 1970s, see recent testimony by Frederick A. O. Schwarz, Jr., "Ensuring Executive Branch Accountability," before the Subcommittee on Commercial and Administration Law of the House Committee on the Judiciary, March 29, 2007, at 4, 10-11.

10. United States v. United States District Court, 407 U.S. 297, 299 (1972).

11. United States v. Sinclair, 321 F.Supp. 1074 (E.D. Mich. 1971).

12. Id. at 1076.

13. Id. at 1077.

14. Id. at 1078 (citing District Judge Ferguson in United States v. Smith, 321 F.Supp. 424, 425 (C.D. Cal. 1971)).

15. United States v. United States Dist. Ct. for E. D. of Mich., 444 F.2d 651, 658 (6th Cir. 1971).

16. Id. at 665.

17. Id.

18. Id.

19. United States v. United States District Court, 407 U.S. at 316.

20. Id. at 316-17.

21. Id. at 317.

22. Id. at 318-19.

23. Id. at 320.

24. Id. at 302-08.

25. Id. at 302-08.

26. "Electronic Surveilllance Within the United States for Foreign Intelligence Purposes," hearings before the Subcommittee on Intelligence and the Rights of Americans of the Senate Committee on Intelligence, 94th Cong., 2d Sess. 76 (1976).

27. "Legal Authorities Supporting the Activities of the National Security Agency Described by the President," Office of Legal Counsel, U.S. Department of Justice, January 19, 2006 (hereafter "OLC Study").

28. Id. at 2.

29. 115 Stat. 224 (2001).

30. OLC Study at 2.

31. Id. For further analysis of the AUMF regarding the TSP, see "Statement of the Constitution Project's Liberty and Security Initiative" (The Constitution Project, Jan. 5, 2006).

32. OLC Study at 1.

33. E.g., see the March 2007 Special Issue of *Presidential Studies Quarterly*, which is devoted to inherent presidential power (37 Pres. Stud. Q. 1 (2007)); Deciding to Use Force Abroad: War Powers in a System of Checks and Balances (The Constitution Project, 2005); David Gray Adler and Larry N. George, eds., The Constitution and the Conduct of American Foreign Policy (1996); and Gary M. Stern and Morton Halperin, eds., The U.S. Constitution and the Power to Go to War (1994).

34. Louis Fisher, "Invoking Inherent Powers: A Primer," 37 Pres. Stud. Q. 1, 2 (2007).

35. Id.

36. Charles Tiefer, "Can Appropriations Riders Speed Our Exit from Iraq?," 42 Stan. J. Int'l L. 291 (2006).

37. Louis Fisher, testimony before the Senate Committee on the Judiciary, hearings on "Exercising Congress's Constitutional Power to End a War," January 30, 2007, at 1-4.

38. 10 Op. Att'y Gen. 74,789 (1861) (emphasis in original).

39. 10 Annals of Cong. 613 (1800).

40. Little v. Barreme, 2 Cr. (6 U.S.) 170, 179 (1804).

41. OLC Study at 1, 6-7, 14, 30.

42. 48 Stat. 1745 (1934).

43. Louis Fisher, "Presidential Inherent Power: The 'Sole Organ' Doctrine," 37 Pres. Stud. Q. 139 (2007). For more detailed analysis, see Louis Fisher, "The 'Sole Organ' Doctrine," The Law Library of Congress, August 2006.

44. Youngstown Co. v. Sawyer, 343 U.S. 579, 655 (1952).

45. "Bush on the Patriot Act and Eavesdropping," New York Times, Dec. 18, 2005, at 30.

46. Id.

47. David E. Sanger, "In Address, Bush Says He Ordered Domestic Spying," New York Times, Dec. 18, 2005, at 30.

48. Press briefing by Attorney General Alberto Gonzales and General Michael Hayden, Principal Deputy Director for National Intelligence, at 2. Available from http://www.whitehouse.gov/news/releases/2005/12/print/20051219-1.html

49. Hearing of the Senate Select Committee on Intelligence on the Nomination of General Michael V. Hayden to be Director of the Central Intelligence Agency, May 18, 2006, transcript, at 35.

50. Id.

51. Id. at 69.

52. Id.

53. Id. at 74.

54. Id. at 88.

55. Id. at 138.

56. Id. at 144.

57. Id. at 68.

58. Id. at 61.

59. Adam Liptak, "Judges Weigh Arguments in U.S. Eavesdropping Case," New York Times, Feb. 1, 2007, at A11.

60. James Risen, "Administration Pulls Back on Surveillance Agreement," New York Times, May 3, 2007, at A16.

*Louis Fisher is scholar in residence at the Constitution Project. He served for four decades as a constitutional scholar for the Library of Congress's Congressional Research Service. He has written many books on constitutional law, in particular the separation of powers between Congress and the president.

Statement of Louis Fisher before the House Judiciary Committee, June 7, 2007 Constitutional limitations on domestic surveillance. 110th Cong.

Discussion Questions

1. Was President Bush justified in creating a secret surveillance program in the wake of September 11, 2001, or
   should he have sought congressional authorization to
   do so? If he had sought authorization, would that have
   undermined the efficacy of the program by revealing
   its existence to al Qaeda?

2. Should the president as "commander in chief" have
   unchecked authority to "engage the enemy" in whatever way he deems appropriate? Alternatively, should
   Congress be free to micromanage the conduct of military operations by enacting statutes that limit the tools
   and tactics the president can use to fight the war?

3. What powers over war making did the Constitution's
   Framers give to Congress? What powers did they give
   to the president? Is it ever permissible for the president
   to act in defiance of express congressional statutes?

4. What does our historical experience with warrantless
   domestic surveillance teach us about the need for separation of powers and checks and balances? Does history
   support President Bush's assertion of unilateral power
   to conduct surveillance of the enemy during wartime?

PART 6:
Privacy and Security

How should privacy protections be weighed against the desire to prevent a future terrorist attack? Privacy is a core constitutional right, central to individual and democratic freedom. The power to spy on suspicious persons is a critical tool in the government's national security arsenal, but may also be abused to target political opponents or critics and to chill and undermine legitimate political mobilization for change. Without privacy, people are not free to develop their personalities, to engage in intimate behavior essential to a fulfilling life, or to engage in political and religious activities free of state intrusion. We say that "a man's home is his castle" for a reason. At the same time, privacy itself can also be abused—as when it is employed as a cover to engage in criminal activity. The long-standing tension between protecting our privacy from unwarranted state intrusion on the one hand and protecting ourselves from criminals by empowering the police to investigate crime on the other remains.

Americans have struggled with these questions since the birth of the Republic. But the modern world poses the questions in new ways. The development of technology has made achieving an evil goal much easier for small groups or even a lone individual. At the same time, technological advances have also radically extended the government's ability to obtain personal information about all of us. Should the government, without any individualized suspicion of wrongdoing, be empowered to collect the private data we share with banks, Internet service providers, credit card companies, businesses, and libraries? Should different rules apply to intelligence gathering for counterterrorism purposes and for ordinary criminal law enforcement? Do the greater risks we face from terrorists justify more substantial intrusions into our privacy? What safeguards can and should be put in place to protect privacy and security in a post-9/11 world?

Richard Posner argues that the vastly increased threats posed by terrorists in the twenty-first century, coupled with the ability to "mine" electronic data by computer and to track government abuse of such information, justify striking a new and different balance between privacy and security. Christian Parenti warns that a culture of fear sparked by 9/11 caused the government to overreact, creating a "surveillance society" at odds with the constitutional principles that have framed our democracy for more than two hundred years.

Security and Rights Against Searches and Seizures in Time of Emergency

by Richard Posner*

Suppose [...] that a [terrorist suspect] was arrested in his apartment in New York City and the apartment was searched and valuable evidence of his terrorist activities or connections was found, or that his phone was tapped. Ordinarily an arrest and a search (and wiretapping and other electronic eavesdropping are now considered searches for Fourth Amendment purposes) are constitutional only if there is probable cause to believe that the person arrested has committed a crime and that the search will turn up contraband or evidence of crime. "Probable cause" is more than a hunch or mere suspicion, even reasonable suspicion, but less than proof sufficient for conviction (proof "beyond a reasonable doubt") or even the lesser amount of proof (proof by a "preponderance of the evidence") that a plaintiff needs in order to win a civil case.

The requirement that searches be based on probable cause is not actually in the Fourth Amendment. It is an invention of the Supreme Court. What the Fourth Amendment actually does is, first, limit the use of warrants and, second, forbid searches and seizures, whether or not pursuant to warrant, if but only if they are unreasonable. Here is the text of the amendment: "The right of the people to be secure in their persons, houses, papers, and effects, against unreasonable searches and seizures, shall not be violated, and no Warrants shall issue, but upon probable cause, supported by Oath or affirmation, and particularly describing the place to be searched, and the persons or things to be seized." The only limitation on the search or seizure itself is reasonableness, a criterion flexible enough to allow the courts to calibrate the government's authority to make an arrest and conduct a search according to the gravity of the concern motivating those actions. Neither probable cause nor a warrant is a precondition found in the text of the amendment to a finding of reasonableness.

The curious structure of the amendment from a modern perspective—how it comes down harder on warrants than on warrantless searches and seizures—reflects the fact that its authors were particularly worried about searches pursuant to warrant because a warrant provided a legal defense to the officer conducting the search if he was sued for trespass. If general warrants, that is, warrants that did not satisfy the amendment's requirements of particularity and probable cause, could justify a search, the police would have carte blanche to search and seize. But in a typical upending of original understandings and disregard of pellucid constitutional text, the Supreme Court in the mid-twentieth century decided that the Fourth Amendment requires, where feasible, that a search be conducted pursuant to a warrant (though of course not a general warrant). This is not much of a filter, because a warrant proceeding is ex parte—the judge or magistrate hears only from the government. But the proceeding creates a written record that makes it easier for a court in which the legality of the search is subsequently challenged to determine whether it was reasonable. It has also spawned a complicated judge-made body of exceptions to the requirement of obtaining a warrant.

Exceptions there must be. Although often a warrant can be obtained within minutes by phone, this is not always possible; events may be moving too fast. If so—if, as the cases say, the circumstances are exigent—the requirement of getting a warrant is excused. And even though the Supreme Court has generally required that a warrantless arrest or search must, like an arrest or search based on a warrant, be supported by probable cause, "generally" is another important qualification. For remember that "probable cause" appears only in the warrant clause and that the legal criterion of a warrantless search is reasonableness. The Court has acknowledged the flexibility of the standard of reasonableness by holding that police can make a brief stop (called a "*Terry* stop" after the case that upheld its constitutionality) of a person, short of a full arrest, on the basis merely of a reasonable suspicion of criminal activity. During the stop they can question him in an effort to confirm or dispel their suspicions, and they can even pat him down to make sure he's not armed.

There are more stops of innocent people than there would be if probable cause were required, and that is a cost. But the cost per *Terry* stop is less than the cost of a full arrest because a brief stop causes less delay and embarrassment to the person stopped. That modest cost is offset by the benefit to law enforcement of allowing the police to make stops on suspicion, because in many cases the suspicion is confirmed and the police have solved one more crime.

Despite general approval of the *Terry* stop, the differential costs of different types or levels of search and seizure are a neglected consideration in discussions of the Fourth Amendment. The neglect is serious because the lower the cost to the person searched or seized, the less important it is to insist on strongly grounded suspicion. This consideration (a generalization from the *Terry* case) is especially important—and especially neglected—with respect to electronic eavesdropping. A physical search imposes costs in time, inconvenience, disruption, fear, and embarrassment on everyone searched; likewise an arrest, and even a *Terry* stop. But surreptitious eavesdropping need impose no costs at all on people who don't know they're being eavesdropped on, or who know but don't care because they have nothing they particularly care to hide from the eavesdropper. The latter is a more common situation than civil libertarians imagine. All manner of e-mail and other Internet "conversations" are monitored and recorded by employers and vendors. Probably most people would prefer to have their communications monitored by an agency interested only in national security than by their employer. And they would prefer either form of surveillance to a police search of their home, let alone to being arrested. It is easy to exaggerate the private as well as social harm from unobtrusive surveillance.

On the benefits side of a cost-benefit analysis (a type of analysis that a standard of "reasonableness" invites courts to conduct) of search and seizure, consider a case in which the police, having learned that a terrorist is driving to a city's downtown area in order to explode a car bomb, throw up roadblocks on all roads leading to the downtown and search every car. Since all the cars they stop except one are not carrying a bomb, they have no probable cause or even reasonable suspicion that a given car is the one they're looking for. Nevertheless, the Supreme Court suggested in *City of Indianapolis v. Edmond* and *Florida v. J.L.*, both decided in 2000, that such a dragnet would be reasonable and therefore lawful under the Fourth Amendment. The aggregate cost to innocent drivers in delay and inconvenience and the (limited) invasion of privacy would not be trivial. But it would be less than the expected cost of the car bombing. When the London transit system was bombed in July 2005, killing more than fifty people, the New York City police began random searches of subway riders' bags and parcels even though there was apparently no evidence that an attack was planned or imminent. The risk of an attack was slight, but so was the cost imposed by the very light searches.

In *Illinois v. Lidster* (2004), the Supreme Court, in an opinion by the liberal Justice Stephen Breyer, went even further, upholding a roadblock set up by the police to stop cars so that the drivers could be asked for information about a recent hit-and-run accident. Not only was there no individualized suspicion of the persons stopped; there was no collective suspicion. The purpose of the roadblock was not to stop the hit-and-run driver but to obtain information that might lead to his being apprehended elsewhere. Yet the Court held that the roadblock did not violate the Fourth Amendment. One factor the Court emphasized is that the stop was less intrusive than an arrest or a conventional search.

The *indiscriminate* character of a roadblock or other dragnet is, paradoxically, one of its redeeming features from a civil libertarian standpoint. Because no one is singled out, the opportunity for abuse by the authorities is reduced. This is an argument against profiling[...].

Lidster is important because it divorces searching from suspicion. It allows surveillance that invades liberty and privacy to be conducted because of the importance of the information sought, even if it is not sought for use in a potential criminal proceeding against the people actually under surveillance. National security intelligence is a quest for information in an analogous sense. Valuable intelligence might be extracted from conversations or other communications between innocent people—for example, one person telling a friend about a new neighbor who, unbeknownst to either party to the conversation, was a terrorist suspect—or at least people too loosely linked to terrorist activities to be prosecutable. Like the searchers in the *Lidster* case, intelligence officers have to cast their net very wide to obtain the information that they need in order to build up a picture of terrorist activities.

Congress overlooked this point when it enacted the Foreign Intelligence Surveillance Act (FISA) in 1978 and even when it amended the act in the USA PATRIOT Act shortly after the 9/11 attacks. The government had long engaged in wiretapping and other forms of electronic surveillance (and sometimes had conducted physical searches), including of U.S. citizens in the United States, aimed at obtaining information concerning possible foreign intrigues or other foreign threats against the nation. It had done these things without seeking warrants or trying to confine surveillance to situations in which there was probable cause to believe that the surveillance would uncover evidence of criminal activity. The Supreme Court in the *Keith* case (1972) had observed that what had become the conventional understanding (though, as we've seen, not always adhered to)—that a search or seizure must be based on probable cause to believe that a crime has occurred or is about to occur—might have to be relaxed when the goal of surveillance was to obtain intelligence information rather than evidence or leads for a criminal prosecution.

It was a prescient observation. The aim of national security intelligence is to thwart attacks by enemy nations or terrorist groups rather than just to punish the perpetrators after an attack has occurred. The threat of punishment is not a reliable deterrent to such attacks, especially when the attackers are fanatics who place a low value on their own lives and when the potential destructiveness of such attacks is so great that even a single failure of deterrence can have catastrophic consequences. That is why, when government is fighting terrorism rather than ordinary crime, the emphasis shifts from punishment to prevention. And prevention requires the intelligence agencies to cast a much wider and finer-meshed net in fishing for information. Once a crime has occurred, a focused search for the criminal and for evidence of the crime is feasible. But if the concern guiding a search is that a crime *might* occur, the focus has to be much broader. [...]

The Foreign Intelligence Surveillance Act authorizes the issuance of warrants to conduct electronic surveillance aimed at obtaining "foreign intelligence information," defined as information relating to foreign threats to U.S. national security. (A warrant is not required in an emergency, but in that case the government must within seventy-two hours of the beginning of the surveillance seek retroactive authorization from the special court that issues FISA warrants.) A warrant may be issued only if there is probable cause to believe that the target of the surveillance is an "agent" of a foreign power or of a foreign group (such as a terrorist gang) or a "lone wolf"—an individual, not necessarily linked to any foreign nation or foreign group, who is engaged or preparing to engage in terrorist activities. If the target happens to be a "U.S. person" who is in the United States, a warrant cannot be issued unless there is probable cause to believe him actually involved in hostile activities against the United States. The category "U.S. person" consists primarily of U.S. citizens and permanent residents of the United States, thus excluding tourists, foreign students, illegal immigrants, and most other foreigners. With respect to those others, a warrant is required if at least one party to the communication is in the United States and the communication is intercepted in the United States.

Probable cause to believe that interception of the target's communications will yield evidence of crime need not be shown (though evidence of crime discovered in the course of a FISA search can be used to prosecute the perpetrators, provided that obtaining foreign intelligence information was a significant purpose of the interception). This departure from the ordinary requirements for getting a warrant is justified by the magnitude of the dangers that national security intelligence seeks to foil. The type of search the act authorizes is an a fortiori example of the category of searches recognized in cases such as *Lidster*. But since 9/11 the government has been making interceptions that FISA doesn't authorize, and we must consider whether such searches violate the Fourth Amendment.

According to the administration, these are just interceptions of communications to and from the United States in which one of the parties is suspected of terrorist connections, though the suspicion does not rise to the probable-cause level that would be required for obtaining a warrant. There may be more to the program, however. Most likely the next terrorist attack on the United States will, like the last one, be mounted from within the country but be orchestrated by leaders safely ensconced somewhere abroad. If a phone number in the United States is discovered to have been called by a known or suspected terrorist abroad, or if the number is found in the possession of a suspected terrorist or in a terrorist hideout, it would be prudent to intercept all calls, domestic as well as international, to or from that U.S. phone number and scrutinize them for suspicious content. But the mere fact that a suspected or even known terrorist has had a phone conversation with someone in the United States or has someone's U.S. phone number in his possession doesn't create probable cause to believe that the other person is also a terrorist; probably most phone conversations of terrorists are with people who are not themselves terrorists. The government can't get a FISA warrant just to find out whether someone *is* a terrorist; it has to already have a reason to believe he's one. Nor can it conduct surveillance of terrorist suspects who are not believed to have any foreign connections, because such surveillance would not yield *foreign* intelligence information.

FISA has yet another gap. A terrorist who wants to send a message can type it in his laptop and place it, unsent, in an e-mail account, which the intended recipient of the message can access by knowing the account name. The message itself is not communicated. Rather, it's as if the recipient had visited the sender and searched his laptop. The government, if it intercepted the e-mail from the intended recipient to the account of the "sender," could not get a FISA warrant to intercept (by e-mailing the same account) the "communication" consisting of the message residing in the sender's computer, because that message had never left the computer.

These examples suggest that surveillance outside the narrow bounds of FISA might significantly enhance national security. At a minimum, such surveillance might cause our foreign terrorist enemies to abandon or greatly curtail their use of telephone, e-mail, and other means of communicating electronically with people in the United States who may be members of terrorist sleeper cells. Civil libertarians believe that this is bound to be the effect of electronic surveillance, and argue that therefore such surveillance is futile. There is no "therefore." If the effect of electronic surveillance is to close down the enemy's electronic communications, that is a boon to us because it is far more difficult for terrorist leaders to orchestrate an attack on the United States by sending messages into the country by means of couriers. But what is far more likely is that some terrorists will continue communicating electronically, either through careless-ness—the Madrid and London bombers were prolific users of electronic communications, and think of all the drug gangsters who are nailed by wiretaps—or in the mistaken belief that by using code words or electronic encryption they can thwart the NSA. (If they can, the program is a flop and will be abandoned.) There are careless people in every organization. If al-Qaeda is the exception, civil libertarians clearly are underestimating the terrorist menace! In all our previous wars, beginning with the Civil War, when telegraphic communications were intercepted, our enemies have known that we might intercept their communi-cations, yet they have gone on communicating and we have gone on intercepting. As for surveillance of purely domestic com-munications, it would either isolate members of terrorist cells (which might, as I said, have no foreign links at all) from each other or yield potentially valuable information about the cells.

FISA's limitations are borrowed from law enforcement. When a crime is committed, the authorities usually have a lot of information right off the bat—time, place, victims, maybe suspects—and this permits a focused investigation that has a high probability of eventuating in an arrest. Not so with national security intelligence, where the investigator has no time, place, or victim and may have scant idea of the enemy's identity and location; hence the need for the wider, finer-meshed investiga-tive net. It is no surprise that there have been leaks from inside the FBI expressing skepticism about the NSA program. This skepticism reflects the Bureau's emphasis on criminal investiga-tions, which are narrowly focused and usually fruitful, whereas intelligence is a search for the needle in the haystack. FBI agents don't like being asked to chase down clues gleaned from the NSA's interceptions; 999 out of 1,000 turn out to lead nowhere. They don't realize that often the most that counterterrorist intelligence can hope to achieve is to impose costs on enemies of the nation (as by catching and "turning" some, or forcing them to use less efficient means of communication) in the hope of disrupting their plans. It is mistaken to think electronic surveillance a failure if it doesn't intercept a message giving the time and place of the next attack.

Whether surveillance outside FISA's limits is reasonable within the meaning of the Fourth Amendment depends not only on the likely efficacy of the surveillance but also on how seriously it invades privacy. Because of the volume involved, massive amounts of intercepted data must first be sifted by computers. The sifting can take two forms. One is a search for suspicious patterns or links; Mary DeRosa gives the example of searching for "use of a stolen credit card for a small purchase at a gas station—done to confirm whether the card is valid—before making a very significant purchase," a pattern suggestive of credit card fraud. The other form is the familiar Google-type search for more information about a known individual, group, subject, activity, identifier, and so on. A search for a social security number, for example, can reveal whether two similar or identical names are the names of two persons or one. The term "data mining" is sometimes limited to the first, the pattern search. But it is often used to embrace the second as well. I shall use the term in the broad sense.

The initial sifting is neither a search within the meaning of the Fourth Amendment nor "surveillance" within the meaning of FISA. Rather than invading privacy, computer sifting prevents most private data from being read by an intelligence officer or other human being by filtering them out. Depending on the search method used, data that are not selected for human scrutiny may not even be recorded and placed in a government database; they may merely be scanned by the computer while the data are being communicated ("packet sniffing").

The data that make the cut and are scrutinized by a human being will be those that contain clues to possible threats to national security, whether or not the clues are solid enough to base application for a FISA warrant on. The human scrutiny of private communications is a search, and most of the communications searched will turn out to be completely innocent. The principal worry about these searches from the standpoint of privacy, besides fear that hackers will gain access to the contents of the intercepted communications, is that those contents might be used to blackmail or otherwise intimidate the administration's critics and political opponents. A secondary fear is that they might be used to ridicule or embarrass. Such things have happened in the past, but they are less likely to happen today. Increased political partisanship, advances in communications technology, the growth of a culture of leaking and whistleblowing, and (related to the preceding point) more numerous and competitive media have converged to make American government a fishbowl. Secrets concerning matters that interest the public cannot be kept for long. The public would be even more avid to learn that public officials were using private information about American citizens for base political or personal ends than to learn that we have played rough with terrorist suspects—a matter that was quickly exposed despite efforts at concealment. Intense, unslaked public curiosity is a magnet to leakers and reporters.

Concerns with privacy could be alleviated, moreover, by adopting a rule forbidding the intelligence services to turn over any intercepted communications to the Justice Department for prosecution for any offense other than a violation of a criminal law intended for the protection of national security. Then people would not worry that unguarded statements in private conversations would get them into trouble. Such a rule would be a modification, urged in a parallel setting by Orin Kerr, of the "plain view" doctrine of search and seizure. That doctrine, another of the exceptions to the requirement of a warrant to search or seize, allows the seizure of evidence that the police discover in plain view in the course of an unrelated lawful search—even though the discovery is accidental and a warrant could not have been obtained to search for the evidence discovered.

But what if an intelligence officer, reading the transcript of a phone conversation that had been intercepted and then referred to him because the search engine had flagged it as a communication possibly possessing intelligence value, discovers that one of the parties to the communication seems to be planning a murder, though a murder having nothing to do with any terrorist plot? Must the officer ignore the discovery and refrain from notifying the authorities? Though the obvious answer is no, my answer is yes.

There is much wild talk in private conversations. Suppose the communication that has been intercepted and read for valid national security reasons contains the statement "I'll kill the son of a bitch." The probability will be very high that the statement is hyperbole, that there is no serious intent to kill anyone. But suppose intelligence officers have been told that if a communication they read contains evidence of crime, they should turn it over to the FBI. The officer in my hypothetical case does that, and the Bureau, since the matter has been referred to it by a government agency, takes the threat seriously and investigates (or turns the matter over to local police for investigation, if no federal crime is suspected). As word of such investigations got around, people would learn that careless talk in seemingly private conversations can buy them a visit from the FBI or the police. At this point the risk that national security surveillance would significantly deter candor in conversation would skyrocket. It is more important that the public tolerate extensive national security surveillance of communications than that an occasional run-of-the-mill crime go unpunished because intelligence officers were not permitted to share evidence of such a crime with law enforcement authorities. But if the evidence is of a crime related to national security, then sharing it with law enforcement authorities is appropriate and should be (and is) required. Other exceptions may be needed. Suppose that what is overheard is a conversation that identifies one of the parties as a serial killer. Serial killing is not terrorism, but it is such a serious crime that clues to it picked up in national security surveillance should be communicated to law enforcement authorities.

If such a rule (with its exceptions) were in place, I believe that the government could, in the present emergency, intercept *all* electronic communications inside or outside the United States, of citizens as well as of foreigners, without being deemed to violate the Fourth Amendment, provided that computers were used to winnow the gathered data, blocking human inspection of intercepted communications that contained no clues to terrorist activity. We know that citizens (and permanent residents) can be terrorists operating against their country, even without any foreign links. The United States has had its share of U.S. citizen terrorists, such as the Unabomber and Timothy

McVeigh and presumably whoever launched the anthrax attack on the East Coast in October 2001. The terrorist bombings of the London subway system in July 2005 were carried out by British citizens. And U.S. persons who are not terrorists or even terrorist sympathizers might have information of intelligence value—information they might be quite willing to share with the government if only they knew they had it. The information that enables an impending terrorist attack to be detected may be scattered in tiny bits that must be collected, combined, and sifted before their significance is apparent. Many of the bits may reside in the e-mails or phone conversations of innocent people, such as unwitting neighbors of terrorists, who may without knowing it have valuable counterterrorist information—one consequence of the jigsaw puzzle character of national security intelligence.

A further question, however, is whether the Fourth Amendment should be deemed to require warrants for such surveillance. The *Keith* case that I mentioned earlier held that warrants are required for conducting purely domestic surveillance even when the purpose is to protect national security, though the Court suggested that perhaps the probable-cause requirement could be attenuated. It would have to be. If the goal of surveillance is not to generate evidence of criminal activity but to detect terrorist threats, including those too incipient to be prosecutable as threats, and even threats of which the persons under surveillance may be unaware because the significance of the clues they possess eludes them, then to insist that the investigators establish probable cause to believe criminal activity is afoot will be to ask too much. The amendment's requirement of particularity of description of what is to be searched or seized would also have to be relaxed for surveillance warrants adequate to national security to be feasible, because intelligence officers will often not have a good idea of what they are looking for.

Given the Fourth Amendment's prohibition against general warrants and warrants not based on probable cause, it is questionable how much watering down of conventional warrant requirements the warrant clause of the Fourth Amendment would permit. Moreover, judicial review of a watered-down warrant application would not be an effective check on abuses. Warrants are intended for situations in which we do not want the police to do something (such as search one's home) without particularized grounds for believing that there is illegal activity going on. (That is true of physical searches, which FISA also authorizes, and there the warrant requirement should be retained.) All that the application for a warrant to conduct the kind of surveillance that I have described could say is that there is reason to believe that the surveillance might yield clues to terrorist identities, plans, or connections. What kind of filter could the court (the FISA court) asked to issue such warrants employ? Moreover, it is a secret court, composed of judges who are appointed by the chief justice of the United States without Senate confirmation, who are willing to undergo the background investigation required for a top-secret security clearance and so presumably are sympathetic to claims of national security, who hear only the government's side of the case because warrant proceedings are ex parte, and who are asked to issue a warrant to protect the nation against potential dangers far greater than that of ordinary crimes for which search warrants are sought. In such circumstances, the warrant would primarily—and perversely—serve its original function of shielding government officers from damages suits, since unless a warrant is procured fraudulently the officers who execute it will normally be shielded from civil liability.

We rightly worry when governmental power is concentrated, but a partial offset is that when power is concentrated so is responsibility. There would be fewer executions if the sentencing judge had to administer the lethal injection. It is better that the president assume the full responsibility for national security surveillance than that responsibility be diffused by enlisting the participation of judges under conditions in which they would be unable to exercise an effective check on executive power. We are not well served by judicial fig leaves.

But [...] calling a practice "constitutional" is not the bestowal of a compliment. Even if comprehensive warrantless electronic surveillance, domestic as well as foreign, would be constitutional in this age of global terrorism, it does not follow that there should be no statutory limitations. The executive branch contains many regulatory structures to channel and check the discretionary activities of civil servants, including national security personnel. The challenge is to design an appropriate structure for electronic surveillance that does not have the crippling limitations of FISA or fetishize judicial warrants.

[...]

*Richard Posner is a judge on the U.S. Court of Appeals for the Seventh Circuit and professor at the University of Chicago Law School. He is the author of many books on a wide variety of legal subjects, including *Not a Suicide Pact: The Constitution in a Time of National Emergency*, from which this essay is excerpted.

Posner, Richard. 2006. Security and rights against searches and seizures in time of emergency. Adapted from *Not a Suicide Pact: The Constitution in a Time of National Emergency.* New York: Oxford University Press. 87–102.

By permission of Oxford University Press.

Fear as Institution: 9/11 and Surveillance Triumphant

by Christian Parenti*

> *Experience should teach us to be most on our guard to protect liberty when the Government's purposes are beneficent. Men born to freedom are naturally alert to repel invasion of their liberty by evil-minded rulers. The greatest dangers to liberty lurk in insidious encroachment by men of zeal, well meaning but without understanding.*

—Supreme Court Justice Louis Brandeis, *Olmstead v. United States* (1928)

> *There are reminders to all Americans that they need to watch what they say, watch what they do. . . .*

—Ari Fleischer, White House spokesman, 2001. This comment was later removed from the official transcript.

Ultimately, 9/11 did not create a technical or legal rupture in the developing infrastructure of everyday superintendence. It did, however, radically accelerate momentum toward the soft cage of a surveillance society, just as it gave the culture of fear a rejuvenating jolt. In many ways the frightening thing about the post-attack crackdown has been how much of everyday life was prefabricated to fit neatly into a new and larger project of intensified state observation and repression. In this we see again that the problem with routine surveillance is not that any single instance is so abhorrent, especially when viewed in isolation, but rather that the cumulative overall effect of such measures is corrosive of popular democratic rights and traditions.

Patriots Galore

As the smoke of the attacks cleared, there emerged in Congress a hastily discussed yet massive schedule of domestic repression: the Uniting and Strengthening America by Providing Appropriate Tools Required to Intercept and Obstruct Terrorism (USA PATRIOT) Act. This hyperbolically named legislation introduced a sweeping arsenal of new federal powers. Put simply, the PATRIOT Act liberalized use of the federal government's four main tools of surveillance: wiretaps, search warrants, subpoenas, and pen/trap orders (which allow investigators to log and map all the telephone numbers called by a suspect). It was the attorney general's ultimate wish list. But in other ways it was just a mopping-up operation that legalized already existing and ongoing, yet illegal, forms of investigation.

Proof of this point came almost exactly a year after the attacks when several major papers ran the story of an internal FBI memo from 2000 that detailed the bureau's routine and widespread violations of privacy laws. Among the memo's many revelations: field agents were improperly tapping and recording phones, illegally videotaping suspects, and, without warrants, intercepting and analyzing e-mails with the data-mining software application formerly known as Carnivore. Furthermore, the memo rooted these transgressions in the pathological permissiveness of the 1978 Foreign Intelligence Surveillance Act (FISA) Under this law agents were permitted easy access to warrants if they could show that there was a substantial "foreign intelligence" angle to their work; the warrants would be granted by a special FISA court. It turned out that the leeway of FISA was being used as cover for otherwise illegal investigations.

Despite the exposé of FBI lawlessness, Ashcroft's PATRIOT Act had as one of its key features a further reduction in FISA's already low standard of proof. Now, even in cases that are entirely criminal in nature, agents can get automatic "administrative" FISA warrants (as opposed to real warrants from potentially hostile judges). As long as the agents assert that there is some foreign intelligence angle to the cases, they receive search warrants on demand. In 2000 alone the docile, highly secretive FISA bench approved 1,012 warrants.[1] And since 9/11 FBI demands for FISA warrants have become so insistent that even the secret FISA court has publicly admonished the FBI for misrepresenting facts on more than seventy-five occasions. This, from a court that civil libertarians ridiculed as an FBI rubberstamp and that approved *all but one* of the warrant requests put before it in the previous *twenty-four years.*[2]

The key distinction to keep in mind about FISA is that the standard of proof in criminal cases is supposed to be much higher than for intelligence cases, the assumption being that criminal cases can lead to prosecution and imprisonment of citizens and thus must be conducted in a restrained and fair fashion. Foreign intelligence, on the other hand, is merely about collecting information on a foreign power; domestic prosecution is not its goal. Since there is less risk of wrongful conviction from foreign intelligence investigations, requests for search warrants in such cases are held to a lower standard of proof.

The PATRIOT Act also allows federal investigators to "shop" for judges nationally when seeking warrants. Instead of being forced to possibly face a liberal judge, agents can now pick the judge of their choice from whichever circuit court they please and that warrant can be used in any part of the country. The raft of new laws also allows for nationwide roving wiretaps. In the past the feds were supposed to get a warrant for each telephone line they tapped. Now one easy warrant allows them to tap all the phones that a single subject might use. Such a warrant could thus cover a person's home phone, work phone, and cell phone, as well as the lines of their friends, family, work associates, and social acquaintances.[3]

Other PATRIOT Act provisions expand the government's automatic access to information stored and generated by Internet service providers. This is done by retooling the parameters of what are called pen registration tap-and-trace warrants. Traditionally such administrative warrants were granted when cops wanted to generate a simple list of all the numbers that had been called from and that had called a particular phone. Because it was deemed that no "content" was revealed by such a list, the standard of proof for a tap-and-trace warrant was very low; agents had only to "certify" or assert that they had a good reason for needing the information—in other words, they didn't have to prove probable cause. After the PATRIOT Act, the same low standard holds true for gleaning information about Web surfing and e-mailing. But Web addresses and e-mail subject lines, unlike simple phone numbers, all contain revealing content.[4] If you visit the Web site of a radical environmental group, this fact will likely be clear from the Web address alone.

Gone too are the firewalls that once prevented the various intelligence agencies from sharing information. Crucially the PATRIOT Act creates a new massively expanded definition of what a terrorist is. Now anyone who breaks the law so as to impact policy or change public opinion and does so in a way that might endanger human life (including their own) can be investigated and prosecuted as a terrorist.[5] An analysis of the USA PATRIOT Act could go on for many pages. The point for our purposes is that it liberalizes the legal environment in which federal cops will be gathering and processing the routine informational detritus of the digital age.

Total Information Awareness: The Logical Next Step

The most explicit and dramatic connection between government spying and the infrastructure of everyday surveillance was the Total Information Awareness (TIA) project of the Pentagon's Defense Advanced Research Projects Agency (DARPA). Begun in January 2002 and defunded in March 2003, DARPA's Information Awareness Office stated that it would "imagine, develop, apply, integrate, demonstrate, and transition information technologies, components, and prototype closed-loop information systems that will counter asymmetric threats by achieving total information awareness that is useful for preemption, national security warning, and national security decision making."[6]

Much like the Transportation Security Agency's airline-oriented CAPPS II, the TIA office was working on a plan to pull together all the disparate records of everyday life. From the digital trails of credit cards, electronic tolls, banking transactions, health records, and library use it sought to create one "virtual, grand database" that could be data-mined for interesting and incriminating patterns.[7] The program was also tasked with inventing "new algorithms for mining, combining, and refining" this information.[8] Connected to this was another DARPA program called Human ID that would mathematically map biometric information from video cameras and other image sources and then use this to track images of people across and through different databases. This would allow the government to identify people with just a photo and to automatically track people as they travel in public space. A rather perturbed-sounding *Fortune* magazine described DARPA's efforts this way: "Every telephone call you make, every credit card transaction, all your e-mail and instant messages, all your medical records, your magazine subscriptions, your police record, driver's license records, gun purchases, travel records, banking records—all would be fed into a hopper and sifted by the TIA spy software."[9]

This complaint from the *Washington Post* was typical: "The potential for abuse is enormous."[10] One could add that the system was abusive by its very nature, that its intended function was to destroy privacy and subordinate the population, above and beyond any "mistakes" that might be made. Heading up this project was the politically radioactive retired rear admiral John Poindexter, who was infamously convicted on five felony counts of lying to Congress and destroying official documents during the Iran/Contra Affair (he was later acquitted on technicalities).[11]

Another important and developing part of the same general project was the administration's "National Strategy to Secure Cyberspace"—essentially an attempt (still in the planning stages) to centralized the World Wide Web. Currently the purview of the president's Critical Infrastructure Protection Board, this cyber enclosure would require all Internet service providers to help build a centralized system for tracking and filtering online traffic. One data-industry specialist compared the system to the FBI's Internet surveillance data-mining program called Carnivore, but added that "it's ten times worse."[12] Eventually the TIA office of DARPA had its funding cut, thanks to popular outcry against the project. But many of these functions continue in modified form under other names.

Friend/Enemy Kulturkampf

Perhaps the most revealing surveillance idea from the Bush team was the failed Terrorism Information and Prevention System (TIPS) program, which sought to turn one in every twenty-four Americans into a snitch. The idea was to recruit meter readers, UPS drivers, and letter carriers to report on "suspicious activities" they witnessed while inside homes. Floated as a serious proposal by Attorney General John Ashcroft in the summer of 2002, TIPS was quickly ripped to pieces by everyone from the mainstream press to the post office, delivery firms, and utility companies it was to rely on. By late fall TIPS had died in its crib. But the program is an important political artifact because of the twisted fundamentals it reveals.

On Planet Ashcroft, society appears as a hub-and-spoke system where citizens mistrust each other, share no popular solidarity, and place all trust in unlimited state and corporate power. Furthermore, this system plays out along the lines of race. Recall Eunice Stone, at best a malicious busy-body, at worst a stone-cold bigot, who called in the Florida police when she overheard three Middle Eastern-looking medical students at a restaurant talking about dates in September. Mrs. Stone insisted they were joking about imminent terrorist attacks. After a huge paramilitary police bust that shut down Alligator Alley, the "terrorists" turned out to be totally innocent, rather square and apolitical medical students who had been talking about how they could return their rental car to Kansas and still get to their residencies in Georgia on time.[13]

This willingness to snitch on anyone who looks remotely Arab is also reflected in polls. A *Newsweek* survey conducted immediately in the wake of 9/11 found that 32 percent of Americans favored putting Arabs under "special surveillance" like that used against Japanese Americans during World War II.[14] A *San Jose Mercury News* poll had 66 percent of respondents favoring "heightened surveillance of Middle Eastern immigrants."[15]

GET THE IMMIGRANTS, AGAIN

So how do such sentiments translate into policy? Jump back to the autumn of 2002, when men from an ever-growing list of countries are required to report for "special registration" requiring them to be photographed, fingerprinted, and interviewed. In Southern California, *la migra* detains hundreds of law-abiding immigrants, many of whom have only minor technical problems with their paperwork. In Los Angeles the mass arrests are so numerous that officials run out of plastic handcuffs and start shipping the estimated four hundred to nine hundred detainees out to more permanent holding facilities.[16] Fear and outrage grip the Arab, Persian, and South Asian communities; soon hundreds of law-abiding Pakistani immigrants are rushing to the Canadian border seeking political asylum.

"I feel sorrow for this society," says a Mr. Pirazdeh, an Iranian political refugee held in an immigration detention facility in San Pedro. "I still believe this society and this country is based on freedom." Pirazdeh was on the verge of getting his residency papers when he was jailed and threatened with deportation.[17] It was all part of ramping up the cumbersome machinery of the new National Security Entry-Exit Registration System, a futuristic version of the methods first used on the Chinese that will now allow the Department of Homeland Security to better monitor all foreign visitors and immigrants.[18]

To begin with, the new immigration program required all residents from Iran, Iraq, Libya, Sudan, and Syria who are not permanent residents or naturalized citizens to register their fingerprints and photos with the local immigration authorities. Next to be called in were all male visa holders over the age of sixteen from thirteen other countries, including Afghanistan, Eritrea, Lebanon, North Korea, and Yemen. Foreign students are also to be tracked with a new and totalizing vigor, thanks to the Student and Exchange Visitor Information System (SEVIS). As the State Department explained, in the newspeak of compassionate xenophobia, "The new system is designed to better maintain accurate records of aliens inside the nation, at the same time it supports a policy of openness toward people from other nations." The DHS will attempt to maintain "updated information on approximately one million nonimmigrant foreign students and exchange visitors" every year.

Thanks to the Internet, universities and colleges will be compelled to do most of the bureaucratic policing and update the feds electronically as necessary. In their new role as the eyes and ears of homeland security overkill, education institutions will be required to report if a foreign student fails to enroll, drops out, has poor grades, changes his or her address or name or field of study. Such data will be electronically transmitted to the immigration cops and the DHS and to the Department of State. "When a student falls out of status, INS will be informed and able to take appropriate action." The goal of all this is more data mining, enabling "the INS to better identify trends and patterns to assist in planning and analyzing risks."[19] Ultimately such security strategies amount to hunting fleas with a sledgehammer. Terrorists are captured when their networks are infiltrated, not when whole populations are harassed.

While the immigration officials were getting SEVIS up and running, the FBI was shaking down schools for voluntary information transfers. According to the law, universities are free to give limited personal student information to law enforcement agencies without a court order. Department of Education guidelines allow all of the following to be handed over to law enforcement: name, address, e-mail address, telephone number, field of study, the weight and height of athletes, and the date and place of birth. However, investigators still need a subpoena to get student ID numbers, Social Security numbers, or information on a student's ethnicity, race, citizenship, and gender.[20]

In the Service of Order

Here again the central question arises: what harm is caused by the proliferation of everyday surveillance? How will carrying a smart-card ID through an environment of swipe scanners, meters, cameras, sensors, and databanks hurt us? Is it just that a few innocent people, like the immigrants discussed above, will be pushed around? That's bad, but is there even more at stake?

Justice Louis Brandeis framed the issue of surveillance in terms of individual quality of life. Recall his famous dissenting opinion in *Olmstead* on the use of police wiretaps, in which he vaunted "man's spiritual nature . . . his feelings" and "his intellect . . ." and saw the Constitution as protecting "Americans in their beliefs, their thoughts, their emotions and their sensations."[21]

Brandeis offers a definition and defense of privacy as eloquent as any before or since, but are these purely individual, experiential parameters enough? What about the political life of the collective? And what about the dangerous implications of privacy? Is not the case for privacy also an argument for lawlessness? Are we protecting the "privacy" to run red lights, steal, abuse children, or kill with airplanes? Put differently, what does one have to fear from total surveillance as long as one obeys all laws? Indeed, total surveillance and total accountability plus total obedience add up to business as usual for the "good citizen."

Already we see signs of this type of ultratrusting, superobedient postmodern subject emerging from within the regime of routine observation and regulation. The *Christian Science Monitor* reports:

> Polls show that kids have been the least surprised by new security measures since they're the most used to having ID cards examined, luggage searched, and jokes screened by authorities. Today's kids trust and confide in authorities, set up Web cams in their rooms, and keep in constant electronic contact with parents and friends. For better or worse, privacy isn't a big issue among teens, and challenges to civil liberties are less of a worry than to older peple.[22]

In other words, the structure of feeling is being transformed by increasingly ubiquitous surveillance. Liberty and autonomy are being replaced by obedience and trust in authority.

Underlying this question of obedience is the implicit assumption that state, corporate, and parental powers are infallible. Thus the heart of the matter emerges: are the rules and laws of this society all rational, benevolent, and just? If they are not, and if many of them serve to reproduce racism, stupidity, exploitation, environmental devastation, and general brutality, then should we not resist them?

Civil Liberties and Resistance

Perhaps a view from the past might help reframe the issue. Milton Mayer, once a well-known essayist, described a similar escalation of surveillance, rules, and obedience in the gathering storm of German fascism. He interviewed a German philologist who described the process in terms that might sound familiar:

> What happened was the gradual habituation of the people, little by little, to be governed by surprise, to receiving decisions deliberated in secret; to believe that the situation was so complicated that the government had to act on information which the people could not understand, or so dangerous that, even if people could understand it, it could not be released because of national security . . . This separation of government from the people, this widening of the gap, took place so gradually and insensibly, each step disguised (perhaps not even intentionally) as a temporary emergency measure or associated with true patriotic allegiance or with real social purposes. And all the crises and reforms (real reforms too) so occupied the people that they did not see the slow motion underneath, of the whole process of government growing remoter and remoter. . . . Each step was so small, so inconsequential, so well explained or, on occasion, "regretted." That, unless one were to detach from the whole process from the beginning, unless one understood what the whole thing was in principle, what all these "little measures" that no "patriotic German" could resist must some day lead to, one no more saw it developing from day to day than a farmer in his field sees the corn growing.

> Believe me this is true. Each act, each occasion is worse than the last, but only a little worse. You wait for the next and the next. You wait for one shocking occasion, thinking that others, when such a shock comes, will join you in resisting somehow. . . . Suddenly it all comes down, all at once. You see what you are, what you have done, or, more accurately, what you haven't done (for that was all that was required of most of us: that we did nothing). . . . You remember everything now, and your heart breaks. Too late. You are compromised beyond repair.[23]

Now, consider again the question of civil liberties: what *are* they for? As far back as the early Greek philosophers we can find notions of "natural law" that transcend the legality of any given state. We find the recurring idea that the law is not the sum total of morality and that at times there must be transgressions against legal norms. Sophocles, for example, has Antigone explain why she willfully disobeyed the king's orders: "Nor deemed I that thy decrees were of such force, that a mortal could override the unwritten and unfailing statutes of heaven. For their life is not of today or yesterday, but for all time, and no man knows when they were first put forth."[24]

Connected to this is the idea that the state's power over individuals may be simultaneously necessary and dangerous. Thus John Locke's argument for legislative government and against the divine right of kings made a similar case for limitations on state power and what is essentially the right to commit illegalities. To his critics who saw dissolving government as a sin Locke answered:

> But if they, who say it lays a foundation for rebellion, mean that it may occasion civil wars, or intestine broils, to tell the people they are absolved from obedience when illegal attempts are made upon their liberties or properties, and may oppose the unlawful violence of those who were their magistrates, when they invade their properties contrary to the trust put in them; and that therefore this doctrine is not to be allowed, being so destructive to the peace of the world: they may as well say, upon the same ground, that honest men may not oppose robbers or pirates, because this may occasion disorder or bloodshed . . . The end of government is the good of mankind; and which is best for mankind, that the people should be always exposed to the boundless will of tyranny, or that the rulers should be sometime liable to be opposed, when they grow exorbitant in the use of their power, and employ it for the destruction, and not the preservation of the properties of their people?[25]

Admittedly, Locke preferred orderly legislative change to open contest and rebellion, but the philosophical door to illegality is open. The ultimate capstone in this tradition of recognizing an implicit right to illegality is of course the US Declaration of Independence.[26] The key passage, once again:

> We hold these truths to be self-evident, that all men are created equal, that they are endowed by their Creator with certain unalienable rights, that among these are life, liberty and the pursuit of happiness. That to secure these rights, governments are instituted among men, deriving their just powers from the consent of the governed. That whenever any form of government becomes destructive to these ends, it is the right of the people to alter or to abolish it, and to institute new government, laying its foundation on such principles and organizing its powers in such form, as to them shall seem most likely to effect their safety and happiness. Prudence, indeed, will dictate that governments long established should not be changed for light and transient causes; and accordingly all experience hath shown that mankind are more disposed to suffer, while evils are sufferable, than to right themselves by abolishing the forms to which they are accustomed. But when a long train of abuses and usurpations, pursuing invariably the same object evinces a design to reduce them under absolute despotism, it is their right, it is their duty, to throw off such government, and to provide new guards for their future security.

The message here is nothing less than an in-your-face proclamation of state fallibility and an assertion of the people's right to commit illegalities. It is from this recognition in part that the Bill of Rights, the first ten amendments to the Constitution, emerges with its potentially meaningful containment of state power. We are given protection against "unreasonable search and seizure" and "security in our personal effects" precisely because the state and the social hierarchies served by the law are neither infallible nor the perfection of morality. Read together with the

Declaration of Independence, the Bill of Rights and the civil liberties it enshrines begin to reveal themselves not just as protection for the innocent who might be wronged by the excess of the law, but also as an ambiguous protection for types of political guilt. There is in the tradition of natural law a space for rebellion.

It is no coincidence then that the women who met at Seneca Falls in 1848 to declare their "natural rights" and their implicit right to commit illegal acts first quoted verbatim the Declaration of Independence before then setting forth the following challenge to existing law:

> Resolved, That such laws as conflict, in any way with the true and substantial happiness of woman, are contrary to the great precept of nature and of no validity, for his is "superior in obligation to any other."
>
> Resolved, That all laws which prevent woman from occupying such a station in society as her conscience shall dictate, or which place her in a position inferior to that of man, are contrary to the great precept of nature, and therefore of no force or authority.[27]

The same subtextual recognition of the right to commit illegalities compelled Henry David Thoreau to write *Resistance to Civil Government*. That book's most libertine lines also recapitulate the essences of the declaration:

> All men recognize the right of revolution; that is, the right to refuse allegiance to, and to resist, the government, when its tyranny or its inefficiency are great and unendurable. . . . Unjust laws exist: shall we be content to obey them, or shall we endeavor to amend them, and obey them until we have succeeded, or shall we transgress them at once?[28]

Mahatma Gandhi and Martin Luther King Jr. both invoked the same obedience to higher laws in defending their disobedience vis-a-vis specific laws. In that light one might ask: would the civil rights movement have been as effective if the world of the 1950s and early 1960s had been as wired with surveillance gear as today's America? If J. Edgar Hoover had something like Total Information Awareness, would his agents have used it, as they did all the other means available to them, to harass civil rights activists, reds, poor peoples' organizations, unionists, and peaceniks? Most certainly.

Much of the history of social progress—from winning the eight-hour workday to women's suffrage to desegregation—was achieved in large part because citizens organized political movements that involved illegal forms of protests. Privacy and civil liberties were essential tools in all these cases. Illegal protests created a nuisance value that served the less powerful as a disposable political resource. The logic was always simple: Agree to a civilized work regime and the strikes and sabotage will stop. Let the ladies vote and they'll stop getting arrested. Desegregate public facilities, and the siege of sit-ins, boycotts, and blockades will stop. Or today: Stop raping old-growth forest and the rugged tree sitters will come down out of their redwoods. At times when government is truly "remote" and unresponsive, disruptive and sometimes illegal protest is the only resource people have.

Similarly, the right to illegality is revealed in the fact that often the only way to get a constitutional test of a law is to violate the statute in question. Viewed from this angle the specter of a totally transparent society in which obedience and self-policing are the ideal is a threat to the basic precondition of oppositional politics and social progress.

What would it take to wind back the "thousand things" that make up the soft cage? Clearly there must be prohibitions against ever-expanding surveillance, but only popular pressure will cause the state to build new firewalls of privacy. Only sustained protest will compel regulators to tell corporations, police, schools, hospitals, and other institutions that there are limits. As a society, we want to say: Here you may not go. Here you may not record. Here you may not track and identify people. Here you may not trade and analyze information and build dossiers. There are risks in social anonymity, but the risks of omniscient and omnipotent state and corporate power are far worse.

ENDNOTES

1. Ted Bridis, "FBI Memo Details Surveillance Lapses in Terror, Spy Cases," Associated Press, October 10, 2002; "One Year Later," *Nation*, September 23, 2002.

2. Dan Eggen, "FBI Misused Secret Wiretaps, According to Memo," *Washington Post,* October 10, 2002.

3. "USA PATRIOT Act Boosts Government Powers While Cutting Back on Traditional Checks and Balances," ACLU Legislative Analysis on USA PATRIOT Act, November 1, 2001; "USA PATRIOT Act—An Analysis by the ACLU," January 12, 2002; "Civil Liberties after 9/11: The ACLU Defends Freedom," September 20, 2002.

4. See Electronic Frontier Foundation, http://www.eff.org/Privacy/Surveillance/Terrorism_militias/20011031_eff_usa_patriot_analysis.html.

5. Ibid.

6. See Defense Advanced Research Projects Agency, http://www.darpa.mil/iao.

7. Jeffrey Rosen, "'Total Information Awareness," in "The Year in Ideas," *New York Times Magazine*, December 15, 2002.

8. The real total for TIA funding comes from Electronic Privacy Information Center (EPIC), http://www.epic.org/events/tia_briefing. In many ways TIA is the worst-case scenario, the end result of proliferating digital everyday surveillance. When I began this book, the attacks of 9/11 had not yet happened, TIA did not exist, and my argument called on readers to *imagine* the digitalized informational landscape that could be centrally monitored with something like TIA. Much has changed

since then, and one need not try and imagine anything, since the critical imagination has once again been overtaken by the implementation of actual policies.

9. Peter Lewis, "At Last," *Fortune*, December 30, 2002; William Safire, "You Are a Suspect," *New York Times*, November 14, 2002; William New, "Back to the Future," *National Journal*, June 14, 2002; William New, "The Poindexter Plan," *National Journal*, September 7, 2002. For one of the earliest mentions, see Dr. Tony Tether, "Statement by Director, Defense Advanced Research Projects Agency," Submitted to the Subcommittee on Emerging Threats and Capabilities, Committee on Armed Services, United States Senate, *Hearings on Fiscal 2003 Defense Request: Combating Terrorism* (April 10, 2002).

10. "Total Information Awareness," *Washington Post*, November 16, 2002.

11. For discussion of this point, see Safire, "You Are a Suspect"; Matthew Engel, "This Perfect System," *Guardian* (London), November 19, 2002.

12. John Markoff and John Swartz, "Bush Administration to Propose System for Wide Monitoring of Internet," *New York Times*, December 20, 2002.

13. Christine Chinlund, "Getting the Rest of the Story," *Boston Globe*, September 23, 2002; Clarence Page, "The Failings of Arab Profiling," *Chicago Tribune*, September 22, 2002; *Democracy Now*, September 24, 2002, http://www.webactive.com/pacifica/demnow/den20020924.html.

14. Daniel Levitas, "The Radical Right after 9/11," *Nation,* July 22, 2002.

15. John Giuffo and Joshua Lipton, "Reverberations," *Columbia Journalism Review*, January 1, 2002.

16. *Chicago Tribune*, December 20, 2002.

17. Henry Weinstein and Greg Krikorian, "Caught between Dueling Policies," *Los Angeles Times*, December 21, 2002.

18. *Los Angeles Daily News,* December 19, 2002.

19. State Department press releases and documents, Federal Information & News Dispatch, Inc., December 13, 2002. According to this press release, "SEVIS implements section 641 of the Illegal Immigration Reform and Immigrant Responsibilities Act (IIRIRA) of 1996. IIRIRA requires the INS to collect current information on an ongoing basis from schools and exchange programs relating to nonimmigrant foreign students and exchange visitors during the course of their stay in the United States. In addition, the USA PATRIOT Act amended section 641 to require full implementation of SEVIS prior to January 1, 2003. In addition, the

Enhanced Border Security and Visa Entry Reform Act of 2002 adds to and clarifies the requirement to collect information, as well as requires an educational institution to report any failure of an alien to enroll no later than thirty days after registration deadline."

20. Ann Davis, "Some Colleges Balk at FBI Request for Data on Foreigners," *Wall Street Journal*, November 25, 2002.

21. *Olmstead v United States*, 277 US 438 (1928).

22. Neil Howe and William Strauss, "Through Prism of Tragedy, Generations Are Defined," *Christian Science Monitor*, September 23, 2002.

23. Milton Mayer, *They Thought They Were Free: The Germans, 1933–1945* (Chicago: University of Chicago Press, 1955), pp. 166–72.

24. Sophocles, cited in Charles Grove Haines, *The Revival of Natural Law Concepts: A Study of the Establishment and of the Interpretation of Limits on Legislatures with Special Reference to the Development of Certain Phases of American Constitutional Law,* (Cambridge: Harvard University Press, 1930), p 5.

25. John Locke, *Second Treatise on Government* (1690, http://www.constitution.org/jl/2ndtreat.htm).

26. Among its fans were Ho Chi Minh and Fidel Castro.

27. Elizabeth Cady Stanton, "The Seneca Falls Declaration, Adopted in Convention, 1848," http://www.constitution.org/woll/seneca.htm.

28. Henry David Thoreau, *On the Duty of Civil Disobedience* [1849, original title: *Resistance to Civil Government*], http://www.constitution.org/civ/civildis.htm.

*Christian Parenti is a contributing editor with *The Nation* and a visiting scholar at the Center for Place, Culture, and Politics at the City University of New York's Graduate Center. He is an award-winning journalist and the author of three books, including *The Soft Cage: Surveillance in America from Slavery to the War on Terror.*

Parenti, Christian. 2004. Fear as institution: 9/11 and surveillance triumphant. Chap. 9 in *Civil Liberties vs. National Security in a Post-9/11 World,* ed. M. Catherine B. Darmer, Robert M. Baird, and Stuart E. Rosenbaum. Amherst, NY: Prometheus Books.

Copyright © 2004 Christian Parenti. Reprinted by permission of Basic Books, a member of the Perseus Book Group.

Discussion Questions

1. Does the fact that we routinely provide a wealth of personal information about ourselves to Internet service providers, credit card companies, and other businesses mean that the government should also have unlimited access to such information? Or should the government be required to demonstrate some objective basis for suspicion before being granted access to such information? If the information is not kept "private" from Google, why should it be kept "private" from the government? Is it more of an intrusion or more dangerous for the government to have access to such information?

2. Did Congress overreact when it gave the government the power, through national security letters, to demand information from Internet service providers without probable cause or judicial authorization?

3. What values does privacy serve? What costs does privacy entail? If the risk of catastrophic attack has increased, should privacy protections decrease? If so, in what situations? Where should we draw the line?

4. Is it less invasive of privacy to have a computer "mine" one's personal data looking for clues of terrorism or crime than to have a government agent do so? When should it be permissible for a government agent to do so?